T0189908

Business Essentials for Strategic Communicators

Business Essentials for Strategic Communicators

Creating Shared Value for the Organization and its Stakeholders

Matthew W. Ragas and Ron Culp

First published in 2014 by PALGRAVE MACMILLAN® in the United States—a division of St. Martin's Press LLC, 175 Fifth Avenue, New York, NY 10010.

Where this book is distributed in the UK, Europe and the rest of the world, this is by Palgrave Macmillan, a division of Macmillan Publishers Limited, registered in England, company number 785998, of Houndmills, Basingstoke, Hampshire RG21 6XS.

Palgrave Macmillan is the global academic imprint of the above companies and has companies and representatives throughout the world.

Palgrave® and Macmillan® are registered trademarks in the United States, the United Kingdom, Europe and other countries.

ISBN 978-1-349-48188-0   ISBN 978-1-137-38533-8 (eBook)
DOI 10.1057/9781137385338

Library of Congress Cataloging-in-Publication Data

Ragas, Matthew W., 1977-
Business essentials for strategic communicators : creating shared value for the organization and its stakeholders / by Matthew W. Ragas and Ron Culp.
        pages cm
    Includes bibliographical references and index.

        1. Business communication.   2. Target marketing   3. Public relations.
        4. Finance.   5. Economics.   6. Communications.   I. Culp, Ron, 1947- II. Title.
    HF5718.R34 2014
    658.4'5—dc23   2014024432

A catalogue record of the book is available from the British Library.

Design by Amnet.

First edition: December 2014

10 9 8 7 6 5 4 3 2 1

Transferred to Digital Printing in 2015

*We dedicate this book to Traci, Sandra,
and our students, who inspire us each and every day.*

Contents

PART IV. Demonstrating and Improving the Business Value of Communication

List of Tables and Figures

Tables

Figures

Foreword

Gary Sheffer

Vice President of Corporate Communications and Public Affairs, General Electric

Chair, Arthur W. Page Society

If anybody asks why I think Matt Ragas and Ron Culp's *Business Essentials for Strategic Communicators* is indispensable for students and professionals alike, the answer comes from personal experience. And it starts with a meeting with Jack Welch.

It was 1999, and I had just started at General Electric (GE), my first "corporate" job.

We were in Jack's conference room, meeting with the Chief Financial Officer to discuss the press release and rollout strategy for the company's quarterly earnings report. The subject turned to organic growth, and I remember to this day exactly what I was thinking. What's organic growth?

I arrived at GE fairly confident in my abilities to handle most communication challenges. I started my career as a journalist, so I could write and edit, according to the *Associated Press Stylebook*, anyway. Reporting for the *Albany (NY) Times Union*, I had some experience asking the questions needed to separate fact from fiction. I also worked in state government as a press aide. I was comfortable with the frantic pace of politics, and I could navigate, or at least tolerate, some bureaucracy.

What more could working at a big company require?

To start, it requires knowledge of the very basics of business—how enterprises actually operate and succeed. That became pretty clear as I was hoping, even praying, that Jack—"Neutron Jack"—wouldn't cast his steely blue eyes my way and ask a question. In college, I studied Chaucer. But at that point, a Twain quote was more fitting. "It is better to keep your mouth closed and let people think you are a fool than to open it and remove all doubt."

I was in the room, but without a depth of understanding and with a lack of business acumen, I wouldn't be there long. I couldn't fill the role of the trusted advisor that I wanted to be or those in the C-suite required.

The meeting convinced me that a communicator should be more than a conveyor of information; a communicator should be a consumer of it; we should work to be the most informed people in the room. I went straight to the investor relations team and asked for a crash course in all things finance, accounting, and governance. As part of that, someone handed me a booklet titled "How to Read a Financial Report." I still refer to the now well-tattered copy, wishing that as a student I had an even more comprehensive resource and, as a professional communicator, waiting for its arrival.

Now it's here—*Business Essentials for Strategic Communicators*. Ragas and Culp are sure to be the Strunk and White for the communication function and industry. They've written a book that every communicator, no matter their level, should keep close. And it couldn't be timelier.

Things move much faster than they did in 1999. To keep up, the function of communication and the role of communicators throughout organizations are also changing both rapidly and radically. Consider the spread of digital and social media, the emergence of global markets, and the financial crisis of 2008–2009. Together, these require that communicators be equipped with a new set of skills and capabilities compared with the skills needed even five or ten years ago. We now need expertise across activities like performing data analytics and metrics, managing social media strategy and implementation, driving an enterprise's ethical orientation, and managing corporate character—all built on a foundation of increased business acumen.

Put another way, in this environment, and to perform at our best level, communicators must be more than just the mouthpieces for our organization. We must be the eyes and ears for our business leaders, too: proactive, not just reactive. Today, and rightfully, transparency is paramount. But to be truly transparent, you need domain expertise and, perhaps, more than anything, the understanding of financial rhythms and reporting: the business of the business.

At GE, and for others, too, communicators used to rotate around the individual enterprises. To allow our people to build the necessary domain expertise—whether it's understanding supply chains, knowing the major players, or navigating regulations—we do that with far less frequency. As for business acumen, it is my intention to make this book required reading. In the pages that follow, Matt Ragas and Ron Culp cover everything from economic indicators and the stock market to governance and corporate social responsibility. They offer the information necessary for communicators to have a basic financial understanding, as well as insight to specific areas in which business and traditional communication intersect. This book also provides communicators with one of the things we've long wanted but for which we were afraid to ask: a glossary. It's an invaluable resource—not for promoting jargon, but for increasing our ability to understand and translate it for ourselves and the various audiences we must reach.

Seven years after that meeting with Jack Welch, his successor Jeff Immelt called me to that same conference room. Jeff briefed me on a potential deal that could be challenging from a reputational standpoint. His order was to "look at it hard."

Jeff Immelt wasn't merely asking his communicators how he and the company should talk about a deal, or what specifically he should say, or even what the press would say about us. He was asking for business counsel. He wanted the perspective of trusted, strategic advisors. Today, communicators don't only wield influence on reputation: we are changing the way major organizations are doing business. And in fact, our suggestions—based on a deep understanding of our company and the environment in which we operated—did lead to some changes in the deal.

As communicators, we cannot be experts on all topics. But we need to ensure that we are always consuming information, always learning, and always building up from a fundamental understanding of business. More and more, organizations are seeing the strategic value of communication. We're in the room. The question is whether we have the foundational knowledge to make the most of that opportunity. With domain expertise and business acumen, we can offer sound counsel and direction on navigating, reacting to, adapting to, and molding stakeholders' perceptions, wherever those stakeholders sit. We can do our part to protect and enhance our organization's reputation, as well as its bottom line.

This book is a great start.

Preface

The communication profession is no longer just about left-brain or right-brain thinking—if indeed it ever was. The most sought after communicators today offer a "whole brain" perspective.

The profession naturally attracts its fair share of right-brain oriented creative minds. But as the field has matured and its responsibilities have increased, strategic communication students and professionals are now more often expected to be not just excellent communicators but also competent businesspeople who can bring a left-brain, analytical mindset to the table. This demands at the very least a fair degree of business acumen.

While most strategic communication students and young professionals will no doubt one day work for or with companies, most receive limited formal training about how the business world actually works. With such a limited understanding of the business environment and an aversion at times to numbers, communicators can find themselves at a disadvantage in offering advice that could result in shared value for the organization and its stakeholders. And that is where this book helps fill the gap.

Our goal in writing this book is to provide foundational knowledge on essential business topics from a strategic communicator's perspective. Incorporating more than 400 references from the scholarly and trade literature, we hope you will find this book to be not only well researched and balanced but also accessible. Strategic communication and business are fast-moving fields, but every effort was made to keep chapter content fresh and current as we went to press.

Each chapter includes insights from interviews with leading strategic communication and business professionals on these subjects. Examples from top brands are frequently used to help illustrate the concepts discussed. If you flip to the back of this book, you'll find a glossary filled with more than 300 key terms that help demystify the language of business, so you are better positioned to serve as an essential translator of such concepts for your stakeholders.

Simply stated, gaining a better grasp on "Business 101" is empowering; it helps a communicator to not only do his or her job better but also make a bigger impact on both the organization and its stakeholders. In the words of billionaire businessperson and serial entrepreneur Mark Cuban (personal communication, April 19, 2014): "If you don't understand the language of business, you're always dependent on somebody else."

MATT RAGAS
RON CULP
Chicago, Illinois

About the Authors

Matt Ragas (PhD, University of Florida) is an assistant professor and academic director of the graduate program for public relations and advertising in the College of Communication at DePaul University, Chicago. An award-winning teacher and researcher, he has authored more than 30 scholarly articles, book chapters, trade articles, and industry research reports, as well as two trade books (Crown Business and Prima). This includes peer-reviewed scholarship in *Journalism & Mass Communication Quarterly, Corporate Communications: An International Journal, Journal of Communication Management, International Journal of Strategic Communication, Public Relations Review,* and *Journalism Studies,* among others. A recipient of the Nafziger-White-Salwen dissertation award from the Association for Education in Journalism and Mass Communication (AEJMC), he has been a fellow of the Donald W. Reynolds National Center for Business Journalism at Arizona State University, The Plank Center for Leadership in Public Relations at The University of Alabama, and a Coleman Foundation faculty entrepreneurship fellow. A member of the founding class of Page Up (where he serves on the operating committee for the organization), he has been the faculty advisor on multiple award-winning entries in the Arthur W. Page Society student case study competition. Matt also holds an MS in management and a BS in marketing from the University of Central Florida. Prior to his career in academia, he worked for close to a decade in online publishing and strategic communication roles, primarily in investment research and business news. He has consulted for a variety of organizations, and he collaborates with industry in his research and teaching. For more information, visit: www.mattragas.com and twitter: @ mattragas

Ron Culp is the professional director of the graduate program for public relations and advertising in the College of Communication at DePaul University, Chicago. He has received numerous awards recognizing his leadership in the field of public relations, and he writes a popular career blog, Culpwrit. His career spans a broad range of communication roles in government and in business-to-business, consumer products, pharmaceutical, and retailing industries. Prior to joining DePaul, Ron was a Ketchum partner and the head of the global agency's North American Corporate Practice. Previously, he headed the Chicago office of financial communication firm Sard Verbinnen and Company after serving as senior vice president of public relations and government affairs for Sears. Earlier in his career, he held senior communication positions at Sara Lee Corporation, Pitney Bowes, and Eli Lilly. He began his career as a reporter for *The Columbus (IN) Republic* before working for the Indiana House of Representatives and then the New York State Assembly, where he served as director of member services. He chairs the Plank Center for Leadership in Public Relations and serves on the boards of Gilda's Club Chicago and the Indiana State University Foundation. He created a Public Relations Student Society of America (PRSSA) scholarship recognizing student mentors, and he also endowed a scholarship for first-generation college students at his alma mater, Indiana State University. He is active in several civic organizations, including the Economic Club of Chicago, where he is a former vice chair and board member. In 2006, he received the Distinguished Service Award from the Arthur W. Page Society, and in 2011 he was honored with the prestigious John W. Hill Award by the New York Chapter of Public Relations Society of America (PRSA). In 2012, he was named PR Professional of the Year by Chicago PRSA. He is featured in the PRSSA book, *Legacies from Legends in Public Relations* (2007), and he was named to the PR News Hall of Fame in 2008.

Acknowledgments

The authors have many people to thank for making this project possible.

The team at Palgrave Macmillan has been fantastic to work with, and we are fortunate to have a publisher that strongly believed in the need for such a cross-market book from the start. Big thanks to Casie Vogel, Bradley Showalter, Leila Campoli, Sarah Lawrence, Chelsea Morgan, Andy Etzkorn, and the rest of the Palgrave team. We also wish to thank Jamie Armstrong of Amnet Systems and ace indexer Lisa Rivero. A special thank you goes out to Arthur Lubow, Sukanya Cherdrungsi, and team at AD Lubow, LLC (http://adlubow.com) for their creative guidance and encouragement on the left brain-right brain cover theme.

We both are proud to call Chicago home and even prouder to be in the College of Communication at DePaul University, where we get to meld theory and practice every day in an entrepreneurial environment that encourages cross-disciplinary work. Our colleagues and students are second to none. Many of the topics herein emerged from discussions with our current and former students, both inside and outside the classroom, concerning trends in the profession. A little part of each guest speaker who passed through our classes is also included.

The support and encouragement we received from friends and colleagues in both the academy and the profession inspired us throughout this process. We are grateful to the several dozen top communicators who agreed to let us interview them for this project. We also thank those who reviewed early chapter drafts or ideas, offered feedback, and helped us strengthen the final product. Our profession, indeed, is so fortunate to have so many individuals who are concerned with helping educate and grow the next generation of leaders. Much of this work is due in part to the excellent academic and professional associations and publications in our field and the talented individuals who help lead them. We particularly wish to thank the Arthur W. Page Center for Integrity in Public Communication, the Arthur W. Page Society, the Association for Education in Journalism and Mass Communication, the

Business Marketing Association, the Commission on Public Relations Education, Council of Public Relations Firms, the Financial Communications Society, the Institute for Public Relations, the International Association of Business Communicators, the International Communication Association, the National Investor Relations Institute, Page Up, the Plank Center for Leadership in Public Relations, the Public Relations Society of America, the Publicity Club of Chicago, and the Strategic Communication and Public Relations Center.

Matt wishes to thank his parents, family, friends, and colleagues. He will never forget waking up as a child early each morning to sit with his dad and read the business section of *The Times-Picayune* (and look up the closing stock quotes from the day before). Matt is blessed to have had wonderful teachers, mentors, and friends through the years, including his dad, who always encouraged him to become a professor and "join the family business"; Ned Grace of Grace Restaurant Partners, who taught him what it really means to be an entrepreneur; Spiro Kiousis and the many professors who encouraged and challenged him to grow as a scholar during his doctoral program at the University of Florida; and his coauthor Ron, who shows him every day that service to others is the essence of being a real leader.

Ron wishes to thank his family, friends, colleagues, and the 1,185 residents of his hometown, Remington, Indiana. Growing up in rural Indiana, Ron was a serial entrepreneur, thanks to parents and neighbors who encouraged his many business ventures ranging from having a neighborhood newspaper and a 5-watt radio station to mowing 50 lawns a week and sharecropping gardens that elderly residents could no longer tend. Ron's commitment to mentoring stems from the many inspirational teachers and mentors from his hometown, college, and business career. Special thanks to Professor Teresa Mastin, who encouraged him to make a perfectly timed life-changing decision to join the faculty at DePaul, where he is surrounded by dedicated academics, professionals, and students who inspire him every day.

Finally, thanks to you, the reader. Your interest in this important subject will enhance your business knowledge, which in turn will no doubt benefit your career and our profession.

PART I

Introduction to Business Essentials
for Communicators

CHAPTER 1

Why Knowledge of "Business 101" Matters

Ask communication students or professionals about their ultimate career goals, and their answers will no doubt be that they seek more than simply "jobs in the profession." Communication professionals today want to become respected voices in their organizations. Most say they strive to create value for society at large, and they want a "seat at the table." That's why this book was written—to equip communication students and professionals with business insights that help make those students and professionals true partners with their management peers.

The public relations, advertising, corporate communication, and public affairs disciplines, now often referred to as components of the more general field of strategic communication (Hallahan, Holtzhausen, van Ruler, Vercic, & Sriramesh, 2007; Holtzhausen & Zerfass, 2014), have grown by leaps and bounds over the past 60 years. Harold Burson, who was named by *PRWeek* as "the century's most influential PR figure" (O'Reilly, 2008, p. 18) and who is the founder of Burson-Marsteller, one of the world's largest strategic communication agencies, describes the communication field as maturing through three main stages (Christian, 1997).

Through the 1950s, or the first stage, the CEO of the organization primarily asked communication professionals, "*How* do I say it?"—*after* organizational decisions had already been made. This question shifted in the 1960s and 1970s as the influence and pressure of the news media and the public on organizational performance grew (Ragas, 2013a). In this second stage, the CEO began to ask, "*What* do I say?" Strategic communication professionals were starting to gain respect from both the senior leadership and the boardroom—at least in terms of *what* messages to communicate and *when*.

In recent decades, strategic communication has entered the third stage of its maturation (Christian, 1997). CEOs increasingly ask communicators not just "what do I *say*?" but also "what do I *do*?" Strategic communication professionals are expected to be just that—*strategic*—which means proactively contributing to both organizational decision making and strategy—and not just simply contributing to the construction and communication of the organization's message (Botan, 2006; Botan & Taylor, 2004; Coombs & Holladay, 2007; Dozier, 1992; Dozier & Broom, 2006; Dozier & Grunig, 1992; Ragas, Laskin, & Brusch, 2014; van Riel & Fombrun, 2007).

Although this is an exciting time for strategic communicators, it also represents a sea change in terms of the knowledge and skills required to fulfill this new "strategic mandate" (Arthur W. Page Society, 2007). Strategic communication, defined as "the purposeful use of communication by an organization to fulfill its mission" (Hallahan et al., 2007, p. 3), has increasingly become a common connection point and shared communication management perspective in the public relations, advertising, corporate communication, and public affairs disciplines. An organization's strategy should be rooted in an organization's values-driven mission and vision (Arthur W. Page Society, 2012, 2013a, 2013b), which in turn serves as the foundation for goal- and objective-setting (R. D. Smith, 2013). Therefore, a major challenge for communication professionals is that contributing at a strategic level generally requires at least a working knowledge of business management concepts, terminology, opportunities, and challenges (Roush, 2006). Most communication professionals probably did not take business school courses in college and, thus, find themselves trying to learn "Business 101" on the job (Duhé, 2013; Kolberg, 2014; Ragas, 2013d).

Unfortunately, if a communicator can't speak the language of business and gain the attention, let alone the respect, of leaders or managers in other established departments (such as marketing, sales, information technology, accounting, or finance), the job becomes difficult (Duhé, 2013). Being a great event planner, copywriter, creative, media relations manager, or social media maven is simply not enough. Although such technical tasks are essential, and one can enjoy a good career by excelling in each of these areas, to truly become a strategic asset to an organization, one must understand "Business 101" (Kolberg, 2014; Roush, 2006). Understanding the world of accounting and financial statements, finance and the stock market, economics and the economy, program measurement and evaluation, intangible assets and nonfinancial information, social responsibility, corporate governance, and corporate reputation is essential. In essence, a strategic communicator should more fully understand how communication helps achieve organizational goals that deliver on the organization's values-driven mission and vision (Arthur W. Page Society, 2012, 2013a, 2013b).

Growing Market Demand and Changing Expectations

The demand and the outlook for communication professionals, particularly those who can speak the language of business and understand business fundamentals, are bright (Kolberg, 2014). Sparked by the digital transformation cutting across every industry, U.S. communication industry spending is expected to reach $1.4 trillion by 2016, growing at nearly double the rate of the previous five years (Veronis Suhler Stevenson, 2012). According to the U.S. Bureau of Labor Statistics (2012), within the United States alone, there are five hundred thirty-seven thousand professionals working in public relations, advertising, promotions, and marketing, and these fields are expected to grow at or faster than the national average over the next decade. On a global basis, there are an estimated three million people working just in public relations (Commission on Public Relations Education, 2012).

The positive, projected growth rate for the field is also reflected in college and university enrollments. Communication is one of the ten most popular majors on college campuses today (Aud et al., 2012). Within the United States, there are 485 university and college programs enrolling more than fifty-one thousand students in public relations, advertising, strategic communication, or integrated marketing communication (Vlad, Becker, Simpson, & Kalpen, 2013). Another fifty-eight thousand students are enrolling in journalism courses, with some of these students poised to pursue a career in strategic communication (Vlad et al., 2013). While it is encouraging that so many universities and colleges around the world now offer undergraduate and graduate degrees in strategic communication–related areas, this means that competition for good jobs is and will continue to be intense—even with the positive growth outlook. Job candidate differentiation is the name of the game (Wright, 2007).

Hiring managers and public relations and advertising agency leaders generally believe that universities and colleges are doing an adequate job of preparing students for careers in public relations but cite several critical areas for needed improvement. More specifically, a survey of senior communicators conducted by the Council of Public Relations Firms (Cripps, 2013), which represents more than one hundred public relations firms, reveals that the members of the profession would like graduates to have a better knowledge of (1) writing, (2) "Business 101"/business strategy, and (3) the business of public relations firms. Specifically, respondents to this industry survey call for a "better understanding of business fundamentals" and for "more general business training. The respondents note that "too many [students] don't understand business" (Cripps, 2013, para. 4).

Kathy Cripps, president of the Council of Public Relations Firms, echoes this sentiment. "I realized a long time ago that public relations professionals with a true understanding of business fundamentals can better serve their clients and their organizations," Cripps says. "In an increasingly hyper-competitive marketplace, the firms that best understand their client's business concerns and challenges will have a decided advantage over competitors" (personal communication, August 28, 2013).

A national survey that the authors of this book conducted of the membership of the Arthur W. Page Society, an association of senior public relations and corporate communication executives and distinguished academics, tells a similar story. A resounding eight out of ten respondents (82 percent) believe that colleges and universities are *not* doing enough to provide students with a basic understanding of business. On the other hand, nearly 85 percent of respondents believe that it is "extremely important" that graduates have a solid grounding in business. This rises to almost 100 percent when those stating that this knowledge is "very important" are included.

Survey respondent and Arthur W. Page Society member Tim Blair, corporate vice president of marketing and communication for Huron Consulting Group, says that business executives fully expect communication professionals today to have strong writing and editing skills, but those skills themselves do not add significant value to an organization (personal communication, August 29, 2013). "The value communicators should strive to add to any business is that of informed counselor," Blair says. "Business leaders will engage communicators at a different level if we can speak their language, understand their pain points, recognize new opportunities, and clearly articulate a strategic, informed point of view."

Qualitative research conducted by talent and performance firm upper 90 consulting and by Holton Research (upper 90 consulting & Holton Research, 2014), consisting of in-depth interviews with a dozen chief communication officers (CCOs), yields similar conclusions on the need for not just communication expertise but also business acumen among communication professionals. According to this study, "CCOs see business fluency/literacy as fundamental for communicators at all levels" (upper 90 consulting & Holton Research, 2014, p. 9).

"Although business knowledge has long been a skill mastered by top corporate communications leaders, the strong emphasis CCOs now place on it suggests that it has become a paramount priority for junior, middle and senior professionals alike," says Mark Bain, president of upper 90 consulting and former global director of communications for Baker & McKenzie, a global law firm, and Alticor Inc., the parent company of Amway and other businesses (personal communication, April 25, 2014).

Counseling Organizational Leadership Means Business

Knowledge of how a business makes and loses money and the intricacies of its industry, the economy, and the stock market simply were not as important for communication professionals to know in years past. *Technicians* and press agents do not need to know such things to do their job well; *strategists* and counselors do—and those are the roles that communicators increasingly play in many organizations (Dozier & Broom, 2006; Duhé, 2013; Ragas & Culp, 2013; Smith, 2013). A national study by the Strategic Communications and Public Relations Center at the University of Southern California's Annenberg School for Communication and Journalism finds that the majority (60 percent) of senior corporate communication professionals are now invited to attend senior-level company-wide planning meetings. Almost 70 percent of these professionals believe their recommendations are being taken seriously (Swerling et al., 2012). If senior communicators are increasingly being asked to counsel leadership and to know about the world of business and about how communication can advance business goals and objectives, then mid- and junior-level communicators on their teams need this knowledge as well.

According to William C. Heyman, president and CEO of communication and public affairs search firm Heyman Associates, recruiters particularly seek out candidates who have a good knowledge of business fundamentals and who understand the opportunities and challenges facing specific industries (personal communication, August 28, 2013) "When I speak to groups of professionals or students, and list what our clients are looking for, the first thing I mention is an understanding of business," Heyman says. "Often one of the great differentiators in candidates applying for top jobs is their understanding of business and the experience they have had working on learning about that business."

A seminal study by the Arthur W. Page Society (2007) of the Authentic Enterprise gauged the perceptions and expectations of the CEOs of America's largest companies regarding strategic communication. According to the surveyed CEOs, communication leaders are expected to be (1) *reactive* (managing press and events, serving as spokespeople, and doing crisis management—the traditional tasks of communicators), (2) *proactive* (developing ideas, shaping messages, and monitoring reputation), and (3) *interactive* (collaborating across the company and its stakeholders, shaping the company's strategic direction, and measuring results in concrete, business-worthy ways). As the report states: "this is no longer about the basics of the communications craft. Those are now taken for granted. Most of the CEOs surveyed expect their senior communication leaders also to possess strong business expertise—knowledge of both the company's industry and business strategy in general" (Arthur W. Page Society, 2007, p. 20).

Again, it is not just senior communicators who need to know "Business 101." Business managers feel strongly enough about the integration of business and communication that there is a push for strategic communication to be taught in more business school master of business administration (MBA) programs (Arthur W. Page Society, 2013d; Public Relations Society of America [PRSA], 2011). In partnership with the Public Relations Society of America (PRSA), ten U.S. universities, including the Tuck School of Business at Dartmouth College and the Kellogg School of Management at Northwestern University, now offer an MBA-level course in strategic communication (Byrum, 2013; Phair, 2013). Additional business schools already offer some coursework in management and business communication. Survey research conducted on behalf of PRSA reveals that business leaders believe "communications has emerged as an essential skill set for corporate-level executives in the 21st century" (PRSA, 2011, para. 4). However, these same leaders feel that only 40 percent of recent MBA hires have an extremely strong skill set in this area (PRSA, 2011). Related research conducted by the Arthur W. Page Society (2013d) finds that business leaders now view communication as a required executive management tool.

It is perhaps both good and bad news for communication students and professionals that more business majors are studying strategic communication and its impact on corporate reputations. This means that business managers will increasingly be conversant in communication concepts and terminology. But the street should go two ways. If businesspeople are increasingly able to speak the language of communication, then there is no excuse for why communication people cannot, in turn, speak and understand the language of business (Claussen, 2008). Successful mid- to senior-level strategic communicators of the future will not need to be factotums of accounting, finance, and economics minutiae, but they will need a working knowledge of "Business 101" and demonstrated business acumen (Ragas & Culp, 2013; Spangler, 2014).

"An organization cannot execute a strategy without effective communication, nor can it implement effective communications without a sound, overarching organizational strategy," says Anthony D'Angelo, senior manager of communications for global, diversified manufacturing company ITT Corporation and cochair of PRSA's MBA program (personal communication, April 23, 2014). "Both business strategists and communication strategists are recognizing that it's a symbiotic relationship between the professions, and the shared goal is to create, lead and manage excellent organizations."

This shift in the knowledge base and skill set required of future communication professionals is also evident in research by the Commission on Public Relations Education (CPRE), a group that represents more than a dozen top industry associations. The CPRE (1999) has long advocated that public relations majors consider double majoring or minoring in business or consider at least taking business classes as electives. After a yearlong program of research into the standards for a master's degree, the CPRE (2012) concludes that students should gain an "understanding of business" (p. 5) and that "basic business principles and processes" (p. 11) should be a part of the core curriculum. Other core areas are strategic public relations management, communication/public relations theory and research methods, global influences on the practice of public relations, and ethics. CPRE (2012) concludes:

> Information gathered by Commission members from both academic and practitioner audiences strongly suggests that all master's degree programs in public relations require graduates to gain an understanding of business principles that would include, but not necessarily be limited to, management, marketing, accounting, economics and finance, plus an understanding of return-on-investment and other strategic business outcomes. (p. 14)

The identified need for more "Business 101"–related coursework is not limited to just U.S. professionals and educators. A global survey of forty-five hundred communication professionals in 23 countries supported by the Plank Center for Leadership in Public Relations identified what approaches should be taken to developing future leaders within the communication management field. Survey respondents assigned above average importance to strengthening the business and economic component of communication education (Berger, 2012; Berger & Meng, 2014).

The Payoff for Learning "Business 101"

So what is the payoff for the communicator who learns the "nuts and bolts" of current business essentials? While having "Business 101" knowledge is only one component of being a successful strategic communication professional—along with having strong writing skills, strong critical-thinking skills, strong problem-solving skills, an adeptness at technology, a strong moral compass, a willingness to work hard, and a natural curiosity about world affairs and globalization, among other skills and traits—it is an increasingly important component, nonetheless. In particular, graduates and professionals with "Business 101" know-how are likely to (1) engender more effective communication and improved understanding between the organization and its stakeholders (because these professionals better understand the business context and setting); (2) get more buy-in from departments and leaders across the organization, thereby having a greater impact and elevating the role of communication; (3) command higher salaries and compensation; (4) have more opportunities for growth and career advancement; and (5) potentially have improved career satisfaction because of a better understanding of the "big picture."

First and foremost, communicators with backgrounds in "Business 101" have a better understanding of the business environment and its various drivers, which is critical for performing their jobs well (Dupont, 2013). Second, these communicators are more likely to gain the respect and buy-in of business managers (Duhé, 2013; Spangler, 2014). Communicators with a grasp of "Business 101" are better positioned to engender more effective communication and a mutual understanding between an organization and its stakeholders. It is difficult to make recommendations that are followed and to communicate effectively on behalf of a client, organization, or specific stakeholders, with only a limited knowledge of how an industry, sector, or the general business environment works (Ragas & Culp, 2013; Roush, 2006).

In many ways, a strategic communicator is increasingly expected to be a business professional first and a communication professional second (or is at least expected to maintain a balance between the two). "The role of a good communications executive or professional is that of a trusted advisor to management," says M. Erik Gonring, former manager of global government and public affairs for McDonald's Corporation. "You have to be on par or close to the level of knowledge held by that executive in order to be credible on any subject or recommendation you make. A working knowledge of the value drivers within a business or industry is critical to that credibility" (personal communication, August 28, 2014).

"Business 101" knowledge has distinct career benefits as well. Everyone likes to be sought after and to have more career growth opportunities. While money is not everything, it doesn't hurt to have the potential to be well compensated and have the opportunity one day to advise or sit with the top decision makers in an organization (or multiple organizations if one is working for an agency). According to the 2014 *PRWeek*/Bloom, Gross & Associates Salary Survey (Daniels, 2014), as shown on figure 1.1, the median salary for corporate communication professionals is $120,000, compared with $85,000 and $80,000 in agencies and nonprofit organizations, respectively (Daniels, 2013). According to this same survey, the median salary for assistant account executives, a junior-level early career position in the field, is $39,300 (Daniels, 2014).

Corporate communication professionals are often expected to demonstrate competence in business fundamentals. Of course, there are also

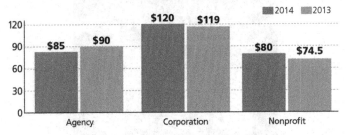

MEDIAN SALARY BY WORK ENVIRONMENT ($000s)

Figure 1.1   2014 *PRWeek*/Bloom, Gross & Associates salary survey: Median salary by work environment for communication professionals

Source: Courtesy of the PRWeek/Bloom, Gross & Associates salary survey.

individuals working inside agencies and nonprofit organizations who make more than their corporate counterparts do. After all, nonprofit organizations and government agencies also benefit from having communicators who bring a business mind-set to the table.

Well-run nonprofit organizations follow the same business principles adhered to by for-profit organizations, says LauraJane Hyde, president of Gilda's Club Chicago, one of the affiliates in the Cancer Support Community, a national organization for people living with cancer, their families, and their friends (personal communication, August 28, 2013). "The need for business basics [among communicators] translates cross-sector. The need in both the for- and non-profit sectors is equally great, and one could argue even greater in non-profits given their reliance on the generosity of others in order to deliver on their mission," Hyde says. "Skilled communicators in non-profits can deliver this message in a way that resonates with all constituencies."

Employers also generally pay more for communicators with a graduate education, particularly for those with a graduate degree that incorporates business knowledge. For example, as shown on figure 1.2, the 2013 *PRWeek*/Bloom, Gross & Associates Salary Survey finds that the median salaries for communicators with an MBA and communicators with a master's degree in public relations and strategic communication are $116,500 and $105,000, respectively, versus a median salary of $90,000 for those with an undergraduate degree. As Phil Carpenter, senior partner and manager of the West Coast offices at Allison+Partners told *PRWeek*: "In our industry, it's the exception rather than the rule to find people with formal business training. As the sector grows, though, it will become advantageous to have that kind of education" (Daniels, 2013, p. 37).

Our own survey of Arthur W. Page Society members finds that a resounding 93 percent of respondents believe that showing competence in "Business

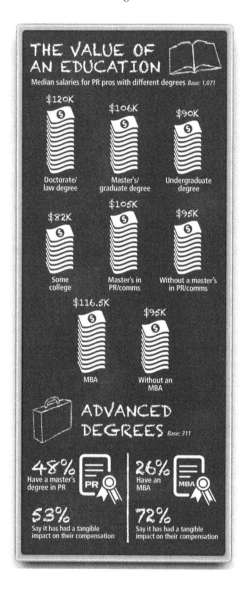

Figure 1.2 The value of an education

Source: Courtesy of the PRWeek/Bloom, Gross & Associates salary survey.

101" contributes to a communicator receiving higher compensation. As survey respondent Peter Marino, chief public affairs and communications officer for MillerCoors, remarks: "Providing communicators with a base understanding of business is critical for our future as a commercial relevant and impactful function" (personal communication, March 14, 2014).

In addition, many of the best-compensated and fastest-growing specializations within the strategic communication field tend to recruit those individuals with an interest in and understanding of business. Research generally finds that areas like investor relations, financial communication, reputation management, crisis communication, employee change and engagement, brand management, and legal communication are among the best paid (Bloom, 2011; Laskin, 2008; StevensGouldPincus LLC, 2012). Ironically, these same areas are often the hardest to fill because there are fewer candidates who have the necessary business know-how. All of the aforementioned areas also tend to be high profile, provide counsel to management, and draw the attention of other departments.

Finally, putting the organizational or stakeholder benefits and personal growth prospects aside, job satisfaction and fulfillment may also be higher in communication positions in which professionals are able to contribute at a strategic level and see how their work connects to the "bigger picture." Even if your goal is to be a specialist or coordinator (and you do not have a burning desire to climb the corporate or agency ladder), there is something to be said for having a better understanding of how the work you do contributes to the organization's overall mission and performance (Arthur W. Page Society, 2012, 2013a, 2013b). "Business 101" knowledge can serve many purposes.

To have a competitive edge, young communication professionals should approach the communication world as strategic thinkers, says Karen Bloom, principal of Bloom, Gross & Associates, a search firm specializing in the areas of marketing, marketing communication and public relations (personal communication, August 28, 2013). Bloom says this means developing business acumen. "There's been an evolution in the way communication pros are viewed. They're expected to be thought leaders and contribute to the process," Bloom says. "That happens best when the investment in education is made as early as possible in one's career and continues for the duration."

Ranking Desired "Business 101" Knowledge

In our national survey of Arthur W. Page Society members, we provided survey respondents with a list of "Business 101" topics and asked them to check off the three most important topics (and to suggest additional topics). It is worth noting that the majority (68 percent) of respondents had 25 years or more of communication industry experience, with the respondents split fairly evenly between those working in corporate (49 percent) and those working in agency (41 percent) positions. This senior group of professionals ranked the following topics as the five most important components of a business education for the strategic communication professional:

- Financial statement basics (75 percent)
- Financial terminology primer (70 percent)
- Communication's contribution to company strategy/goals/objectives (39 percent)
- U.S. Securities and Exchange Commission (SEC) and the communication requirements of public companies (34 percent)
- Corporate governance basics (21 percent)

See table 1.1 for a complete ranking of the various topics. As the findings above clearly indicate, senior communication professionals place a particularly high value on their junior- and midlevel colleagues having at least a basic knowledge of financial statements and reports and the "in's and out's" of financial terminology. Communicators should also be able to demonstrate how communication contributes to organizational strategy, goals, and objectives. Further, communicators should be conversant with the role of the SEC and the reporting and disclosure requirements for publicly held companies. Other topics also attract attention, including having a knowledge of corporate reputation management, corporate governance, stock market basics,

Table 1.1 Essential "Business 101" knowledge for strategic communicators

"Business 101" topics	Percentage (%)
Financial statement basics	74.8%
Financial terminology primer	69.6%
Communication's contribution to company strategy	39.1%
SEC and public company disclosure requirements	33.9%
Corporate governance basics	20.9%
Basics of the stock market and its various players	19.1%
Corporate reputation management basics	15.7%
Economic indicators primer	10.4%
Review of the major types of stakeholders	8.7%
Relationship of PR/advertising with corp. comm.	6.1%
Corporate social responsibility/sustainability basics	5.2%
Careers for communicators with business knowledge	3.5%
Major differences between public and private companies	3.5%
Employee compensation terminology	2.6%

Note: n = 116 respondents. Respondents were asked to "check off what you believe are the three most important topics to cover as part of a 'Business 101' for strategic communicators curriculum." The percentages represent these totals.

economy essentials, stakeholder identification and management, corporate social responsibility (CSR) and sustainability, and public relations and advertising linkages with corporate communication.

A review of the open-ended comments shows that additional topical areas identified by these senior communicators include program measurement and evaluation, corporate law, business models and business drivers, basic accounting, crisis management, executive counseling, business news and financial journalism, and globalization and international trade.

Building a Base of "Business 101" Knowledge

So how does a communicator go about gaining a solid foundation in the above topics? Well, you have already taken an important first step by picking up this book. The contents of this book were specifically designed with the feedback we received through the responses that senior communicators shared with us in our national survey; through our many conversations over the years with industry leaders, current and former students, and fellow educators; and through our own professional and teaching experiences. This is a book written primarily for current and aspiring strategic communication professionals. Anyone with a liberal arts or social sciences background who has not received formal training in business but who works for or with companies (or intends to do so one day) is likely to benefit from reading this book. Even those with such training may gain value from it.

While this book is a starting point, there are a variety of additional ways to build your business knowledge. First, broaden your news diet and, if you have not already done so, start regularly reading major business news publications like *The Wall Street Journal, Financial Times, Fortune, Forbes, The Economist*, the business sections of *The New York Times*, and your local newspaper or city business journal. Major news wires like Bloomberg News, Dow Jones News, Reuters News, and the Associated Press also produce high quality business journalism and are available online. The Yahoo! Finance website is a free way to access many of these quality news sources. Through reading about business, you will become more conversant in business concepts and terminology, and you will see how this world connects back to communication opportunities and trends for your organization or clients. Do not stop with reading business, though; sample adjacent areas like politics, health, science, and popular culture. Business obviously intersects with all of these areas, and a multisided, broad view is important.

If you are still in school or perhaps thinking of going back to college, take business classes. Introduction to marketing, management, finance, accounting and economics classes are all possibilities. If you are out of school, look for continuing and professional education offerings on topics like financial literacy for nonbusiness managers. Professional associations like the Public Relations Society of America (PRSA), the International Association of Business Communicators (IABC), the Arthur W. Page Society, the Business Marketing Association (BMA), the National Investor Relations Institute (NIRI), and the Financial Communications Society (FCS) offer relevant resources and training. Centers affiliated with universities like the Plank Center for Leadership in Public Relations at the University of Alabama, the Institute for Public Relations (IPR) at the University of Florida, the Arthur W. Page Center for Integrity in Public Communication at Pennsylvania State University, and the Strategic Communication and Public Relations Center at the University of Southern California Annenberg School also offer valuable programming and research.

Finally, look for someone who has a strong business mind that you respect and who has the heart of a teacher. Ideally, this person works or teaches in the communication field. Even if the person is outside that field, it is invaluable to have a sounding board for business-related topics. Gaining competency in business fundamentals is like learning any other subject. The more time you invest in stretching outside your comfort zone, the more proficient and confident you become. The payoff for you, your organization, your organization's stakeholders, and society is substantial.

Key Terms

Arthur W. Page Center
Arthur W. Page Society
Harold Burson
Business Marketing
    Association (BMA)
Business model
Commission on Public
    Relations Education
Council of Public Rela-
    tions Firms
Financial
    Communication
    Society (FCS)

Goal
Institute for Public
    Relations (IPR)
International Association
    of Business Commu-
    nicators (IABC)
Mission
National Investor Rela-
    tions Institute (NIRI)
Objectives
Plank Center for
    Leadership in Public
    Relations

Public Relations
    Society of America
    (PRSA)
Strategic communication
Strategic Communication
    and Public Relations
    Center
Strategy
U.S. Securities
    and Exchange
    Commission
    (SEC)
Vision

Discussion Questions

1. How far along do you feel we are in the third stage (i.e., the "what do we do?" stage) in the evolution of the strategic communication profession? Are we even in the third stage? What might the profession and field look like in another ten years?

2. Can you think of examples of situations in your own job (or a previous job) in which it is or would have been helpful to be conversant in "Business 101" concepts, language, and perspectives?

3. What do you think the future holds for strategic communication, public relations, and advertising graduates? What knowledge and skills will set candidates apart and help them make the greatest contribution to the organization and its stakeholders?

4. Do you want to counsel the organizational leadership or even become a member of the organizational leadership or the board of directors one day? Why or why not?

5. Do you agree with the benefits that the authors stated for communicators with "Business 101" knowledge? What other benefits do you see and why? What about the downside?

6. Besides the ideas shared by the authors, how else might strategic communicators gain a good grounding in the business fundamentals that are beneficial to their job and career?

PART II

*Foundational Business Knowledge
for Communicators*

CHAPTER 2

Economics and Economic Indicators

"It's the economy, stupid!"

This internal campaign slogan developed by Democratic political strategist James Carville helped propel Bill Clinton to his victory over incumbent George H. W. Bush in the 1992 U.S. presidential election (Clinton, 2004). At the time, the U.S. economy was mired in a recession, and the American public held a cautious economic outlook. Carville smartly realized that people often make decisions based largely on how they feel about the world around them. In this case, the economy was sluggish, and some blamed then-president Bush for being out of touch. Ultimately, a majority of voters believed that Clinton represented a change and a fresh start.

Similarly, businesspeople, organizations, and stakeholders make strategic decisions every day based—at least in part—on how they feel about the world around them, specifically, the health of the economy. When deciding to make investments and allocate resources, business managers look for signs that the economy is improving, holding steady, or declining (Constable & Wright, 2011). Organizations do not make these decisions in a vacuum because they know that their fortunes are interconnected with the decisions that current and prospective stakeholders, competitors, the government, and other organizations are making as well (Ragas, 2013a).

As part of their roles, communication professionals have long engaged in environmental scanning (Smith, 2013), which is monitoring the environment in which their organizations and clients operate for potentially influential issues, trends, and other factors. As such, to truly be a *strategic* asset to an organization, a strategic communication professional should incorporate their knowledge of the economy and their monitoring of relevant economic indicators into their communication activities and advice (Arthur W. Page Society, 2007; Cripps, 2013; Dupont, 2013).

Having likely studied economics and finance, many business professionals and managers pepper their conversations with references to economic concepts and the latest economic reports. Strategic communication professionals who are comfortable with this terminology, know how to interpret at least the major economic indicators, and understand what impact the indicators may have on the business environment or a particular industry are more valuable to their organizations and their stakeholders (Duhé, 2013; Ragas & Culp, 2013; J. Spangler, 2014).

"The movement of complex markets within which corporations operate is among the most important and challenging external factors in determining a company's performance," says Tom Davies, senior vice president of Kekst and Company Incorporated, a top strategic, corporate, and financial communication firm (personal communication, September 10, 2013). "I can't imagine attempting to craft a comprehensive communications plan to support a business strategy without understanding the critical impact the economy is having on current performance and future prospects. A company's stakeholders are certainly following economic developments so effective communicators must as well."

The Economy and Economics in a Nutshell

Organizations, both companies and nonprofits, compete each day in the marketplace for limited resources, including attracting and retaining high quality employees, securing or retaining investors, or generating word-of-mouth recommendations from satisfied customers. This marketplace, whether studied at an industry, local, regional, national or even global level, represents an economy—the aggregate sum of all goods and services produced among market participants (Wheelan, 2010). Economics is the study of the cause-and-effect relationships in an economy. Economists study the consequences of decisions that people make about the use of land, labor, capital, and other resources that go into producing the products and services that are bought and sold (Sowell, 2011). Macroeconomics is concerned with the economy as a whole, while microeconomics focuses on individual firms and households.

Much of classic economic theory is based on the assumption of rational decision making by the various participants in a market. However, people are not always fully rationale; they also make decisions in part on the basis of their emotions, feelings, and other factors. In recent years, the fields of behavioral finance and behavioral economics have grown in stature, both in academia and in the business world (Akerlof & Shiller, 2009; Shiller, 2005). People possess what John Maynard Keynes (2011) called "animal spirits"—noneconomic motives and feelings that influence their decisions.

This shouldn't come as a surprise to strategic communicators; we have long known that people at times make decisions based largely on their feelings and that outside factors like the news media, public relations, advertising, and social media can shape these feelings.

That being said, there are core economics concepts that haven't changed much over the years and that are as relevant as ever. For example, a touchstone concept underlying economics is that of supply and demand (Slavin, 1999). In a free market, supply and demand interact and influence the pricing of products and services. In short, when there is more supply than demand for a product or service, prices tend to go down, whereas when there is more demand than supply, prices generally go up. Take, for example, tickets to a major league baseball game. More people want to buy tickets to see a winning team in the heat of a pennant race, which drives up ticket prices, whereas there is less demand to see a losing team, even one as beloved as, say, the Chicago Cubs, which results in lower prices. At times, companies will even purposely release a limited amount of a product to try to generate buzz and higher prices. However, if market demand isn't there, prices will ultimately need to be reduced for the inventory to be sold.

Key Interconnected Economic Indicators

There is no shortage of economic indicators that are released by government agencies, associations, trade groups, private market research firms, and other organizations each month and even every week. However, some indicators are much more widely followed and more influential than are others.

Gross domestic product (GDP) is the most frequently used measure of a country's standard of living and general economic health (Slavin, 1999). GDP represents the market value of all goods and services produced within a country over a set time. Economies go through economic cycles, in which an industry or a country is either growing or declining. When an economy is growing, it is said to be "expanding"; when it is declining, it is said to be "contracting." U.S. GDP is measured and reported quarterly. If GDP is negative for two quarters in a row, an economy is officially in a recession. This was the case for the U.S. economy from December 2007 through June 2009, following the collapse of the real estate market and mortgage crisis (National Bureau of Economic Research, 2013). A particularly severe recession is known as a depression, the most infamous one being the decade following the stock market crash of 1929.

Although the U.S. economy remains the largest economy in the world, it is a developed, mature market, and in recent decades it has grown at a slower pace than many emerging economies, such as the so-called BRIC countries—Brazil, Russia, India and China. For example, U.S. GDP has grown at a 2–3 percent annual rate in recent decades, while China has averaged 9 percent annual growth over this same period (Trading Economics, 2013). Table 2.1 provides a ranking of the world's largest economies according to GDP data from the World Bank.

These faster-growing emerging economies, although more volatile, have become major new markets and growth opportunities for many North American and European companies, agencies, consulting firms, and nongovernmental organizations. For example, all of the leading international communication groups have operations in Brazil today, says Willer Velloso, planning director at Giacommeti Comunicação in São Paulo (personal communication, December 31, 2013). "Brazil has a stable democracy, no serious social upheavals, and no wars, plus it has an American-friendly business culture," Velloso says. "The prospects for the coming years are positive for economic growth, and, consequently, Brazil is part of most expansion plans of international companies."

Table 2.1 Ranking of the world's largest economies by GDP

Rank	Country	GDP (in billions USD)
1	United States	$16,800.0
2	China	$9,240.3
3	Japan	$4,901.5
4	Germany	$3,634.8
5	France	$2,735.0
6	United Kingdom	$2,522.3
7	Brazil	$2,245.7
8	Russian Federation	$2,096.8
9	Italy	$2,071.3
10	India	$1,877.0
11	Canada	$1,825.1
12	Australia	$1,560.6
13	Spain	$1,358.3
14	South Korea	$1,304.6
15	Mexico	$1,261.0
16	Indonesia	$868.3
17	Turkey	$820.2
18	The Netherlands	$800.2
19	Saudi Arabia	$248.3
20	Switzerland	$650.8

Note: Data are in current U.S. dollars. Dollar figures for GDP are converted from domestic currencies using single year official exchange rates.
Source: The World Bank Group (2014).

Another closely followed economic indicator is the employment report, also known as the jobs report or the jobs number (Constable & Wright, 2011; Slavin, 1999; Sowell, 2011). Each month, the U.S. Bureau of Labor Statistics releases the number of jobs added to or lost in the U.S. workforce in the prior month. The employment report shows specific sectors of the economy, such as professional services or leisure and hospitality, in which jobs were gained or lost. This report also includes the widely quoted unemployment rate, which measures the percentage of Americans who are currently looking for work and unemployed. Economists and investors on Wall Street estimate the monthly jobs figure in advance of its release, thereby setting expectations before the official results are released. A better than anticipated gain in jobs and a drop in the unemployment rate below the forecasted level are generally taken as positive signs by business people, while a weaker than expected jobs report is often viewed as a negative.

While the monthly employment report receives the most attention from the business world, there are two other employment indicators that also receive investor and media attention. Ahead of the employment report each month, giant payroll processing company ADP and ratings agency Moody's jointly release a jobs report based on private sector hiring by ADP customers. Finally, each week, the U.S. Department of Labor releases a report on initial jobless claims, which shows how many people have filed for unemployment benefits in the prior week. The week-to-week results tend to be volatile and generally receive less attention than do the monthly employment reports.

Business managers also keep tabs on inflation, or the rate at which prices rise for products and services. While it might seem that companies would actually like to see prices rise, more than a very modest increase in inflation is considered a bad thing for the economy. Inflation decreases the value of money and reduces its purchasing power, which is bad not just for consumers but for all stakeholders. In short, inflation means that a dollar buys *less* than it used to (Wheelan, 2010). Take box office receipts, for example. While *Avatar*, released in 2009, is the so-called highest grossing film of all time, with a gross of $2.78 billion, when that amount is adjusted for inflation (i.e., the steady increase in ticket prices over the decades), *Gone with the Wind*, released in 1939, actually surpasses it, having posted $3.3 billion in inflation-adjusted sales (Pincus-Roth, 2011).

The most widely followed measure of inflation is the consumer price index (CPI). Calculated by the U.S. Bureau of Labor Statistics, the monthly CPI is a measure of the average prices paid by urban consumers for a basket of goods and services, including everything from clothing and household goods to entertainment and housing (Wheelan, 2010). In the United States, an annual inflation rate of less than 2 percent is generally viewed as acceptable (Spicer,

2012). Most countries have their own version of the CPI and set inflation targets in an attempt to manage their economies. The opposite of inflation is deflation or falling prices, which can be even worse than inflation. Deflation leads to consumers delaying purchases and makes consumers feel poorer, as the value of their assets, such as home prices and real estate, fall. In short, business managers and financial-oriented stakeholders generally want to see steady prices for products and services.

Closely related to inflation and employment are interest rates. Interest rates are critical because this is the rate at which interest is paid by people to borrow money from lenders, such as banks. Interest rates affect the price and availability of credit to purchase cars, homes, and even other businesses (Slavin, 1999). Interest rates also impact the pricing of stocks, bonds, and other financial instruments. Generally speaking, low interest rates equal "cheap money" and promote economic growth, whereas high interest rates result in less lending demand and, in turn, reduced consumer purchases and lower economic growth. For the U.S. economy, the Federal Reserve, a government entity that is discussed in more detail later in this chapter, plays a leading role in influencing interest rates. The Federal Reserve sets the "federal (fed) funds rate" or the rate at which other banks lend to each other. Following the financial crisis of 2008, the Federal Reserve (Fed) aggressively lowered interest rates in an attempt to spark U.S. economic growth and reduce the effect of the recession.

In the United States, interest rates, while slowly rising, remain around historic lows. The fed funds rate, a gauge of short-term rates, stood at just 0.25 percent as of October 2014, compared with 5.25 percent before the financial crisis (Board of Governors of the Federal Reserve System, 2014). Interest rates and inflation tend to be inversely related; in other words, as interest rates decline, inflation tends to rise and vice versa (Wheelan, 2010). Higher interest rates tend to reduce inflation but also slow down economic growth, whereas lower interest rates could encourage inflation but also promote economic growth. Employment is, of course, related to economic growth. As the economy grows, more jobs are created, or conversely, as the economy declines, jobs are reduced or eliminated (Slavin, 1999; Sowell, 2011). As one can see, there is a tricky balancing act between interest rates, inflation, and employment. Business managers and other financial-oriented stakeholders regularly monitor these economic indicators for signs of where the economy is heading and for signs of how the actions of bankers and policymakers may impact their organizations.

Hard economic numbers are fine and good, but how does the economy actually affect how people *feel*? A popular measure of public opinion toward the economy is called consumer confidence (Sowell, 2011). In the United States, there are two primary indicators of consumer confidence: the consumer confidence index, produced by The Conference Board, and the Thomson Reuters/University of Michigan consumer sentiment index. Both consumer confidence measures are based on surveys of a representative sample of the American public. As the names imply, these surveys measure how confident or optimistic consumers feel about the overall state of the economy. Consumers often act how they feel. If they feel good about the economic outlook, they are likely to spend more, whereas if they feel cautious or negative, they are likely to spend less. Businesses use this information to adjust their production and investment on the basis of the notion that consumer confidence is predictive of future demand. As with other economic measures, like the employment report, economists estimate the monthly consumer confidence number in advance of its release. The actual number is then evaluated in relation to these forecasts.

Figure 2.1 provides a historical view of the Thomson Reuters/University of Michigan consumer sentiment index, with the shaded grey areas indicating periods in which the U.S. economy has gone into recession. As one can see, consumer sentiment and broad economic performance are generally linked. A limitation of both the Thomson Reuters/University of Michigan and The Conference Board indexes is that they are available only monthly, leaving large gaps between polling. A newer index called the Economic Confidence Index by Gallup tracks sentiment on a daily and weekly basis. It is worth noting that research (e.g., Blood & Phillips, 1997; Hester & Gibson, 2003; Ragas, 2013a, 2014a) finds that consumer confidence responds not just to prevailing real-world economic conditions but also to media reporting about the economy and stock market. As such, it is important to also monitor the

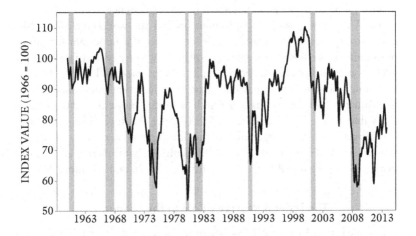

Figure 2.1 Historical view of U.S. consumer sentiment index

home pages of top media outlets like *The New York Times* and *The Wall Street Journal* to see how they are interpreting economic news.

In an increasingly interconnected, globalized world, it is not enough to simply track U.S. economic barometers. Much of the growth for public relations and advertising agencies, corporations, nongovernmental agencies, and other organizations has come—and will continue to come—from additional international expansion. All established and many emerging economies have available measures of employment, inflation, and consumer confidence. By working with colleagues and partners on the ground in markets in which the organization has a presence, communication professionals can learn which economic indicators are most credible, reliable, and meaningful for the organization as it sets and adapts its business strategy and goals in response to the environment.

Speaking of globalization, currency exchange rates are now relevant to not only international currency traders and business managers but also communication professionals. An exchange rate is the rate at which one currency is exchanged for another. In recent years, the U.S. dollar (USD) has been weak against other major currencies, like the euro (EUR) of the European Union (EU), an economic and political partnership between nearly 30 primarily European countries. For example, in recent years, every one EUR has been equal to at least USD $1.20 and as much as USD $1.50. While a weaker dollar means it is more expensive for U.S. tourists to visit Europe, it is not necessarily a bad thing for businesses that sell products in USD. In fact, when a currency is weaker relative to other currencies, that weakness promotes exports from the currency's home country (Glinton, 2011). Conversely, a weaker currency makes imports more expensive. Yahoo! Finance (http:// finance.yahoo.com) is a good free site for tracking currency rates.

For U.S. companies with operations around the world, including the major strategic communication agencies and firms, it is important for communication professionals to be able to explain how currency fluctuations may affect overall business results. For example, London-based WPP PLC, one of the world's largest communication agency holding companies, announced in February 2014 that it was lowering its financial projections due to currency fluctuations in some of its markets (Bender, 2014; K. Holton, 2014). More specifically, the strengthening of the British pound against currencies in fast-growing emerging markets for WPP like India, South Africa, and Brazil negatively impacted WPP's profit margins (Bender, 2014; K. Holton, 2014).

The Federal Reserve's Role in the Economy

Established in 1913 by the U.S. Congress, the Federal Reserve is the central bank of the United States, which gives it responsibility for setting the country's monetary policy (Board of Governors of the Federal Reserve System, 2005). In plain terms, this means that the Federal Reserve attempts to steer the U.S. economy forward. The policy of the Fed is guided by what is known as "a dual mandate"—to promote maximum employment (i.e., low unemployment) and stable prices (i.e., low inflation). The Federal Reserve has many tools at its disposal to try to speed up or slow down the economy, but the most visible is its impact on interest rates. As discussed earlier in this chapter, the Fed influences interest rates through adjusting the fed funds rate. The Federal Open Market Committee (FOMC), headed by the Fed chair, meets formally eight times per year to set policy, such as adjusting rates. The written statement issued by the FOMC following each meeting is closely followed by the markets. In recent years, the Fed has added quarterly news conferences to boost transparency (Di Leo, 2011).

The current chair of the Board of Governors of the Fed is economist Janet Yellen, who took office in 2014, becoming the first woman to hold this position. The Fed chair is widely regarded as the most powerful appointed official in the country, if not the world, as the United States remains the world's largest economy. The mere words of the Fed chair can impact global financial markets and the decisions of businesspeople (Hilsenrath, 2011; Sorkin, 2013). In fact, the use of public statements by the Fed and other policymakers to try to shape economic behavior even has its own name—jawboning.

Most countries or economic regions have central banks that perform a function that is similar to the Fed. This includes the People's Bank of China, the Bank of Japan, the Bank of England in the United Kingdom, the Bundesbank in Germany, and the European Central Bank, which oversees monetary policy for the European Union (EU). In the increasingly globalized world that we live in today, the policy changes and pronouncements of the central banks of the world's top economies are increasingly relevant, regardless of where an organization or client may be headquartered and have its operations.

In addition to the Federal Reserve, the U.S. stock market and businesspeople also closely follow comments made about the economy and about business policies by the president and the White House, as well as the heads of the executive departments of the federal government. Public statements by the secretary of the treasury about the dollar and international trade can be particularly influential. During the 2008–2009 bailout of Wall Street and of the Detroit auto companies, then–treasury secretary Hank Paulson and then–Fed chair Ben Bernanke were particularly visible. Finally, business executives and financial stakeholders also monitor public comments made by policymakers at the national and state level, as well as track proposed and pending legislation and regulations that could impact their industry and business environment.

Sorting Through Industry-Specific Indicators

There are literally dozens of different economic indicators that business managers, investors and other financial-oriented stakeholders use for detecting potential shifts in the business environment. In addition to some of the broad economic indicators we have reviewed in this chapter, there also are many economic indicators and market forecasts that are specific to certain sectors and industries. Whether you work or serve clients in the real estate, semiconductor, automotive, hospitality, or pharmaceutical industries, there are trade associations, private market research firms, investment banks, and other organizations that release specific forecasts and projections that are closely tracked by the professionals working in these fields.

For example, a strategic communication professional working in the real estate sector is likely well acquainted with the release schedule for statistics from the National Association of Realtors, while a communicator working in high-tech may follow the Semiconductor Industry Association's monthly reports on global semiconductor industry revenue. Michael Trevino, assistant vice president of external communications for Berkshire Hathaway's BNSF Railway, tracks a variety of general and industry-specific economic indicators as part of his job (personal communication, December 9, 2013). "I always know the current yield of the 10-year U.S. Treasury bond, where the unemployment rate stands in the United States, the price of a barrel of West Texas Intermediate crude oil, as well as the average rate my competitors are growing their revenue," Trevino says. "In retail, it's about knowing the performance of same-store sales. For airlines, you want to understand revenues and expenses on a seat-mile basis, and railroads care about velocity of freight movement, on-time performance and how long the freight sits at a terminal waiting to be moved."

Within the communication industry, there is no shortage of sources that generate industry forecasts. For the broad communication field, private equity firm Veronis Suhler Stevenson is well known for providing very detailed multiyear forecasts and research on the communication industry, down to specific sectors like mobile and digital spending. Strategic communication professionals, especially those working specifically in advertising, follow and react to the ad spending forecasts provided by firms like Zenith Optimedia, Nielsen, Kantar Media and eMarketer. Digital advertising–specific forecasts are provided by the Interactive Advertising Bureau. Private market research firms like Forrester Research, IDG, Gartner and comScore specialize in the information technology field, producing research that is increasingly relevant to strategic communicators. Finally, the leading professional associations for strategic communication, marketing, public relations, and advertising professionals are also rich sources of actionable market data. These associations include the Public Relations Society of America (PRSA), the International Association of Business Communicators (IABC), the Council of Public Relations Firms, the American Advertising Federation (AAF), the American Association of Advertising Agencies (4A's), and the American Marketing Association (AMA).

Putting It All Together

Learning about economics and learning how various economic indicators work and how they impact an organization and its stakeholders is like anything else—the more time you spend learning about it, the better you get, and the more these often-interconnected concepts become clearer. Economics has been derisively called "the dismal science" because many economists use arcane terminology to explain concepts that, in reality, are not nearly as complex as they might seem at first.

Concepts like supply and demand, economic cycles, inflation, the employment rate, interest rates, and consumer confidence get at the very heart of business and of how business managers decide to allocate their limited resources in a competitive marketplace to create value for stakeholders. Strategic communication professionals who understand core economics terminology are already ahead of the game when they step into a meeting with managers from other business units (Dupont, 2013). By following broad economic indicators, as well as industry-specific barometers, a strategic communication professional is able to anticipate in advance how business leaders are likely to set or adapt organizational strategy, goals, and objectives. Further, the strategic communication professional is better positioned to recommend appropriate communication programs that match the shifting business environment.

Finally, a good grasp of basic economics and of how to monitor the economic environment are just as important for managing interactions with other stakeholders (Duhé, 2013). The strategic communication function frequently serves as the interface and conduit between the organization and its stakeholders. By staying on top of economic and industry trends, a strategic communication professional is able to anticipate stakeholders' questions and concerns, whether they are reporters' questions about what the latest economic report might mean for a company or client's industry or are explanations to shareholders about how changes in the economic environment and a specific industry might impact the financial outlook for the company.

Ann Barkelew, the retired former vice president of corporate public relations for retailer Dayton Hudson Corporation (nka Target Corporation), says it is critical for strategic communicators to understand the economics of the industries in which they work and advise (personal communication, September 4, 2013). With this knowledge in hand, Barkelew says her team was able to educate journalists new to the retail beat. Further, Barkelew says this knowledge allowed her team to share reports with the company's executives in a language that resonated with them. Barkelew adds: "We weren't just corporate public relations people. We were retailers. We understood the business. We cared about the business. We took pride in the fact that we were making a difference."

Nonexecutive, internal stakeholders like frontline employees also want to know what the business environment means for them and the future of the organization. Strategic communicators who intimately know the economics of their business are able to explain the environment to employees. In short, these answers are frequently not as simple as "it's the economy, stupid," but the answer often has its roots in the prevailing economic backdrop.

Key Terms

Behavioral economics	Economics	Inflation
Consumer confidence	Economists	Interest rate
Consumer price index	Employment report	Jawboning
(CPI)	Environmental scanning	Macroeconomics
Currency exchange rate	Federal Reserve	Microeconomics
Deflation	Federal Open Market	Recession
Depression	Committee (FOMC)	Supply and demand
Economic cycle	Gross domestic product	Unemployment rate
Economy	(GDP)	

Discussion Questions

1. In your opinion, of the economic indicators covered in this chapter, what do you think is the most important indicator for a strategic communication professional to track? Why?
2. Review the business section of your local newspaper or a national newspaper like *The Wall Street Journal* or *The New York Times*. Which economic ideas and terms do you see mentioned in these articles? Which terms have you not seen before?
3. Run a Google News or Yahoo! News search for the term "Federal Reserve." How many news stories did you find? What economics topics and concepts are found in these stories? What might this news mean for organizations and communication professionals?
4. Besides using official indicators like the Thomson Reuters/University of Michigan consumer confidence index and The Conference Board consumer

sentiment index, how else might you determine the level of people's optimism about the economy and your particular industry or sector?

5. The leadership of your organization or client wants your opinion. Your primary market is experiencing rapid GDP growth with low inflation, high employment, and modest interest rates. How might this information influence your strategic communication efforts?

6. You work in strategic communication for an international hotel brand. What are the economic indicators that you would pay attention to for your industry? Why? Now change things and assume you work for an office supplies retailer with locations around the United States. What economic indicators would you pay attention to? Why?

CHAPTER 3

Finance and the Stock Market

Not much has changed from when the Beatles sang 50 years ago: "Money (That's What I Want)" (Bradford & Gordon, 1963). In a capitalist system, as found in many countries around the world today, money often still makes the world go round (Shiller, 2005). Ready access to money, more formally known as capital, is the essential lifeblood of any business, whether that organization is a multinational corporation, a young start-up company, a nongovernmental organization, or even a university.

With the possible exception of government, every organization needs to balance its revenue and expenses over time and at least figure out how to "break even"; otherwise, the organization will ultimately be forced into bankruptcy and may cease to exist. While all stakeholders are important, financial stakeholders, namely, investors, continue to hold outsized sway at most organizations since they control what organizations want and need—money (Goodman & Hirsch, 2010; Lev, 2012; Rawlins, 2006; van Riel & Fombrun, 2007). Without the support of such stakeholders, most organizational goals and objectives are unattainable.

For corporations, the stock market and its investors are an essential source of capital. Strategic communication can play an important role in an organization garnering and maintaining the support of the financial community, as well as other stakeholder groups concerned with company finances. However, many communication professionals have not taken courses in finance or investing, thereby making the stock market unfamiliar terrain (Ragas, 2013d). While communication professionals do not need to fully speak the language of a Wall Street analyst, if they want to have a strategic impact on financial matters across the organization and with all stakeholders, whether they are investors, employees, or regulators, then communication professionals do need to understand the basics of corporate finance, the stock market, and its various players.

Michael Trevino, assistant vice president of external communications for Berkshire Hathaway's BNSF Railway, says that several of the Fortune 500 CEOs he has worked for have previously served as chief financial officers (CFO) before getting promoted to the top jobs (personal communication, December 9, 2013). "Most all corporate leaders, especially those working for public companies, have a solid grasp of their company's financials and are measured based on how they are able to contribute to improved financial results," Trevino says. "If financial results intimidate you, then you're operating with one hand tied behind your back."

Corporate Finance and Making Money

The field of finance is essentially about the management of money. Corporate finance is specifically concerned with the raising and managing of funds (i.e., capital) to meet the goal of maximizing value for stakeholders (Stern & Chew, 2003). Priority is often given to shareholders since it is their capital that is at risk and for which companies compete (Appleby, 2010). There are several different ways that a company management team may go about raising capital and growing a business. These options include (1) reinvesting retained earnings, also known as retained profits, back into the operations of the business, (2) borrowing money from banks and other lenders to finance growth, (3) taking on debt by selling bonds to investors, or (4) selling stock in the company to investors. It is important to differentiate between stocks and bonds. When someone buys stock (i.e., equity) in a company, they actually become an owner, a shareholder, in the underlying business. On the other hand, a bond is a form of debt. When a company issues bonds, it is essentially borrowing money from investors at an agreed upon interest rate and must pay back the borrowed funds at an agreed upon date in the future.

Most large companies issue both stock and bonds as sources of financing. Often, large companies choose to list their stock on a stock exchange, which makes the shares in the company easier for investors to buy and sell. A public stock exchange listing also tends to reduce the company's cost of capital (Rosenbaum & Pearl, 2013), as investors are generally willing to pay more for stock in companies that are easier to trade, an idea known as liquidity (Amihud & Mendelson, 2006, 2012). Company chief financial officers (CFOs) and treasurers are eager to reduce a company's cost of capital because this helps improve the profitability of the business and provides for more opportunities for growth. As a general rule, larger companies tend to be publicly traded and listed on a stock exchange, whereas younger or smaller companies tend to be privately held and to not be listed on an exchange. However, there are exceptions. Very large, successful businesses like Cargill, Koch Industries, Mars, SC Johnson, Meijer, Aramark and Fidelity Investments choose to remain private and closely held, meaning they typically have fewer total shareholders than their publicly traded counterparts do (A. Murphy, 2012).

Table 3.1 outlines some of the major differences between public and private companies. Simply stated, from a communication perspective, private companies may choose to disclose limited information about the inner workings of their business and financial performance, whereas public companies must file quarterly and annual reports with the U.S. Securities and Exchange Commission (SEC) and provide audited annual financial statements (Gentry, 2011). In short, because of these reporting requirements, public companies are held to a higher level of transparency.

Stock Exchanges and Stock Listings

There are two major stock exchanges in the United States today: the New York Stock Exchange (NYSE) and the NASDAQ, both of which are located in New York, the world's financial capital. Intercontinental Exchange Group Inc., based in Atlanta, acquired the parent company of the NYSE for $8 billion in December 2012. The NYSE, also known as the "Big Board," is much older than the NASDAQ and remains the larger of the two exchanges, having been established in 1817. The NASDAQ was founded in 1971 and for many years was known as the preferred stock exchange for technology and younger growth companies. As of year-end 2013, there were approximately five thousand companies listed on major U.S. exchanges (Strumpf, 2014). In addition to the NYSE and the NASDAQ, there are hundreds of typically higher risk firms that are traded on the less regulated over-the-counter (OTC) bulletin board and pink sheets. A rise in the costs associated with public companies

Table 3.1 Differences between public and private companies

Private company	Public company
• Small number of shareholders	• Larger number of shareholders
• Not listed on a stock exchange	• Listed on a stock exchange
• Lower liquidity (hard to buy/sell shares)	• Higher liquidity (easier to buy/sell shares)
• More limited access to more expensive capital	• Broader access to less expensive capital
• Limited information flow—can be more secretive	• Reporting requirements of SEC and stock exchanges—higher information flow

complying with securities laws has contributed to an overall decline in the number of publicly-traded companies in the U.S. markets (Krantz, 2013; Lucchetti, 2011).

A stock exchange provides a market for investors to purchase and sell shares of stock in a company. In many ways, a stock exchange is like eBay, in that it matches up buyers and sellers in order to get the best price on a particular item. In this case, the items for sale five days a week, Monday through Friday (9:30 a.m. EST–4:00 p.m. EST), except for major holidays, are shares of stock in thousands of America's most well-known companies, ranging from Apple to Xerox. Financial professionals known as designated market makers (previously called specialists) ensure the orderly buying and selling of company shares during market hours. The traders gesturing on the iconic trading floor of the NYSE around market maker posts near the center of the room are engaging in "open outcry" trading. However, approximately 80 percent of the trading volume on the NYSE today is conducted electronically via computerized systems (Strasburg & Das, 2012). The NASDAQ has always been an electronic-only market.

Although New York is the center of the stock market in the United States, Chicago, the home of the Chicago Board of Trade, the Chicago Mercantile Exchange, and the Chicago Board Options Exchange, is the hub for the trading of complex financial instruments like futures and options. A futures contract is a standardized agreement that requires the delivery of an asset, such as a physical commodity, of a specified quantity at a specified future date and price. Conversely, an option is a contract that offers the buyer the right—but not the obligation—to buy ("call") or sell ("put") a security at a specified future date and price during a certain time period.

Initial Public Offerings and "Going Public"

An initial public offering (IPO) is a high profile, seminal event in a company's history. Strategic communication is front-and-center throughout the IPO process (Sherk, 2004). An IPO marks the first time that a corporation sells stock to the public and that the corporation's shares are listed on a stock exchange, either the NYSE or the NASDAQ (if it is a U.S.-based IPO). Companies choose to conduct an IPO and "go public" for a variety of reasons: (1) to raise capital to grow the business, (2) to reward early investors, founders, and company employees by providing them with a way to sell shares, (3) to incentivize management and employees through the issuance of stock options exercisable for shares in the public company, (4) to have a stock "currency" that may be used for future acquisitions, and (5) to raise the company's profile with current and prospective stakeholders.

While the actual IPO takes place on just one trading day, it is the culmination of an elaborate process that is up to several years in the planning (Ernst & Young, 2012). To initiate the IPO process, a company hires an investment bank, such as Goldman Sachs, Morgan Stanley, or JPMorgan Chase & Co., to estimate the value of the company and assess the interest in its stock. In conjunction with the investment bank, which serves as the underwriter, the company files an initial S-1 registration statement, called a prospectus, with the SEC if the IPO is a U.S. offering or with the comparable securities regulator in another country if the IPO is a non-U.S. deal.

As part of the Jumpstart Our Business Startups (JOBS) Act of 2012, U.S. companies with less than $1 billion in annual revenue are now allowed to confidentially file the initial prospectus if they so choose. This has the benefit of giving a company more time to work out its plan to go public before disclosing its financials and other details to the public (M. Murphy, 2014). It can take up to six months for the SEC to review a firm's prospectus, ask for changes, and ultimately approve it (Krantz, 2006). The prospectus document is crafted by a team of lawyers, accountants, investment bankers, and investor relations professionals; it outlines the company's operations and past financial performance, the risks the company faces, and what the company intends to do with any funds from the offering.

Investor relations professionals have more specialized knowledge of the financial markets and securities regulations than more general interest strategic communication professionals do, says Steve Collins, former executive vice president and chief financial officer (CFO) of ExactTarget (personal communication, August 19, 2013). "In the lead up to the IPO, investor relations works extensively with accounting and finance to craft the S-1," says Collins, who helped lead the IPO process at ExactTarget, which was later acquired by Salesforce.com Inc. "Accounting typically takes the lead on the MD&A (management discussion and analysis) section of the S-1, while finance and IR take more of a lead in describing the company's business, industry sector, competitors and strategy."

Once a company has filed its prospectus, it has entered what is known as its "quiet period." As mandated by U.S. federal securities laws, a prepublic company is not allowed to selectively share information with stakeholders, which could change investors' opinions of the company's stock value (U.S. SEC, 2011). The point of this rule is to prevent companies from hyping their stock. Strategic communicators and other representatives of the company must be especially careful to not make forward-looking statements about the company or comment specifically on the offering (Weise, 2012). So as to have a balanced playing field, the SEC requires that all information about a company's investment prospects and outlook be filed with the SEC via the

Electronic Data Gathering, Analysis, and Retrieval (EDGAR) system, a freely available and searchable online disclosure system. The quiet period generally extends for 40 days after the IPO, at which time the company can once again speak more freely. The quiet period rule can be tricky; well-known companies like Google, Salesforce.com, and Groupon were all investigated for possible inadvertent quiet period violations ahead of their IPOs (Berr, 2012).

In the lead up to an IPO, a company's management team goes on what is called a road show with its underwriters (Ritter & Welch, 2002). The road show consists of a series of meetings in major cities with large prospective shareholders, such as professional money managers. Some of these meetings may also be conducted virtually. Communication professionals are often tasked with helping to prepare the presentation slides, helping to prepare the management team for likely questions, and helping to coordinate the travel schedules. Company management must be careful at these meetings to share only information that has already been made available in the company's prospectus and in the supplemental information filed with the SEC's EDGAR system. On the actual day of the IPO, company management, along with advisors such as communication professionals, often celebrate by ringing the opening bell of the exchange on which the firm has decided to list its shares (Mitchell & Fitzpatrick, 2013). If the IPO is particularly well received, a company may decide down the line to conduct a secondary offering, also called a follow-on offering, in which it sells additional shares to the public.

The opposite of "going public" is "going private." If a publicly traded company is facing operating difficulties or other business challenges, it may find it beneficial to fix its operations beyond the glare of the public markets and shareholders' inclination toward short-term performance. In this case, an investor group, often in conjunction with company management, may decide to acquire the firm and buy out the stock held by public market shareholders. Typically, the purchase is financed partially with debt in what has traditionally been known as a leveraged buyout (LBO). Well-known companies like Dell, Harrah's Entertainment, Hilton, and HJ Heinz have all been the subject of going private transactions (Bobkoff, 2013; Thomson Reuters, 2013). During an LBO, a key role of the corporate communication professional is to persuade shareholders that they are receiving a fair price for their shares and that they should support the proposed transaction.

After having "gone private" and restructured its operations over a period of several years, a company's management and investors may then decide that it would be beneficial to rejoin the public markets. For example, Hilton World-wide Holdings Inc. was taken private by Blackstone Group LP in an approximately $25 billion debt and equity transaction in 2007 (Jarzemsky, 2013).

In December 2013, after restructuring its debt and refining its franchising model, Hilton returned to the public markets by raising $2.35 billion in a record IPO for a hotel operator. At the IPO price of $20 a share, the entire company, when factoring in outstanding debt, was valued at approximately $31 billion, generating a substantial profit for Blackstone (Jarzemsky, 2013).

The Financial Community and Wall Street

Quite a cast of characters make up the financial community, which is commonly referred to in the U.S. financial markets as "Wall Street" (or simply "the street") since this street is the location, in lower Manhattan, of the NYSE and many investment firms. Although most communication professionals are not likely to interact with *all* of the players who make up the financial community, it is still helpful to understand both the names of the players and what they do.

"In preparing external communications, companies rely on internal expertise residing in their corporate communications, investor relations and corporate governance teams," explains Patrick Tracey, senior vice president of business development for Georgeson, a Computershare company and a top provider of strategic shareholder consulting services (personal communication, April 7, 2014). "In certain cases, they may seek out advice and obtain services from additional outside providers to augment their efforts." Tracey says this may include corporate and investor relations advisory firms, graphics design companies, proxy solicitors, investment banks, and firms that specialize in regulatory disclosure.

References to these and other financial players may emerge in company news coverage, annual reports, shareholder meetings, employee town halls, memos, and even day-to-day informal communication with employees, suppliers, and other stakeholder groups. With strategic communication serving as the interface and boundary spanner between the organization and its stakeholders, having a better grasp of the stock market's players can contribute to more effective overall organizational communication (Burton, Grates, & Learch, 2013; Cripps, 2013; J. Spangler, 2014).

Investor Relations

Most public companies have an investor relations department. Offering a mix of finance, legal, and communication expertise, an investor relations professional serves as the point person when it comes to communication with the street. Investor relations focuses on relationship building directly with institutional investors and analysts (Laskin, 2009, 2011).

Investment Banks

As discussed earlier, investment bankers are hired to help take companies public and advise them on financial matters such as reviews of strategic alternatives. This could include everything from selling a division of a company to buying another firm. Top investment banking firms include Bank of America, Merrill Lynch, Citi, Credit Suisse, Deutsche Bank, Goldman Sachs, JPMorgan Chase, Morgan Stanley, and William Blair (*Financial Times*, 2013).

Corporate Law Firms

In addition to investment bankers, public companies typically work with outside corporate law firms, which provide counsel on legal and strategic matters. They may recommend outside strategic communication firms to hire. Top corporate law firms include Baker & McKenzie; Cravath, Swaine & Moore; Jones Day; Kirkland & Ellis; Mayer Brown; Sidley Austin; Skadden, Arps, Slate, Meager & Flom; Sullivan & Cromwell; and Watchtell, Lipton, Rosen & Katz (Corporate Board Member, 2012).

Regulators

In the U.S. market, the SEC regulates the stock market at the federal level. However, each state also has its own securities regulator. The SEC also collaborates with the U.S. Department of Justice on some investigations. Finally, The Financial Industry Regulatory Authority (FINRA) self-regulates member brokerage firms and exchange markets.

Corporate Communication

In smaller public companies, the general corporate communication or corporate affairs functions may also be responsible for investor relations. Even in large public companies, corporate affairs professionals are typically the first point of contact for financial journalists and often work closely with their colleagues in investor relations.

Financial Communication Firms

Public companies often hire outside financial communication advisors to counsel them on major corporate issues like restructurings, bankruptcies, crises, shareholder activism, IPOs, and mergers and acquisitions. Top firms in this specialized area include Abernathy MacGregor Group; Brunswick Group; FTI Consulting (formerly Financial Dynamics); ICR; Joele Frank,

Wilkinson Brimmer Katcher; Kekst and Company; Finsbury; and Sard Verbinnen & Co (Holmes Report, 2013).

Institutional and Individual Investors

Institutional investors are large professional investors, such as mutual funds, hedge funds, pension funds and endowments, which typically buy large blocks of stock. *Individual* investors are smaller, private investors who tend to buy smaller amounts of stock at a time. Institutional investors today own on average more than 70 percent of the stock in the top one thousand largest U.S. corporations (Tonello & Rabimov, 2010).

Venture Capital Firms

These professional investors provide equity capital to young, fast-growing, emerging private companies. Venture capitalists hope the start-up companies they invest in will grow into larger companies that will ultimately conduct an IPO or be acquired. Well-known venture capital firms include Accel Partners, Andreessen Horowitz, Benchmark, Kleiner Perkins Caufield & Byers, New Enterprise Associates, and Sequoia Capital (Geron, 2013).

Private Equity Firms

While venture capital firms concentrate on investing in start-up companies, private equity firms tend to invest in older, more established companies. Investing using a mix of debt and equity, private equity firms ultimately hope to generate a return on their investment through either having the stock sold in an IPO or having the business acquired. Top private equity firms include Bain Capital, The Blackstone Group, The Carlyle Group, GTCR, Kohlberg Kravis Roberts, Madison Dearborn Partners, TPG Capital, and Warburg Pincus (Private Equity International, 2013).

Information Intermediaries

While investors do their own research, they also rely on the expertise and opinions of information intermediaries, such as Wall Street analysts and financial journalists, when deciding to buy, hold, or sell their stock in companies (Golz, Zivin, & Spero, 2012). Wall Street analysts are employed by brokerage firms (known as the "sell side"). They publish investment research recommendations, which are read by institutional investors (known as the "buy side"). The goal is for this research to generate trading commissions for the brokerage firms. Individual investors typically have only limited access or no access to Wall Street analyst reports. Therefore, smaller investors are more influenced by financial media reporting.

Proxy Solicitors

Every year, shareholders in public companies vote on corporate matters such as electing the board of directors and deciding for or against company- or shareholder-submitted proposals. Proxy solicitors are specialized communication and research firms that are hired by company management or by a dissatisfied shareholder group to persuade shareholders to vote for or against ballot issues and to project voting outcomes. In the U.S. market, the top proxy solicitors include AST Phoenix Advisors, D. F. King & Co., Georgeson, Innisfree M&A Incorporated, MacKenzie Partners, Morrow & Co., and Okapi Partners (Stewart, 2010). Proxy solicitors are discussed more in chapter 7, which is about corporate governance.

Proxy Advisers

Many institutional investors turn to specialized investment research firms known as proxy advisers to advise them on how to vote their stock holdings on company ballot issues, such as board of director elections, corporate transactions, or shareholder proposals. In the U.S. market, the two top proxy advisers are Institutional Shareholder Services (ISS) and Glass Lewis. Public companies actively court the support of proxy advisers (Lublin & Grind, 2013). Proxy advisers are discussed more in chapter 7, which is about corporate governance.

Barometers of Company and Stock Market Performance

The United States is the home to the world's two largest stock exchanges–the NYSE and the NASDAQ. See table 3.2 for a list of the world's ten largest equity markets ranked by the combined market values of the companies listed on each exchange. Investors, business managers, and other financial-oriented stakeholders monitor the performance of a stock market by tracking a stock index. A stock index comprises a collection of stocks and tracks the overall change in price of the stocks that make up the index. In the United States, the most famous stock index is the Dow Jones Industrial Average (DJIA), also known as simply "the Dow." The Dow index is a collection of the stocks of 30 very large, well-known "blue chip" U.S. corporations. The companies that make up the Dow represent a microcosm of the components of the overall U.S. economy. The Dow includes retailers like Wal-Mart and The Home

Depot, energy companies like Exxon Mobil and Chevron, and manufacturers like Caterpillar and Boeing. The change in the price of the Dow each day is widely covered by the general news media (Schnurr, 2013).

There are many other indexes that investors, business managers, and financial stakeholders interested in the U.S. markets track. Perhaps the three most well-known are the Standard & Poor's 500 (S&P 500), the NASDAQ Composite, and the Russell 2000. The S&P 500 index is based on the performance of five hundred large capitalization or "large cap" U.S. firms as selected by Standard & Poor's. The NASDAQ Composite, on the other hand, is an index comprising the approximately three thousand firms listed on the NASDAQ stock exchange. Finally, the Russell 2000 is an index of two thousand smaller capitalization or "small cap" U.S. companies.

As shown in table 3.2, the U.S. stock market is far from the only game in town. Europe is the home of several top exchanges and, because of increasing globalization, stock markets in Asia and Latin America have grown rapidly in recent years. As within the U.S. market, each of these international markets has one or more stock market indexes that are tracked by global investors and managers at multinational corporations. For example, major international indexes include the FTSE 100 in the United Kingdom, the Deutscher Aktien Index (DAX) in Germany, the CAC 40 in France, the Nikkei 225 in Japan, the Hang Seng in Hong Kong, the Straits Times index in Singapore, and the Bovespa in Brazil. The performance of a stock market is generally viewed as a leading indicator of the health of a country's economy, and that indicator has an impact on business decisions and the allocation of capital.

Stock indexes are good for getting a big picture view of how a stock market and, more indirectly, an economy are performing. The most visible and

Table 3.2 Ranking of the world's largest equity markets by market capitalization

Rank	Exchange	Market capitalization (in billions USD)
1	NYSE Euronext (U.S.)	$17,950
2	NASDAQ OMX (U.S.)	$6,085
3	Japan Exchange Group (Japan)	$4,543
4	London Stock Exchange Group (U.K.)	$4,429
5	NYSE Euronext (Europe)	$3,584
6	Hong Kong Exchanges (China)	$3,101
7	Shanghai SE (China)	$2,497
8	TMX Group (Canada)	$2,114
9	Deutsche Bourse (Germany)	$1,936
10	SIX Swiss Exchange (Switzerland)	$1,541

Note: Data are based on largest domestic equity market capitalizations at year-end 2013.
Source: World federation of exchanges (2014).

direct way to track the actual market performance of a specific public company is to monitor the change in its stock price. The stock price, also called the company share price, serves as a day-by-day gauge of how shareholders collectively feel about the company's current and future financial prospects. Generally speaking, the better investors feel about the future of the company, the more they will be willing to pay for its shares and the higher the stock price. Conversely, the less positive that investors feel about the company's prospects, the less they will generally pay and the lower the price.

Over the longer term, the company's stock price tracks underlying company financial performance, such as increases or decreases in profitability, but over the short term, the company's stock price and actual financial performance may not fully align. Company news, rumors, the overall economy, and other factors may play a larger role. As famous investor Warren Buffett has been quoted as saying about the stock market: "in the short run, the market is a voting machine and sometimes people vote very unintelligently. In the long run, it's a weighing machine and the weight of business and how it does is what affects value over time" (CNNMoney.com, 2002, para. 5).

Simply looking at the price change in an individual company's stock by itself can be misleading. It is more instructive to look at the performance of a company's share price in relation to the overall stock market and/or its peer group (i.e., the other public companies in its industry or sector). For example, the stock prices of Southwest Airlines and JetBlue Airways increased approximately 114 percent and 18 percent, respectively, during the five-year period that ended in 2013. During this same time period, the NYSE Arca Airline Index, an index that measures the performance of passenger airline stocks as a whole, rose approximately 175 percent, and the S&P 500, a broad measure of large U.S. stocks, increased nearly 100 percent. These comparisons show that, on a relative basis, while Southwest handily outperformed JetBlue, both companies underperformed relative to the airline sector as a whole. JetBlue also underperformed, compared with the broader stock market, while Southwest did slightly better (114 percent versus 100 percent). It is important for strategic communication professionals to put stock price performance in its proper context.

The Stock Market Matters for Strategic Communicators

Whether it is called money or capital, every business competes for it, and the stock market and the financial community is often at the center of this money hunt. Unfortunately, some communication professionals do not feel comfortable discussing the stock market and corporate finance. This is regrettable because it is hard to develop effective communication strategies and tactics for financial-oriented stakeholders and counsel business managers regarding policy in this important area if one does not take the time to understand finance and the stock market.

Tom Davies, senior vice president of Kekst and Company Incorporated, a leading strategic, corporate, and financial communication firm, says that finance and stock market terminology are simply "part of the basic vocabulary of business" (personal communication, September 13, 2013). "Communicators must understand these critical elements for virtually any corporate communications project," Davies says. "Other executives in business or leadership roles at the companies of which they are a part certainly do understand them, and communicators' effectiveness will be based on their ability to engage and convince their colleagues of the merits of their position."

Similarly, it is difficult for a communicator to interpret and translate company financial news into plain English for the nonfinancial stakeholders of an organization if the communication professional does not possess a base level of understanding about finance and the stock market.

The world has gotten smaller and the audiences that strategic communicators reach has become larger, says Matthew Sherman, president of Joele Frank, Wilkinson Brimmer Katcher, a top strategic communication advisor (personal communication, October 5, 2013). "Gone are the days when speaking to a trade magazine meant that you were just reaching your customers. Likewise, it is not just investors anymore who read *The Wall Street Journal* or watch CNBC," Sherman says. "Your customers, employees, and partners may understand that your company is a publicly traded company and they may understand that your company's market capitalization and stock price can influence business outcomes; shouldn't you as a communicator have this understanding as well?"

In short, communication professionals, particularly those working in corporate settings, risk marginalizing themselves and limiting their opportunities to contribute at a truly strategic level if they choose to ignore the stock market and the financial community. This one chapter alone does not make you an expert on the world of corporate finance, the stock market, and its players. We hope, though, that it does spark your interest in learning more on this topic and that you then bring this knowledge to the table the next time a financial communication issue arises.

Key Terms

Capital	Corporate finance	Dow Jones Industrial
Cost of capital	Debt	Average (DJIA)

EDGAR	Liquidity	Road show
Equity	Market maker	Russell 2000
Individual investor	NASDAQ	Secondary offering
Information intermediary	New York Stock	Standard & Poor's 500
Initial public offering	Exchange	(S&P 500)
(IPO)	Over the counter (OTC)	Stock exchange
Investment bank	Public company	Stock index
Investor relations	Private company	Stock options
Institutional investor	Private equity firm	U.S. Securities &
Jumpstart Our Business	Prospectus	Exchange
Startups (JOBS) Act	Proxy adviser	Commission (SEC)
of 2012	Proxy solicitor	Venture capital firms
Leveraged buyout (LBO)	Quiet period	Wall Street

Discussion Questions

1. Think of three of your favorite companies. Now visit Yahoo! Finance and type in each of their names into the search box. Are they publicly traded or private? If they are public, how has their stock price performed over the past year? Is this what you expected?

2. Visit the corporate home pages of these same three companies. If they are public, click on the investor relations link on their websites. What sort of information do you find in the investor relations section? If you were a financial stakeholder in this company, would you be happy with the quality of the information provided?

3. Visit Google News, Yahoo! News or another online news source and type in the term "IPO." What kind of news stories come up? What companies have gone public recently or are in the process of going public? Are you familiar with these companies?

4. Turn on a financial news cable channel (CNBC, FOX Business, Bloomberg) or watch the evening news. What stock market terminology and financial players did you see mentioned during the broadcast? What terms and concepts mentioned were new to you?

5. Out of the various financial players profiled in this chapter, which type of player do you think is the most important to a publicly traded company? Why? Explain your reasoning.

6. Do you think financial stakeholders like shareholders have too much influence and power at many publicly traded corporations? Why or why not? Explain your reasoning.

CHAPTER 4

Accounting and Financial Statements

Accounting has often been called the language of business (Piper, 2013). Through the debits and credits, revenues and expenses, and assets and liabilities found on financial statements, companies communicate to stakeholders the financial health of the organization and the progress it is making in achieving its financial-oriented goals and objectives (Botan, 2006; Coombs & Holladay, 2010; Hallahan, Holtzhausen, van Ruler, Vercic, & Srirmesh, 2007; Smith, 2012).

Public company accounting, finance, and legal professionals, often working in conjunction with communication professionals, prepare and release financial statements to the public a minimum of four times a year. These statements serve as a kind of quarterly performance scorecard for the organization and its management team (Gentry, 2011; Taparia, 2004). Whether the stakeholders are shareholders, creditors, frontline employees, suppliers, or community organizers, virtually all stakeholders have some level of interest in understanding the financial health of the organization with which they have a relationship. This is not just a public company issue. Private companies and nonprofit organizations may choose to release less detailed financials and may do so less frequently, but some level of financial information is still likely to be shared with the public. This means there is still a need for the strategic communicator to understand and be able to interpret this information in plain language for the organization's stakeholders (Claussen, 2008).

Accounting terminology and financial statements are topics that make some strategic communicators uncomfortable and put those communicators outside of their comfort zones. This is understandable to some extent, as accounting and finance are topics that have traditionally received limited attention in universities' communication curriculums and continuing education programs for communicators (Ragas & Culp, 2013). Further, some communicators think they have a built-in aversion to numbers (Roush, 2006). This idea is unfortunate because this risks limiting the role of the communication function in interpreting financial information and in engendering mutual understanding between the organization and the stakeholders on financial topics, as well as in participating in financial decisions and strategy (J. Spangler, 2014).

As our survey of senior communication professionals in chapter 1 found, knowledge of financial statements and financial terminology were viewed as the top two most important components of "Business 101" knowledge for successful strategic communicators. According to Michael Buckley, vice president of global business communication for Facebook Inc., financial statements serve as the "scorecard for achieving business objectives" (personal communication, December 9, 2013).

"Absolutely all practitioners should take the time to understand corporate finance. It is the language of business," says Buckley, previously the U.S. managing partner at Brunswick Group LLC, a top international corporate communication partnership (M. Buckley, personal communication, December 9, 2013). "It is what boards and investors pay attention to. It is ultimately how public companies are judged. And it should be one part of how all communicators think about the impact they can have on their organization. Building a brand or reputation must ultimately have value among a set of broader business objectives."

Learning how to read a financial statement also has the added benefit of preparing the communicator for managerial positions and growth opportunities. Just like professionals in other departments, strategic communication professionals are expected to prepare and manage budgets (Roush, 2006). A communicator who knows his or her way around a financial statement is better positioned to contribute at budget meetings and to earn more budgetary responsibility. In short, with accounting a leading language of business, whether that "business" takes place in a major corporation or a nongovernmental organization, knowledge of financial statements is likely to open new doors (Kolberg, 2014; J. Spangler, 2014).

Quarterly Financial Reporting

A public company is required by the U.S. Securities and Exchange Commission (SEC) and the stock exchange upon which its shares are listed to report its financial performance every three months (i.e., quarterly). This is known as a quarterly earnings report (Gentry, 2011). First quarter earnings are referred to as Q1, second quarter earnings are referred to as Q2, and so on. These quarterly reports typically attract stakeholder attention, and the corporate communication function (and sometimes an outside agency or consultant) is front and center in preparing and communicating these quarterly results. If a company doesn't report its quarterly financial results in a timely manner, its stock can be delisted (removed) from the stock exchange, and the company can face other actions. Many companies use the calendar year as their fiscal year (i.e., January 1—December 31), but companies in some industries, such as retail, may choose a fiscal year that better fits seasonality patterns (Quinn, 2010). For example, the fiscal year for Macy's Inc. (NYSE: M) closes each year at the end of January or the start of February, so as to fully incorporate the holiday shopping season, which represents its more natural "end of the year."

There are several key players that set the standards for public company reporting of financial results and provide oversight into this process. The SEC grants authority to the Financial Accounting Standards Board (FASB), an independent private organization, to set the standards used in U.S. financial reporting and accounting (Taparia, 2004). These rules set by FASB are known as Generally Accepted Accounting Principles (GAAP). Outside the United States, the International Accounting Standards Board (IASB) is responsible for developing the International Financial Reporting Standards (IFRS). Public companies are required to file their GAAP-compliant quarterly financial statements with the SEC's EDGAR online system, where these filings are then freely available for review by the public. The vast majority of companies also choose to release these financials through an earnings news release, in which management attempts to contextualize the results and provide supplemental information (Ragas, 2010).

Types of Financial Statements

Financial statements are a snapshot-in-time look into a company's business model (Lev, 2012)—essentially the drivers behind how it tries to make money and whether it has been successful in doing so. While many public companies choose to release additional supplemental financial and nonfinancial information as part of their disclosures, there are three major types of financial statements that all public companies are required to release on a quarterly basis:

1. **Income statement:** This statement, also known as a profit and loss statement or "P&L," tracks what a company made or lost and spent over a period in time.
2. **Balance sheet:** This statement tracks a company's assets, liabilities, and net worth; it essentially summarizes what a company owns and owes at this point in time.

3. **Cash flow statement:** This statement literally "follows the money." It shows the amount of cash generated or spent by a company in its course of business over a period in time.

For nonfinancial professionals, it is arguably most important to understand the basics of income statements and balance sheets, as these are the two types of statements that communicators are most likely to encounter in their jobs and in the press. Therefore, this chapter goes more in depth into income statements and balance sheets.

The financial disclosure document that a public company files with the SEC's EDGAR system for the first three quarters of its fiscal year is known as a 10-Q or, simply, a "Q" (Leder, 2003). These quarterly filings provide the company's quarterly financial performance for the prior year as a source of comparison. Once per year, for its fiscal fourth quarter (i.e., year-end), a public company will file a more detailed document known as a 10-K filing or "K" (Leder, 2003). This document discloses the financial performance not only for the past quarter but also for the full fiscal year. Again, the financials for the prior quarter and year are provided as reference points. The 10-K document provides the basis for the more broadly disseminated company annual report, which also includes a letter from the CEO to shareholders.

An important difference between a 10-Q and 10-K report is that 10-Q reports are *unaudited*, while the 10-K is *audited*, meaning the financials are prepared in accordance with GAAP and "certified" by an outside accounting firm (Gentry, 2011). Following the accounting scandals of the late 1990s and the passage of the Sarbanes-Oxley Act of 2002, nicknamed "SOX," the company CEO and CFO must personally certify the accuracy of the financial information and face severe penalties for misstatements (Lev, 2012; Roush, 2011).

The Income Statement

Simply stated, an income statement shows whether a company is making or losing money and, when compared with a prior quarterly or annual period, reveals whether a company's performance is improving or declining. Even with GAAP standards, the titles of categories and number of subcategories included on an income statement vary somewhat from company to company. However, the major categories that are included and the concepts remain unchanged. To walk through the categories typically found on the income statement of a large corporation, we use the income statement of Fortune 500 company Yum! Brands Inc. (NYSE: YUM). Yum!, the world's largest restaurant company based on the number of locations, is the owner of the KFC, Pizza Hut, and Taco Bell brands.

Table 4.1 YUM! Brands Inc. income statement (2011–2013)

Revenues (amounts in millions, except per share data)	2013	2012	2011
Company sales	$11,184	$11,833	$10,893
Franchise and license fees income	1,900	1,800	1,733
Total revenues	**13,084**	**13,633**	**12,626**
Company restaurant expenses, net			
Food and paper	3,669	3,874	3,633
Payroll and employee benefits	2,499	2,620	2,418
Occupancy and other operating expenses	3,333	3,358	3,089
Company restaurant expenses	9,501	9,852	9,140
General and administrative expenses	1,412	1,510	1,372
Franchise and license expenses	158	133	145
Closures and impairment (income expenses)	331	37	135
Refranchising (gain) loss	(100)	(78)	72
Other (income) expense	(16)	(115)	(53)
Total costs and expenses, net	11,286	11,339	10,811
Operating profit	**1,798**	**2,294**	**1,815**
Interest expense, net	247	149	156
Income before income taxes	**1,551**	**2,145**	**1,659**
Income tax provision	487	537	324
Net Income—including noncontrolling interest	1,064	1,608	1,335
Net Income—noncontrolling interest	(27)	11	16
Net income—YUM! Brands Inc.	**$1,091**	**$1,597**	**$1,319**
Basic earnings per common share	**$2.41**	**$3.46**	**$2.81**
Average shares outstanding	452	461	469
Diluted earnings per common share	**$2.36**	**$3.38**	**$2.74**
Average shares outstanding	461	473	481
Dividends declared per common share	$1.41	$1.24	$1.07

Revenue

Also known as gross sales or the "top line," revenue is found near the top of the income statement. A company may choose to break out its revenue into multiple subcategories. As shown on table 4.1, Yum! reported 2013 total revenue of nearly $13.1 billion.

Cost of Goods Sold

Also known as COGS or COS, the cost of goods sold line, or series of lines, comes directly under revenue and lists the *direct* costs that go into producing the product or service and generating revenue. For Yum!, this is titled "Company restaurant expenses" and includes food, paper, payroll, occupancy, and other expenses, which totaled approximately $9.5 billion in 2013. Gross profit is the revenue minus the cost of goods sold, or nearly $3.6 billion for Yum! in 2013.

General and Administrative Expense

Also called "G&A," the general and administrative expense line includes items like sales, marketing, and public relations expenditures; research and development; salaries of headquarters personnel; and other related expenses that do not go directly into producing the product or service. As displayed on table 4.1, G&A totaled $1.4 billion for Yum! in 2013.

Operating Income

Sometimes called operating profit or income from operations, the operating income line shows how much money the firm made or lost after it takes into account all operating expenses (i.e., COGS, G&A, depreciation and amortization, and any miscellaneous expenses), but *before* it pays its taxes and *before* it pays any interest expense or income tied to financing the business (i.e., *non*operating expenses). Yum! reported an operating income of $1.8 billion in 2013.

Net Income

The literal "bottom line," net income, or net earnings, is found on a line near the bottom of the income statement. This critical line on the income statement shows the company's bottom-line profit (or loss) for the period after *every expense* has been taken into account. As shown on table 4.1, the net profit for Yum! totaled nearly $1.1 billion for 2013.

While growing top-line revenue is important, it is even more essential to understand the decisions that drive bottom-line profits. With this in mind, Beam Inc., the global premium spirits company that is home to brands like Jim Beam, Maker's Mark, and Sauza, established the Beam Business Academy in 2012 to instill greater business acumen across the organization.

"Most PR practitioners can talk about things that impact the top line," says Clarkson Hine, senior vice president of corporate communications and public affairs for Beam Inc., a division of Suntory Holdings (personal communication, August 28, 2013). "Unfortunately, far fewer in the profession understand—or even care about—what's happening at the bottom line. That puts them at a disadvantage and can limit how far they can go and the value that they can add."

Profit Margins

Business managers and financial-oriented stakeholders frequently talk in terms of a company's "profit margins," not simply the company's *absolute* net earnings or profitability (Skonieczny, 2012). Managers want to see a company's relative profit margins hold steady or expand each year, rather than decline. Stable or growing margins are generally evidence of a healthy underlying business. A range of different profit margins may be calculated from a company's income statement. Two important indicators are operating margin and net margin.

Operating Margin

The operating margin, a measure of operational efficiency, shows how much money a company makes (i.e., has left over) on each dollar of sales it generates (before interest, taxes, dividends). This ratio is operating income (profit) divided by net revenue. So in 2013, the operating margin for Yum! was 13.7 percent ($1.8 billion/$13.1 billion), which means Yum! made nearly $0.14 on every dollar of sales. This represented a decline from the prior year, in which the operating profit margin was 16.8 percent ($2.3 billion/$13.6 billion), indicating Yum! made nearly $0.17 on every dollar of sales. This so-called "margin contraction" is generally negative and attracts the scrutiny of financial-oriented stakeholders.

Net Margin

Unlike operating margin, net margin takes into account not just operating expenses but also *nonoperating* expenses, such as interest and taxes (i.e., all possible expenses are included). This ratio is net income (profit) divided by net revenue. In 2013, Yum! posted a net margin of 8.3 percent ($1.1 billion/$13.1 billion), a decline from a net margin of 11.7 percent in the prior year. This means that both the absolute ($1.6 billion vs. $1.1 billion) and the relative (11.7 percent vs. 8.3 percent) level of profitability of Yum! declined year-over-year. Financial-oriented stakeholders would likely want to know what the drivers behind this decline are and what is being done to fix this situation.

Earnings Per Share (EPS)

Every public company not only reports its net income or earnings on its income statement but also converts this figure to an earnings per share (EPS) basis (Piper, 2013; Skonieczny, 2012; Taparia, 2004). This figure essentially tells investors how much in the way of a profit (or a loss) shareholders would receive for each share of stock they own if the company was to distribute all of its earnings for this period. EPS is calculated by dividing the net income (i.e., earnings) of the company by the total number of shares of stock outstanding. The company share count for making this calculation is generally found near the bottom of the income statement below the net income line. The conservative approach is to use the average shares outstanding total listed under the *diluted* earnings per share line (rather than *basic* share count), as the diluted share count number takes into account all possible additional shares (e.g., stock options, warrants, preferred shares) that could be issued in the future (Schoen, 2013).

For example, Yum! posted diluted earnings per common share of $2.36 in 2013. This figure was calculated by dividing the net income of nearly $1.1 billion in 2013 by its diluted average total shares outstanding of 461 million. This represents a 30 percent decline from the $3.38 in diluted earnings per share that Yum! posted in the prior year. Investors in public companies are typically more concerned with a company's earnings on an EPS basis than the absolute net income figure since they think in terms of the stock they own representing a per share ownership percentage of that company's profits (or losses). The EPS figure provides the basis for several important financial valuation metrics, such as the price-to-earnings (P/E) ratio, which are widely used by financial stakeholders. The P/E ratio is revisited in more detail later in this chapter.

Balance Sheet

While an income statement shows how much money an organization made or lost on an accounting basis, the balance sheet provides an assessment of what a company owns that is a source of value (i.e., assets) and what it owes (i.e., liabilities). The balance sheet also shows approximately how much money would be left over for shareholders (i.e., shareholders' equity or net worth) if the organization sold off all of its assets and paid off all of its liabilities. The balance sheet is so-named because the company's total assets must equal or "balance" relative to the company's total liabilities plus shareholders' equity (Piper, 2013; Skonieczny, 2012; Taparia, 2004). For example, as shown on table 4.2, for 2013, Yum! reported total assets of approximately $8.7 billion and corresponding liabilities and shareholders' equity of the same amount (total liabilities of $6.4 billion and total shareholders' equity of approximately $2.2 billion).

Assets

An asset is something a company owns that has value and that has the potential to generate revenue and contribute to earnings. An asset may either be

Table 4.2 YUM! Brands Inc. balance sheet (2011–2013)

Assets(amounts in millions)	2013	2012	2011
Current assets			
Cash and cash equivalents	$573	$776	$1,198
Accounts and notes receivable	319	301	286
Inventories	294	313	273
Prepaid expenses and other current assets	286	272	338
Deferred income taxes	123	111	112
Advertising cooperative assets, restricted	96	136	114
Total current assets	**1,691**	**1,909**	**2,321**
Property, plant and equipment, net	4,459	4,250	4,042
Goodwill	889	1,034	681
Intangible assets, net	638	690	299
Investments in unconsolidated affiliates	53	72	167
Restricted cash	—	—	300
Other assets	566	575	475
Deferred income taxes	399	467	549
Total assets	**$8,695**	**$9,013**	**$8,834**
Liabilities and shareholders' equity			
Current liabilities			
Accounts payable and other current liabilities	$1,929	$2,036	$1,874
Income taxes payable	169	97	142
Short-term borrowings	71	10	320
Advertising cooperative liabilities	96	136	114
Total current liabilities	**2,265**	**2,279**	**2,450**
Long term debt	2,918	2,932	2,997
Other liabilities and deferred credits	1,244	1,490	1,471
Total liabilities	**6,427**	**6,701**	**6,918**
Shareholders' equity			
Common stock, no par value	—	—	18
Retained earnings	2,102	2,286	2,052
Accumulated other income (loss)	64	(132)	(247)
Total shareholders' equity—YUM! Brands	**2,166**	**2,154**	**1,823**
Noncontrolling interests	63	99	93
Total shareholders' equity	**2,229**	**2,253**	**1,916**
Total liabilities and shareholders' equity	**$8,695**	**$9,011**	**$8,834**

sold by the company or be used by the company to produce its product or service. Examples of assets include cash and securities; accounts receivable (i.e., money owed the company); inventory; real estate (property and buildings); equipment; trucks; intangibles, such as copyrights, trademarks, patents, and the like; tax credits; and any prepaid expenses. Current assets are assets that the company expects to convert to cash in a year or less, whereas noncurrent assets are longer term in nature. Typically, these long-term assets include factories, stores, buildings, equipment, and fixtures (Piper, 2013).

Liabilities

A liability is some sort of monetary obligation that a company owes to others. This includes everything from money borrowed from a bank on a short-term basis to a mortgage on a company building or funds owed to suppliers and vendors (i.e., accounts payable). Other common liabilities include future income taxes payable and any outstanding long-term debt, such as money borrowed through a corporate bond offering, which must eventually be repaid by the company. Current liabilities are liabilities that the company expects to pay within a year, whereas noncurrent liabilities have a payback duration of beyond a year. Long-term debt and long-term lease obligations are common examples of noncurrent liabilities (Piper, 2013).

Shareholders' Equity

This figure is the amount that stockholders have invested in the company (through buying stock and other securities) and the retained earnings (profits) since inception. Shareholders' equity is also known as net worth or book value. If all assets were sold and liabilities were settled, shareholders' equity would hypothetically be the amount of value or money left over for shareholders. If a company's balance sheet shows "negative equity," this could be a sign that the company risks becoming insolvent and being unable to continue as a so-called "going concern," in accounting parlance—unless it is able to find new investors to help finance its operations. Auditors are required to state in their audit opinion of a public company's financial statements whether they believe there is "substantial doubt" about the company's ability to continue as a going concern (M. Murphy, 2012). Bankruptcy is a risk for such companies.

Financial Valuation Metrics

There are literally dozens of financial valuation metrics and ratios that businesspeople, investors, and other financial stakeholders use to determine the investment value and financial health of publicly held companies. Many valuation metrics and financial ratios are beyond the scope of this book. A detailed knowledge of such metrics and ratios are probably only necessary for those strategic communicators working in investor relations or financial communication. However, any strategic communicator (regardless of their specialization) who works for or with a corporation, particularly a publicly traded company, would benefit from understanding the following two financial valuation concepts: market capitalization and price-to-earnings ratio.

Market Capitalization

Also known as simply "market cap," this measure determines the total market value of the firm based on all of its shares of stock outstanding. Market cap is calculated by taking the current value of the company's stock and multiplying it by the total number of issued shares (Roush & Cloud, 2012). As you may recall, this share count figure is provided near the bottom of the income statement. A firm's stock price is available on any number of free investment websites like Yahoo! Finance or Google Finance. In the case of Yum! Brands, the diluted share count of 461 million found on the 2013 income statement multiplied by the closing stock price of $72.06 per share on February 4, 2014, the day after the release of its 2013 earnings report, results in a market capitalization of roughly $33.2 billion. A company's market cap is not static because it adjusts to changes in a company's stock price and an increase or decrease in the amount of shares. Enterprise value, a more detailed measure of company value, takes into account a company's stock market value plus a company's net cash/debt and any preferred stock (Roush & Cloud, 2012). Enterprise value represents the minimum price people would generally have to pay if they wanted to buy the entire company.

Price-to-Earnings Ratio

Also known as a P/E ratio or simply the "earnings multiple," the price-to-earnings ratio is perhaps the most widely used and most basic measure of a company's stock market valuation (Roush & Cloud, 2012). The P/E ratio is the company's stock price per share divided by its earnings per share (EPS). This allows a business manager, investor, or other financial stakeholder to look at how much value the stock market is assigning to the company's current or projected earnings on a per share basis. It is particularly useful in comparing the value of a company's stock relative to its peer group (i.e., competitors) or the overall stock market (Roush, 2011). A company with a stock price of $2.00 per share isn't necessarily "cheap," just as a stock that trades for $100 per share isn't necessarily "expensive." To make an apples-to-apples comparison regarding the value of two or more stocks, they must be analyzed on an EPS basis.

For example, the stock price for Yum! Brands the day after it reported its 2013 earnings results was $72.06 per share, and earnings per share were $2.36. Recall that company stock price data are available on many free investment websites like Yahoo! Finance and Google Finance and that EPS data are included near the bottom of a company's income statement. Given this information ($72.06 /$2.36), Yum! has a trailing P/E ratio of 31. The forward P/E ratio, a calculation based on how much money financial analysts expect the company to earn in the next year ($72.06/$3.65), is 20. For comparison, shares of companies in the U.S. restaurant industry have historically traded for up to 20× earnings (Hamburger, 2014). These valuation measures show that the stock price for Yum!, even assuming a rebound in the firm's future earnings, is valued at the high end of restaurant stock values, perhaps because of the company's traditionally strong record.

Investors are generally willing to pay a higher multiple of earnings (i.e., higher P/E ratio) for companies that have an established track record of earnings growth and/or a positive outlook for future growth. Going back to the example used in this chapter, Yum! has a track record of very respectable long-term earnings growth. However, in 2013, the company suffered a temporary setback in profitability due to a decline in sales at its China division, an important growth market and profit driver. Most business managers and investors would like to see a public company achieve a stock market valuation that is at least comparable to its peer group. This is quite different from simply trying to obtain the highest possible stock price (Ragas, Laskin, & Brusch, 2014). Company management, strategic communicators, and stakeholders all benefit long term from a company obtaining a market valuation that is appropriate and sustainable.

Table 4.3 Review of financial formulas

Key Term	Definition
Income statement	
Gross profit	Net revenue – Cost of goods sold = Gross profit
Operating income	Net revenue – Operating expenses = Operating Income
Net income	Net revenue – Operating and nonoperating expenses = Net income
Operating margin	Operating income/Net revenue = Operating margin
Net margin	Net income/Net revenue = Net margin
Earnings per share	Net income/Total shares outstanding = Earnings per share
Balance sheet	
Total assets	Total liabilities + Shareholders' equity = Total assets
Shareholders' equity	Total assets – Total liabilities = Shareholders' equity
Financial valuation	
Market capitalization	Stock price × Total shares outstanding = Market capitalization
Enterprise value	Market cap + Preferred shares + Debt – Cash = Enterprise value
Price-to-earnings ratio	Stock price/Earnings per share = Price-to-earnings ratio

See table 4.3 for a review of the key financial formulas discussed in this chapter.

Practice Makes Perfect and Is Worth It

Susan Hoff, retired senior vice president and chief communication officer of consumer electronics retail giant Best Buy Co. Inc., credits her willingness to "wear many different hats" and develop business acumen as the keys to her career growth (personal communication, December 31, 2013). Hoff says that successful communication professionals on her team sought to gain accounting and financial knowledge that was more akin to that of an investor relations executive. Communicators that did not seek out this knowledge were less likely to be promoted or to stick with the team long term.

"Some communicators felt they were specialists in a particular area of communications and didn't care to learn anything else about the company nor communicate with other teams within communications," says Hoff, who joined Best Buy when it only had six locations (S. Hoff, personal communication, December 31, 2013). "They felt they deserved a raise simply for a well-covered release, or delivering a special written project on deadline—yet they didn't understand the first thing about the company's P&L, why we couldn't hire more communicators that year, or what our company's competitive advantage was."

As with learning about finance and the stock market, gaining familiarity and comfort with accounting, financial statements, and basic financial valuation metrics takes time, practice, and some patience. A good way to gain greater familiarity with accounting concepts is to search for business news stories discussing the quarterly earnings reports of public companies in industries that are of interest and then visit the investor relations section of a company website to read the earnings release discussing the company's earnings. This release also will contain the company's most recent financial statements. Looking up the key financial numbers referenced in the news stories and in the earnings release as presented on the company's actual income statement or balance sheet is a good way to practice the concepts and calculations reviewed in this chapter. A friend or colleague with a financial or accounting background who enjoys discussing these topics can also be a valuable resource for discussing what you have read and how you interpret this information.

The payoff for the strategic communicator who knows his or her way around financial statements and basic financial terminology can be substantial. Financial information remains the core of most companies and is of interest to not just management or investors but also employees, suppliers, regulators, customers, and other stakeholders. Simply stated, strategic communicators with competencies in accounting and finance are better positioned to explain and contextualize company financial performance for these various stakeholder groups and then convey the financial-oriented concerns and priorities of these stakeholders back to management.

"A well-educated, contemporary, business-savvy communications professional is far more likely to become a true trusted advisor to a company's board and C-suite executives," says Edward P. "Ned" Grace III, a senior advisor to private equity firm Angelo, Gordon & Co. and the founder, CEO, or director of more than a half dozen public companies over his career (personal communication, August 26, 2013). "They understand the expected market and internal employee reaction to the communicated news, are well prepared, and help prepare management for any eventuality that may develop."

Further, financially literate strategic communicators are better qualified to have such discussions on these topics with the managers of other business units and departments. At a time when the financial literacy rate of the American public is low (FINRA Investor Education Foundation, 2013; Library of Congress, 2011; U.S. SEC, 2012c) but interest in organizations being transparent about their financial performance and strategy is high, communicators have more responsibility than perhaps ever before to effectively translate this "language of business" for stakeholders.

Key Terms

Accounting	Enterprise value	Income statement
Accounts payable	FASB	Liabilities
Accounts receivable	Financial statement	Market capitalization
Asset	Fiscal year	Negative equity
Balance sheet	Form 10-K	Net income
Bottom line	Form 10-Q	Net margin
Cash flow statement	GAAP	Operating income
Cost of goods sold	General and administra-	Operating margin
Credit	tive expense	Sarbanes-Oxley Act
Debit	Gross profit	Shareholders' equity
Earnings	IASB	Shares outstanding
Earnings per share	IFRS	Top line

Discussion Questions

1. Visit the investor relations section of the website of a public company that interests you. Pull up the company's most recent *annual* earnings report. Look at the income statement. How much revenue did the company report? What about its net income? Did the company report make more or less money than you expected? Explain.

2. For the same company, look at the annual financial results the company reported in the prior year. According to the company's income statement, did its revenue and net income increase, decline, or essentially stay the same from the prior year? Would you be happy with this performance if you were a financial stakeholder in the company?

3. For the same company, find the company's reported annual earnings per share (EPS) on its income statement or within the earnings release. Next, visit a free investment website like Yahoo! Finance or Google Finance and look up the firm's stock price. Use this stock price and the EPS figure to calculate the P/E ratio. The long-term average P/E ratio of the stock market is 16. Would you invest in this company's stock? Why or why not?

4. Objectively read through the news release provided by this same company about its recent annual earnings report. What did the quote from the CEO say about the company's performance? Did you find the information provided by the company helpful in understanding its financial performance? How might the language be improved?

5. Visit a free investment website like Yahoo! Finance or Google Finance and search for news stories about this same company's most recent annual earnings report. What financial information did business journalists highlight in their stories about the company? How is this information similar to or different from the information in the company news release?

6. Do you think the interpretation and communication of financial information to stakeholders will become more or less important for companies in the future? Why?

CHAPTER 5

The Law and Corporate Disclosure

Today, organizations of all types and sizes increasingly recognize the value in being more transparent (DiStaso & Bortree, 2012; Rawlins, 2006b, 2008, 2009). This said, large corporations, particularly public companies, cannot simply say *what they want, when they want,* to *whomever they want* through *whatever channel* they so please. Business managers and strategic communicators must carefully follow the rules of the game, specifically the web of securities laws, rules, and regulations that guide the disclosure of mandatory and voluntary information about companies to investors and other stakeholders. Further, these same companies must guard against shareholder lawsuits and other litigation as a result of what they say and share (Lev, 2012).

The benefits of effective corporate disclosure are clear. Research shows that companies that consistently release *more* and *better quality* information about their businesses are generally rewarded by both investors and the stock market with greater liquidity and less volatility in their shares, a lower cost of capital, and a better valuation (Amihud & Mendelson, 2003, 2006, 2008, 2012; Blankespoor, Miller, & White, 2012; Bushee, Matsumoto, & Miller, 2003; Bushee & Miller, 2012; Bushee & Noe, 2000). Further, efforts to demonstrate greater transparency can also result in positive nonfinancial outcomes with stakeholders, such as better reputations (Hutton, Goodman, Alexander, & Genest, 2001), enhanced trust (DiStaso & Bortree, 2012; Rawlins, 2008, 2009), and improved organization-public relationships (Seltzer & Zhang, 2011; Strömbäck & Kiousis, 2011). In short, stakeholders typically favor transparency over opaqueness in the companies that they choose to do business with, whether that is buying stock in a firm, working for it, or purchasing its products and services.

Strategic communicators are often on the front lines of information disclosure. Therefore, it is critical that every strategic communication professional is well versed in the basics of the theories, research, laws, and regulations that guide corporate disclosure. Communicators must understand what financial and company information public companies are required to disclose to the public on an ongoing basis, how and when this information must be disclosed to meet legal requirements, and what communication channels are available for both required and voluntary disclosure. With this knowledge in hand, a communicator is better positioned to more intelligently advocate for greater transparency within the organization-stakeholder relationship, while keeping their client or organization within the legal boundaries of disclosure regulations.

According to Chris Hodges, founder and CEO of Alpha IR Group, all strategic communication professionals working for public companies should understand the rules and regulations that come with public ownership (personal communication, December 9, 2013). "Employee, customer and other stakeholder-specific communication will ultimately end up in shareholders' hands," says Hodges, previously a senior managing director and the head of the North American industrials practice with FTI Consulting. "If that communication varies significantly from prior investor communications, a company could have a major shareholder issue on its hands and possibly a shareholder lawsuit. So even if a communications initiative is not intended for shareholders, the professional that's creating the communication should be aware of how it might impact shareholders."

Securities Laws for Public Companies

In the wake of the stock market crash of 1929 and the ensuing Great Depression, the U.S. government passed a series of landmark laws designed to reform the financial markets and provide investors with more timely, accurate, and complete corporate information. Ahead of the stock market crash, some company insiders, such as company executives that were privy to the deteriorating conditions of the businesses they were running, quietly sold their stock en masse. This selling was done unbeknownst to other shareholders and the public (Taparia, 2004). Corporate securities regulations and corporate disclosure requirements in the United States trace back to The Securities Act of 1933, also known as the Truth in Securities Act, and the Securities Exchange Act of 1934 (National Investor Relations Institute [NIRI], 2012b, 2014). The 1934 Act established the Securities and Exchange Commission (SEC) as the federal regulator responsible for overseeing the integrity of the nation's security markets. The first chair of the SEC was Joseph P. Kennedy Sr., father of U.S. president John F. Kennedy. Mary Jo White, the current chair of the SEC, was appointed to the position in 2013. Information is the lifeblood of markets (Morrill, 1995). Therefore, a major focus of both the initial corporate securities laws and the laws implemented later has been ensuring that investors receive timely, accurate, and complete information before they choose to invest in a company's stock or other securities. As discussed in chapters 3 and 4 of this book, by virtue of being a public company and listed on a stock exchange, companies are required to disclose their financial performance on a periodic basis (usually quarterly). In between these periodic reports, public companies are required to keep investors current as to any developments that are "material" in nature (U.S. SEC, 2012). The U.S. Supreme Court defines "materiality" as when there is a substantial likelihood that a reasonable investor would consider such information to be important in making an investment decision (Davidoff, 2011; NIRI, 2012b, 2014). Beyond making these required informational disclosures, many public companies also choose to make *voluntary* disclosures that provide additional information about the status of the business and its plans.

For strategic communication professionals, the passage in August 2000 of Regulation Fair Disclosure, commonly known as Reg. FD, marks the most significant change in corporate disclosure practices at public companies since the formation of the SEC (Lynn, 2012; Monks & Minow, 2011). Prior to the advent of the Internet and the widespread adoption of the Web as a tool for investment research and news, individual investors were largely reliant on their stockbroker for information about their investments. The rise of online stock brokerages and free investment websites made smaller investors more aware of important company information sources, such as quarterly earnings conference calls, which were only available to professional investors. Reg. FD sought to further democratize the release of corporate information; bring greater transparency into the public company reporting and disclosure process; and eliminate so-called "selective disclosure," in which professional investors received market-moving, material information from companies ahead of smaller investors (Davidoff, 2011; NIRI, 2012b, 2014). Under Reg. FD, if a company inadvertently discloses material, nonpublic information to a select group of investors, a company must quickly take corrective action by broadly sharing this information.

According to Lou Thompson, who was president and CEO of the National Investor Relations Institute (NIRI) for more than 20 years, including during the development of Reg. FD, some investment professionals were initially concerned that Reg. FD would result in less—not more—disclosures by public companies (personal communication, March 14, 2014). Thompson says some feared that SEC actions for violating this new regulation would "diminish the availability of quality investment information." Instead, the opposite occurred. "In 2005, I appeared before the Federal Reserve annual financial markets conference on Sea Island, Georgia, with Harvard Business School Professor Paul Healy, who presented his paper showing that the opposite had occurred. The quantity and quality of material information had been enhanced under Reg. FD," says Thompson, now principal of Thompson Value Creation & Governance Strategies LLC.

All communication professionals that work on behalf of public companies, regardless of their communication specialization, must have at least a baseline understanding of disclosure rules, says Jeffrey Morgan, the president and CEO of NIRI from 2008 through 2014 (personal communication, September 11, 2013). "The stakes are simply too high to operate without this knowledge," Morgan says. "We are now in an age where communications are immediate and indiscriminate with respect to specific audiences. Any corporate communication—sales, marketing, public relations, investor relations, even internal [communication]—considering blogs and sites like Glassdoor, has the potential, intentionally or otherwise, [to be a] 'material disclosure' subject to stock exchanges rules and state and federal securities regulation."

Material, Nonpublic Information and Insider Trading

There are significant, negative repercussions for companies and individuals that violate the securities laws, including the misuse of material, nonpublic information. Company insiders, such as officers, members of the board of directors, and large shareholders, are not allowed to profit from such information or to make selective disclosures. For this reason, public companies often have self-imposed "quiet periods" around the end of a quarter and before quarterly earnings have been announced (U.S. SEC, 2011). During these "quiet periods," company executives and communication professionals limit their communication with the financial community (NIRI, 2010). To reduce the risk of insider trading, public companies also typically have "blackout periods" around quarterly earnings reports. During these periods, company insiders cannot buy or sell shares of company stock (NIRI, 2010). As per SEC regulations, even when company policies allow insiders to legally trade in their own stock, they must disclose these activities on a timely basis through Form 4 filings with the SEC's EDGAR online filing system (U.S. SEC, 2013).

Company officers, directors, key employees, and other insiders who profit on material, nonpublic information or even pass along this information to others who then trade on this information have engaged in insider trading (Tseng, 2010). A very well-known insider trading case involved Martha

Stewart's sale of shares in biotech company ImClone one day before the public learned that the Food and Drug Administration would not review ImClone's application for its cancer drug (CNNMoney.com, 2006). Stewart's stockbroker also handled the account of ImClone founder Sam Waksal, who tipped off select friends and family to the forthcoming bad news. Even outside consultants, such as accountants, lawyers, and communication advisors, whom receive confidential information in the course of their business, can be prosecuted for insider trading if they misuse material, nonpublic information for personal profits or for the ill-gotten gains of others (Tseng, 2010). Penalties for insider trading include serving jail time, paying fines, and being barred from serving as an officer or director of public companies.

Even if company insiders or consultants do not profit from material, nonpublic information, they could be charged with a Reg. FD violation if they selectively disclose such information to others. For example, in October 2010, Office Depot's then CEO and chief financial officer (CFO) were charged with violating fair disclosure regulations by selectively conveying to analysts and large investors that the firm would likely miss analysts' earnings projections. Other investors did not receive this same information in advance of the company's official release of quarterly earnings. Office Depot agreed to settle the charges without admitting or denying wrongdoing and paying a $1 million penalty. In addition, the CEO and CFO each agreed to pay $50,000 fines (Human, 2010).

Corporate Disclosure Theories and Research

Corporate securities laws and regulations are geared toward minimizing the amount of imperfect information (Stiglitz, 2000, 2002) on publicly traded companies, so as to provide for a more level playing field for all market participants. This increased informational transparency benefits not only the general investing public but also corporations and their stakeholders. As noted in the introduction, companies that make efforts to boost transparency through more frequent and better informational disclosures tend to enjoy both tangible *financial* (i.e., better liquidity, lower volatility, lower cost of capital, better valuations) and *nonfinancial* benefits (i.e., heightened trust, better relationships, strengthened reputations). While competitive concerns must be taken into account when it comes to disclosure (Amihud & Mendelson, 2003), it generally pays for companies to be more—not less—transparent in their business activities.

Over the past 20 years, there has been an explosion in the amount of business research focused on the effects of imperfect information on the decision making of organizations, stakeholders, and individuals (Lofgren, Persson, &

Weibull, 2002). Research into information asymmetry (Akerlof, 1970)—situations in which one party (i.e., an insider) has more and better information than the other (i.e., an outsider)—demonstrate that these information gaps lead to less than optimal outcomes for both parties. In such situations, one party is likely to know more than the other does about the underlying quality and value of the object in the prospective transaction, whether it is a car, a house, an investment security, or some other product or service. Sensing heightened risk due to limited public information, the other party will pay less or nothing at all. Sometimes the seller feels better informed. Other times, the prospective buyer feels better informed. Whatever the case, whenever one side of a market believes the other side of a market is better informed, mutually advantageous transactions and relationships are stifled.

There are many examples of the negative effect of information asymmetry on pricing and other behavioral outcomes. In the used car market, the seller often knows more than the buyer knows about the quality of the car. The C-suite and the board of directors typically know more about the long-term value of the company than outside shareholders know. In the mortgage market, the borrower knows more than the lender knows about the borrower's creditworthiness. In the job market, job applicants know more about their ability and future performance than prospective employers know. To improve market outcomes, market participants will engage in observable and costly actions and behaviors, known as "signals" (Connelly, Certo, Ireland, & Reutzel, 2011; Spence, 1973, 2002), which credibly signal private information to less informed market participants. This is why home inspections and warranties are typical components of the sale of a home and why certified vehicle history reports are often included in used car transactions. These aforementioned signals reduce the level of information asymmetry.

Both intentional and unintentional actions taken by corporate leadership serve as signals to the market and a company's stakeholders [i.e., signal receivers] (Connelly et al., 2011). For example, the announcement of a dividend increase is generally viewed as a positive vote of confidence by company insiders in the company's long-term health. Conversely, the departure of a key executive or board member could be interpreted positively or negatively, depending on the explanation and context provided around the news. It has often been said that "actions speak louder than words." The reality is that actions (nonverbal communication) and words (verbal communication) are most effective when they are used together and are coordinated from the start. Ideally, this means that strategic communicators should have the opportunity to advise business managers *before* they make policy decisions that send signals to the market and stakeholders. At a minimum, communicators can help stakeholders better interpret both the intent of these signals and the stakeholders' reception to such signals (i.e., countersignaling) for business managers.

An examination of research that focuses on agenda-building theory (Turk, 1985, 1986) and information subsidies (Gandy, 1982; Lieber & Golin, 2011) shows that strategic communicators can impact how organizational information is used and interpreted by stakeholders, depending upon the presentation and dissemination of such information. Information subsidies are prepackaged materials (e.g., news releases, earnings conference calls, investor presentations, websites, social media messages) produced by strategic communication professionals that lower the cost of information, thereby increasing consumption by stakeholders and influencers, such as journalists (Kiousis, Kim, McDevitt, & Ostrowski, 2009; Kiousis, Popescu, & Mitrook, 2007). In the context of corporate disclosures and the desire to reduce information asymmetry, organizations and communicators have a variety of communication channels and formats (i.e., information subsidies) at their disposal for contextualizing and explaining company signals.

Communication Channels for Corporate Disclosure

A variety of communication channels are recognized by the SEC for meeting Reg. FD reporting requirements. These recognized disclosure methods include SEC filings, news releases, posts made to a recognized and open corporate website, and open conference calls (NIRI, 2012b, 2014). For this latter disclosure channel, the financial community and other interested stakeholders should receive advance notice before a conference call, typically done by the company sending out a news release with call details.

In April 2013, the SEC updated its previous instructions on the use of corporate websites for disclosure to include company social media channels (Goldstein, 2013). A company may use a social media channel such as Facebook or Twitter as a means of disclosure only if the company has already widely notified investors that these channels will be used to disclose such information (Zilka, Myers, & Gomes, 2013). The *personal* social media accounts of company executives would not ordinarily be assumed to meet this requirement. As shown in table 5.1, a National Investor Relations Institute survey found that the most used social media channel for disclosure is the corporate Twitter account (NIRI, 2013a). This same survey (see figure 5.1) also found that the top reason social media is not used for disclosure is the lack of financial stakeholder demand (NIRI, 2013a).

Many companies continue to play it safe and rely on company news releases distributed by a paid wire service, such as Business Wire or PR Newswire, and/or rely on SEC filings with EDGAR to definitively meet

Table 5.1   Usage of social media by investor relations professionals

Rank	Social media platforms/tools
1	Twitter
1	Webcasts
3	LinkedIn
3	Facebook/Like buttons
5	StockTwits
6	YouTube
7	RSS feed or other web feeds
8	Slideshare
9	Social media network/message boards investor relations-oriented corporate
10	blog

Note: In this table, '1' indicates the highest ranked social media tool, a '2' indicates the second highest ranked tool, and so on.
Source: Social Media Use in Investor Relations 2013 Survey Results.

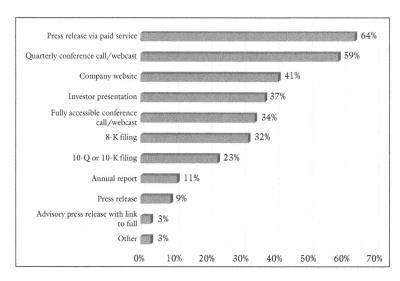

Figure 5.1   Communication channels used for financial guidance disclosures
Source: Social media use in investor relations 2013 survey results.

Reg. FD disclosure requirements. Specifically, Form 8-K filings play a key role in the disclosure of both required and voluntary information about public companies (U.S. SEC, 2012a). A Form 8-K filing must be made whenever there is a material event that occurs at a public company in between its required periodic reports (10-Qs and 10-K). Such current events would include the acquisition or sale of assets, the departure of a company officer or director, a default on a loan or major change in financial obligations, or an entry into or termination of a major agreement. As a precautionary measure and to broaden dissemination, companies may file copies of conference call transcripts, investor presentations, and related materials through Form 8-Ks. A company also may use an 8-K to voluntarily share additional information that it feels is important but is not necessarily "material" information.

While news releases and SEC filings remain critical tools for disclosure and usage of social media is growing (NIRI, 2013a), there are a variety of additional channels that are core components of communicating with the financial community. These channels include the following.

Earnings Conference Calls

Virtually all U.S. public companies hold an earnings call each quarter (NIRI, 2012b, 2013b, 2014). These calls, typically lasting around an hour, feature prepared remarks by the CEO and CFO discussing quarterly performance, followed by a question and answer session. Since such calls are typically open, the media, competitors, and any interested stakeholder may dial into the call and listen in. Many companies webcast and then archive the calls. Additional calls may be held for major events like a merger or an acquisition.

Analyst/Investor Day

More than seven out of ten U.S. public companies periodically hold an analyst/investor day, most often on an annual basis (NIRI, 2011). Such a day allows financial analysts and large investors to meet with multiple company executives to gain a more sophisticated understanding of company strategy and future plans. Analyst/investor days are typically held in a large financial center like New York or London or at a company facility. Often analyst/investor days are webcast, which open up such days to a broader audience.

Investment Conferences

A member of the company management team, often accompanied by an investor relations professional, will typically make presentations throughout the year at a variety of conferences sponsored by investment banks. These conferences are attended by Wall Street analysts and large investors. The format is often a short set presentation followed by a limited question and answer session. Increasingly, such presentations are webcast.

Nondeal Road Shows

In addition to investment conferences, company management teams and investor relations professionals typically go on a series of "road shows" throughout the year in which they meet with current and prospective professional investors in major cities. Typically, these road shows are sponsored and organized by investment banks. Unlike conference appearances, which are frequently announced in advance, road shows are kept more private.

Regardless of the above venue, a company must issue a news release and/or make an 8-K filing if a company executive inadvertently discloses *new* material information in the course of such investor interactions. To remain Reg. FD compliant, this corrective release and filing must generally be made within 24 hours of the inadvertent selective disclosure (NIRI, 2012c).

Corporate communication and investor relations professionals are typically very involved in the planning and execution of earnings conference calls, analyst/investor days, investment conference appearances, and nondeal road shows. "How a CEO or CFO is perceived by the listeners on the [earnings conference] call is important, and proper planning and preparation of the executives is essential," says Patrick Tracey, senior vice president of business development for Georgeson, a Computershare company and a top provider of strategic shareholder consulting services. "Corporate communication professionals help in training the executives on presentation techniques and identifying questions in advance and preparing the answers."

Earnings Guidance and Forward-Looking Statements

No discussion of corporate transparency and disclosure is complete without a review of earnings guidance practices. Markets and financial stakeholders are forward looking. They are just as—if not more so—interested in what a company intends to do in the future with its corporate strategy and financial performance as they are in what it is doing currently. The large majority of public companies provide forecasts about future financial performance, a practice known as earnings guidance. Survey research by BNY Mellon (2012) shows that nine out of ten publicly traded global companies provided some sort of guidance in 2012. This represents an increase from three years earlier, in which six out of ten companies provided some sort of guidance (BNY Mellon, 2009). Guidance is nearly as prevalent among U.S. companies, with 88 percent providing some form of guidance as of 2012. That figure is, however, down slightly from recent years (NIRI, 2012a). As of 2009, 93 percent of U.S. firms were providing guidance (NIRI, 2012a).

Proponents for providing guidance give several main reasons. They argue that providing such forecasts has become an expected best practice, which provides stakeholders with greater insight into future, anticipated performance (NIRI, 2012a, 2013b). By sharing such expectations, it also helps make company management more accountable. Further, professional investors and analysts will make company financial projections anyway, so companies should attempt to manage such expectations through sharing their own forecasts (Lev, 2011, 2012a, 2012b). Critics of earnings guidance frequently argue that such forecasts encourage management and stakeholders to focus on short-term quarterly performance to the detriment of longer-term value creation (Financial Executives Research Foundation, 2009). This could lead to management misallocating resources or even playing accounting games to meet or exceed short-term performance metrics. While there is empirical evidence that providing guidance boosts and protects company market valuation (e.g., Marempudi & Wolff, 2012; Lev, 2012b), some large, well-known firms like Coca-Cola, Costco, Google, Sears, and Unilever abstain from such practices (Judd, 2013).

The amount, type, and frequency of guidance information provided by public companies can vary substantially. As shown on figure 5.2, larger companies are more likely to provide some form of guidance than smaller firms are (NIRI, 2012a). For companies providing guidance, the most common time horizon is an annual forecast, and the most frequent time span for updating such estimates is quarterly (NIRI, 2012a). On a global basis, providing guidance on capital expenditures (CapEx)—how much money a

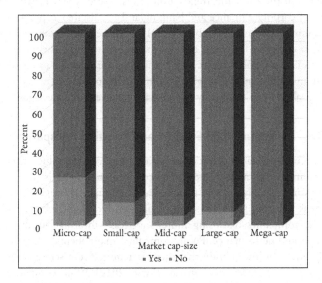

Figure 5.2   Financial guidance by company market capitalization
Source: NIRI guidance practices and preferences survey-2012. Compiled by NIRI, August 2012.

company anticipates investing in long-term assets like buildings and equipment—is most prevalent, followed closely behind by revenue forecasts (BNY Mellon, 2012). Other top categories for guidance include earnings projections, nonfinancial goals, and profit margins. Guidance priorities in the United States are similar; however, revenue guidance is slightly more prevalent, followed by capital expenditures, anticipated company tax rate, and earnings (NIRI, 2012a).

There is, of course, litigation risk that comes with providing guidance as a public company. The Private Securities Litigation Reform Act of 1995 represents an attempt to limit frivolous lawsuits if an SEC reporting company misses a previously released forecast. Whenever a public company makes a forward-looking statement (i.e., provides guidance), it should include with such information what is called "safe harbor language" (Hodges, 2012). This language discusses company-specific risk factors that could impact its future expected performance. Such language is frequently included at the bottom of earnings releases, at the start of investor presentations or earnings calls, and at other places and times, wherever and whenever forward-looking information is shared with the public. The strategic communication professional who is aware of the rules and limitations around earnings guidance and forward-looking statements is ahead of the game.

The explosive growth of online communication has increased the velocity of changes in the rules and trends around disclosure, says Christine Ieuter, director of corporate finance and banking at The Allstate Corporation (personal communication, September 11, 2013). "It's very important to be aware of the ever-changing landscape of rules and trends in your industry and communication as a whole," Ieuter says. "Knowing the rules for using all forms of communication, as well as what is common in your industry and for your audience, allows you to directly and concisely deliver your message."

Disclosures in "Plain English" and Boosting Transparency

Strategic communication professionals have long seen the value in transparent communication and business practices. The good news is that business managers increasingly see the financial and nonfinancial benefits of transparency as well. Securities laws and regulations like Reg. FD have resulted in public companies disclosing more—not less—information about their operations and performance. Public companies that adhere to disseminating only the material information that they are required to disclose are increasingly atypical in the U.S. stock market (Lynn, 2012). While companies must always consider the competitive implications of disclosures, financial stakeholders expect more and better quality information.

A strategic communication professional who has a solid grounding in the laws, rules, regulations, and practices surrounding corporate disclosures can add value both internally and externally. Internally, most public companies have Reg. FD disclosure policies and training programs. Strategic communicators with an understanding of this area can develop communication that helps better educate employees and advisors on these rules. Externally, far too often, disclosure materials are dense and confusing (Levitt, 2011). Even a sophisticated investor like Warren Buffett has lamented that, at times, he is unable to decipher from corporate disclosures what if anything is being said (U.S. SEC, 1998). Strategic communicators are more accustomed to writing in "plain English" and can ideally bring this know-how to the table when collaborating with other departments on the wording of disclosures.

Finally, strategic communication professionals are better positioned to advocate for greater transparency surrounding corporate practices and information when the professionals demonstrate their understanding of the legal and regulatory boundaries to managers. The rise of the Web and digital communication promises many new channels for corporate disclosure in the years ahead (NIRI, 2013a). In turn, the laws, policies, and practices surrounding corporate disclosure are likely to grow more complex. It is important that strategic communication professionals are poised to contribute to these discussions within and outside of organizations.

Key Terms

Agenda-building theory	Form 8-K	Road show
Analyst/investor day	Great Depression	Safe harbor language
Blackout period	Imperfect information	Signaling theory
Capital expenditure	Information asymmetry	Securities Act of 1933
Disclosure	Information subsidies	Securities Exchange Act
Earnings call	Investment conference	of 1934
Earnings guidance	Material information	Securities law
EDGAR	Quiet period	Selective disclosure
Form 4	Regulation FD	Transparency

Discussion Questions

1. Visit the investor relations website of a public company that you find interesting. Does the company post a link to archived, recent quarterly earnings calls on this website? What about recent investment conference presentations? Are copies of the slides available?

2. For the same company's investor relations website, listen to the first 10–15 minutes of a recent quarterly earnings call or investor presentation if an archive

of the call or presentation is available. What seemed to be the presenter's key message points?

3. For the same archived earnings call or investor presentation, critique the performance of the executive(s) presenting. Were they presenting the information in "plain English"? What words and phrases were unfamiliar? How would you improve the presentation?

4. Visit the SEC's EDGAR online system (www.sec.gov/edgar.shtml). Type in the name of the same public company that you used in the previous questions. Scan the resulting company filings, and click on the five most recent Form 8-K filings. What are the topics of these filings?

5. Go back to the results page on the EDGAR online system for the same company. Scan the resulting company filings, and click on the five most recent Form 4 filings. Determine from these filings whether company insiders seem to be buying or selling company stock (or both).

6. Does this public company use social media channels like Facebook and Twitter to disclose corporate financial and business information? If yes, what information is it disclosing? If no, should it be using these channels for disclosure? Why or why not?

CHAPTER 6

Intangible Assets and Nonfinancial Information

A seismic shift has occurred in recent decades regarding how organizations create value and achieve sustained competitive advantage (R. S. Kaplan & Norton, 2001, 2004a, 2004b, 2007; Low & Siesfield, 1998). Organizations increasingly outperform competitors through the strategic ownership, management, and growth of intangible assets, such as people; processes and systems; environmental, social, and governance policies; stakeholder relationships; reputations; patents; brand names; and other intellectual property, rather than through the ownership and management of industrial era physical assets like buildings, machinery, and property (DiPiazza et al., 2006; Lev, 2004, 2005, 2012b; Rassart & Miller, 2013).

In today's knowledge and information-based economy, value increasingly accrues to those organizations that are allocating more of their resources toward intangible assets and keeping their stakeholders informed of these critical investments. Traditional physical assets, such as factories and equipment, have largely become commoditized because of (1) globalization and greater competition that require a faster pace of innovation and (2) the many physical assets that are now available to a large number of companies at a low cost (Hand & Lev, 2003).

The consumer electronics industry is an excellent case in point. The world's top consumer electronics brands used to focus on owning and operating their own manufacturing equipment and factories. Now, much of the production and manufacturing and even some of the design of iconic products like the iPod, iPhone, Kindle, PlayStation, and Wii are outsourced to behind-the-scenes electronics manufacturing services companies like Foxconn, Flextronics, and Jabil (Hagerty, 2013; Luk, 2013). In turn, a sustained competitive advantage is much less likely to be gained through manufacturing and production. Instead, consumer electronics brands focus on innovating and creating value through investing more in research and development; attracting, retaining, and developing the best managers and employees; and building unique brands and reputations that will differentiate themselves from competitors (Silvestrelli, 2010).

A range of stakeholders is increasingly interested in learning about how organizations are investing in and managing their intangible assets (Deloitte, 2013). Intangibles are defined as those sources of future benefits that lack a direct physical embodiment (Lev, 2005). Research across various disciplines finds that stakeholders tend to "undervalue" the contributions these intangibles make to the long-term success of the organization (e.g., Amir, Lev, & Sougiannis, 2003; Eberhart, Maxwell, & Siddique, 2004; Edmans, 2011; Lindemann, 2004; Rindova, Williamson, & Petkova, 2010). Unlike tangible asset values, which must be reported regularly on financial statements, the performance of intangibles often remains murky to stakeholders unless an organization chooses to voluntarily share this nonfinancial information on an ongoing basis (Chan, Lakonishok, & Sougiannis, 2001; Hoffmann & Fieseler, 2012; Laskin, 2008).

Strategic communication professionals often are tasked with advising business managers on what types of nonfinancial information the organization should share with various stakeholder groups and how best to present and interpret this information for stakeholders (Hoffmann & Fieseler, 2012). While knowledge of traditional accounting and financial reporting is essential, in an increasingly information and knowledge-driven economy, it is arguably just as important that communicators understand at least the basics of intangible assets and nonfinancial information. Simply stated, intangibles are key drivers of future organizational success (Lev, 2001, 2011, 2012b). In other words, how intangibles are managed and communicated has a direct impact on very tangible longer-term organizational performance, including future financial results and stock market valuations (e.g., Chan et al., 2001; R. S. Kaplan & Norton, 2004, 2007, 2008).

Tangible, Intangible, and Financial Assets

As discussed in chapter 4, an asset is something a company owns that is a source of value, meaning that the asset has the potential to generate revenue and contribute to profits. Tangible assets and intangible assets are sometimes defined as "hard" and "soft" assets, respectively. More formally, an intangible asset is a source of future benefits that *lacks* a direct physical embodiment. Classic examples include patents; trademarks; copyrights; brands and reputations; organizational strategies; and unique processes, procedures, and organizational cultures. Sometimes intangible assets are called knowledge assets or intellectual assets. On the other hand, a traditional tangible asset has a physical embodiment, such as real estate, factories, equipment, vehicles, or product inventory. Financial assets, such as stocks, bonds, and cash, also lack a direct physical embodiment, but such assets are not considered intangibles since they basically represent claims on organizational assets, both tangible and intangible (Lev, 2005). Finally, human capital, such as a company's management and employees, is generally treated as a type of intangible asset.

Intangible assets such as company culture draw on an organization's character, mission, and values. "With more and more products becoming commoditized, corporate character becomes a key competitive differentiator," says Wendi Strong, chief communications officer of USAA, which not only is a top brand in financial services but also is among the most visible brands in the United States (Harris Interactive, 2013). "At USAA, strong values and passionate advocacy for our members are what distinguish us. It's baked into our DNA. Our CEO and all of our senior executives start every meeting by reinforcing our mission, brand and core values" (W. Strong, personal communication, February 15, 2014).

GAAP Reporting and Intangible Assets

As discussed in chapter 4, all public companies in the United States are required to report their financial performance according to Generally Accepted Accounting Principles (GAAP). These standards were developed following the Great Depression of the 1930s, an era in which economic power was largely derived from amassing physical assets rather than nurturing nonphysical assets. As such, these standards do not require companies to share much—if any—information about various classes of intangible assets. Although some progress has been made (Interbrand, 2001), GAAP standards are inadequate for informing stakeholders about corporate investment and performance of intangibles. The situation on the reporting of intangibles and nonfinancial information is better internationally but is not perfect (Lindemann, 2004).

An exception to GAAP reporting's exclusionary treatment of intangibles is that research and development (R&D) is a required line on financial reports. However, R&D is *expensed* (i.e., treated as a cost on the income statement) rather than *capitalized* (i.e., treated as an asset on the balance sheet). Capital expenditures are assets that are expensed over time rather than all at once, under the view that the asset will provide future benefits over a number of years. While research clearly shows that investing in intangible assets often yields long-term benefits, this is not how GAAP standards treat this area. As another example, investments in advertising, public relations, training programs, and related activities are all lumped together under one expense line—selling, general, and administrative expense (SG&A)—on the income statement. Again, this investing is treated as an expense rather than a source of future value.

Additionally, categories called "goodwill" and "intangibles" (with estimated monetary values for each) generally only appear on a company's balance sheet if the company made an acquisition in which it paid above so-called book value, an accounting measure of the net asset value carried on the acquired company's books. In other words, a company does not generally receive formal accounting recognition on its balance sheet for the value of its intangibles unless it engages in acquisitive behavior (Lev, 2012b). Companies that choose to grow organically (i.e., not engage in mergers or acquisitions) are inadvertently penalized.

Even the accounting profession acknowledges the inadequacy of current GAAP reporting standards and the lackluster information provided in corporate reports. As the heads of the six largest global audit networks wrote in a white paper for the industry (DiPiazza et al., 2006):

> Clearly, a range of "intangibles" that are not well measured, or not measured at all, under current accounting conventions are driving company performance. Investors and other stakeholders in business information understandably want to know what those intangibles are, and how they might plausibly affect how businesses perform *in the future*." (p. 16, italics in original)

Just in the United States alone, companies invest over a trillion dollars annually into intangible assets, comparable to the amount invested in traditional tangible assets (Lev, 2004, 2005). Intangibles now account for well over half of the market value of public companies (Lev, 2005). The growing gap between how the stock market values corporate assets and what accounting rules say a company is worth is most evident when looking at the market-to-book (M/B) ratio (R. S. Kaplan & Norton, 2001). The M/B ratio is calculated by taking a company's total market capitalization (i.e., stock market value) and dividing it by the company's book value—the stated net value of the company's assets on its balance sheet. Before the stock market crash of 2008, this ratio was 3× (Lev, 2012). In other words, investors were willing to pay a two dollar "premium" for every dollar of book value. This premium reflects an imprecise attempt by investors to calculate the value of these missing intangible assets from corporate balance sheets.

Research by Ocean Tomo, LLC, an intellectual property-focused merchant bank, paints an even more vivid picture of the rise of intangible assets in contributing to the total market value of publicly traded companies. "The last decade has seen a continual rise in investor attention to intangible assets, particularly intellectual property (IP)," says James E. Malackowski, chair and chief executive officer of Ocean Tomo (personal communication, April 29, 2014). "At a macro level, this can be seen in the growing proportion of company value represented by intangibles."

As shown on figure 6.1, research conducted by Ocean Tomo (2014) finds that as of 2010, approximately 80 percent of the total stock market value of the component companies that make up the S&P 500, a widely followed index of five hundred of the largest U.S. publicly traded companies, is based on intangible assets. Just 20 percent of this market value is attributable to tangible assets. This represents almost a complete reversal from 1975, in which 83 percent of the total market value of S&P 500 components was attributed to tangible assets and just 17 percent was attributed to intangibles.

A More Holistic Approach to Evaluating Performance

From investors and financial analysts to business managers and directors on corporate boards, a range of stakeholder groups increasingly feel that organizational performance should be measured and evaluated by much more than simply a profit and loss statement. Financials are important, but they tell stakeholders more about the *past* (i.e., previous financial performance),

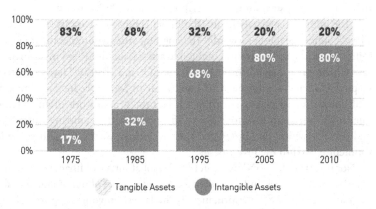

Figure 6.1 Historical view of drivers of S&P 500 market value
Source: Ocean Tomo, LLC.

rather than how the organization will perform in the *future*. There is growing recognition that the management (or mismanagement) of intangible assets is a leading indicator of future financial performance (Hoffmann & Fieseler, 2012; R. S. Kaplan & Norton, 2001; Laskin, 2008; Lev, 2012b). As a result, stakeholders expect greater access to nonfinancial information so that they may better monitor whether an organization is successfully managing and growing its intangibles or whether it is underperforming in this regard. Research by Rassart and Miller (2013) of the Deloitte Global Center for Corporate Governance finds that organizations often fall short in this area:

> Today, people look to organizations to provide them with a broad range of information—from traditional financial topics to non-financial subjects including the environmental behavior, workplace practices, community social responsibility, and more. Organizations that meet these expectations not only build greater trust with their stakeholders, but . . . they may also be better performing organizations as well. (p. 3)

Research shows that *more than a third* (35 percent) of the typical professional investor's investment decision making is significantly influenced by the nonfinancial information about a company, particularly its strategic vision, its perceived ability to execute on its stated strategy, and the credibility of its management team (Ernst & Young, 1997; Light, 1998; Low & Siesfield, 1998). Environmental, social, and governance (ESG) performance and the risk of regulatory or legal responses related to ESG performance are also being taken into account by more investors when evaluating companies (Ernst & Young, 2014). Collectively, such information is increasingly viewed as sending signals about an organization's future profitability and the potential risks surrounding the attainment of such future financial results (Ernst & Young, 2014).

"The minute a quarterly financial number is missed, investors ask, 'should I have confidence going forward?' The ongoing articulation, depth and credibility of the discussion around intangible assets is an important investment," says Christopher Galvin, the cofounder, CEO, and chair of Harrison Street Capital LLC and the former CEO and chair of Motorola Inc., a company well known for its patent portfolio. "It lays the groundwork to answer the question, 'should an investor have confidence that the company can adapt and drive to win in an unpredictable future business and competitive environment related to the investment?'"

Not surprisingly, a BNY Mellon (2012) global survey of financial communication professionals finds that demand for disclosures of nonfinancial goals, such as corporate ESG performance, is the fastest growing category among the types of information desired by investors and analysts. While roughly 40 percent of Western European and Latin American companies now report making ESG disclosures, only 20 percent do so in the United States (BNY Mellon, 2012). Looking more broadly, about half of U.S. public companies issue some sort of nonfinancial guidance, ranging from trend information to factors that may drive future earnings (NIRI, 2012a).

A global survey of institutional investors conducted by Ernst & Young (2014), in collaboration with *Institutional Investor* magazine, revealed that nine out of ten respondents felt that nonfinancial information played a pivotal role in *at least one* of their investment decisions in the past 12 months. This survey also found that almost two-thirds (64.5 percent) of respondents conducted some kind of evaluation of nonfinancial information when making their investment decisions (Ernst & Young, 2014). Mirroring the findings of the BNY Mellon (2012) global survey, Ernst & Young (2014) found that investors in the United States and Canada were far less likely to use nonfinancial data in investment decision making than in other parts of the world.

The desire for nonfinancial information about intangible assets is not limited to financial-oriented stakeholders. Business managers, employees, and boards of directors also show a growing interest in monitoring the performance of intangible assets. The landmark work of R. S. Kaplan and Norton (1992, 1996, 2001, 2004a, 2004b, 2007, 2008) on "balanced scorecards" over the past 20 years has ingrained in corporate cultures the concept that financial data alone are not an accurate gauge of organizational performance. The original balanced scorecard (R. S. Kaplan & Norton, 1992, 1996) judged organizational performance toward achieving an organization's vision on the basis of four broad categories of performance data: (1) financial, (2) customers, (3) internal business processes, and (4) learning and growth. Balanced scorecards remain one of the most widely used tools by business managers around the world to gauge performance (Rigby & Bilodeau, 2013).

Corporate directors also show greater affinity for nonfinancial information. A global survey, conducted by Deloitte (2013), of directors in 19 countries found that the six out of ten (63 percent) directors serve on boards in which company performance is reviewed against nonfinancial indicators. All U.S. directors reported using some form of nonfinancial information to gauge performance. Deloitte (2013) credits this growing interest in nonfinancial information among directors to the external pressure over the past decade for organizations to disclose metrics on the environment, the handling of social issues, and corporate governance.

Categories of Intangible Assets and Nonfinancial Information

There is no definitive typology regarding the various classes of intangible assets. Rather a range of classification schemes have been developed and used by scholars and professionals working in this area (e.g., Chareonsuk & Chansa-ngavei, 2008; Ernst & Young, 1997; Hill & Knowlton, 2006; Hoffmann & Fieseler, 2012; R. S. Kaplan & Norton, 1992; Laskin, 2008; Lev, 2005; Low & Siesfield, 1998; Young, 1998). The classification of intangibles is made more difficult by the fact that intangibles are interconnected. For example, company strategy and company management (i.e., the designers and overseers of the strategy) are closely related but are not one and the same. As another example, environmental, social, and governance performance are often included as dimensions of corporate reputation but are also important intangibles on their own. Based on a review of these schemes, the authors introduce the following major categories of intangibles, which collectively contribute to an organization's net intangible asset value (see figure 6.2):

1. Vision and Strategy
2. Management
3. Employees
4. Reputation, Brands, and Relationships
5. Research and Development
6. Environmental, Social, and Governance (ESG) Performance

The following sections briefly explore each of these classes of intangibles, as well as provide possible key performance indicators (KPIs) that may be used to track the performance of each asset class (Low & Siesfield, 1998).

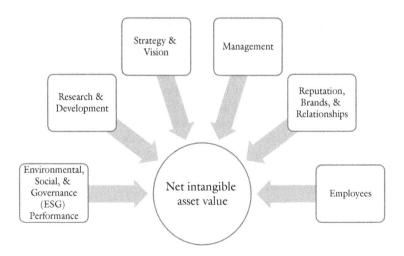

Figure 6.2 Categories of intangible asset value creation

Regardless of the level and quality of communication, a specific class of intangible asset may be valued more or less by a stakeholder, depending on the industry the organization is in, the type of stakeholder (for example, a consumer versus an investor), the life stage of the organization (i.e., a fast-growing earlier-stage company or a more mature entity), and other situational factors (Chareonsuk & Chansa-ngavei, 2008; Chasan, 2012).

Vision and Strategy

All stakeholders have an innate interest in where an organization plans to head in the future—its vision and how it plans to get there—its strategy. Research shows that in assessing nonfinancial information, investors, analysts, and directors consistently place a high level of importance on the company's strategic vision and perceived ability to execute against it (Deloitte, 2013; Laskin, 2008; Low & Siesfield, 1998; Roach, 2013). A strategy should be straightforward and simple to articulate. Google CEO Larry Page, for example, says that the company's strategy is to only invest in and develop products that pass the "toothbrush test," meaning that the products must be important enough to use at least twice a day (Helft, 2013). Relevant KPIs for tracking the efficacy of a strategy could include customer-centric data points like product/service launch and upgrade milestones, sales order backlogs or same store sales figures (as applicable), market share measures, and customer adoption and loyalty rates.

Management

While this is no longer the era of the "celebrity CEO," many stakeholders remain interested in who is steering the ship—the CEO and the C-suite, as it is this executive team that is most responsible for setting and overseeing organizational strategy (Park & Berger, 2004). There is widespread recognition of the ability of a CEO and executive team to create or destroy value for the organization and its stakeholders. For example, the stock price of JCPenney initially surged by 17.5 percent, adding more than $1 billion in market value, simply on the surprise news in June 2011 that former Apple executive Ron Johnson had been hired as the new CEO of the retailer (Holmes & Lublin, 2011). Johnson was later ousted after his strategy proved unsuccessful. In terms of KPIs, the CEO and executive team grow, maintain, or lose credibility, particularly among financial stakeholders, on the basis of their ability to meet or exceed the financial guidance and performance targets that they have provided (Roach, 2013). Guidance is discussed in chapter 5.

Employees

While executives set and oversee a strategy, it is an organization's midlevel managers and frontline employees who actually implement it. Research shows that greater employee morale, satisfaction, and engagement drives increases in employee productivity and innovation, which in turn often translate into superior performance (Chareonsuk & Chansa-ngavej, 2008; Edmans, 2011; Gerpott, Thomas, & Hoffmann, 2008; Liebowitz & Wright, 1999; Sveiby, 1997). As a result, organizations are investing more in employee training, leadership development, and related initiatives that nurture and grow their human capital. Recognizing the importance of employees, stakeholders want to better understand the success of such efforts. Relevant KPIs include appearances in reputable "best places to work" lists, receiving awards related to employees and organizational culture, and tracking metrics on employee retention, engagement, and diversity.

Maril MacDonald, CEO of leading strategy execution and employee engagement firm Gagen MacDonald, sees a growing global trend among her clients. "As what we do becomes more and more commoditized, the intangible assets of who we are and how we do it become even more critical. Investors recognize that while current value may be based on the tangible assets you have now, future value will be based on your ability to do something even greater with those assets," MacDonald says (personal communication, May 9, 2014). "That potential lies in the hands of any organization's people, the leaders and employees who can best execute, innovate and adapt to an ever-changing world. Smart companies know that those who excel at attracting, retaining, developing and aligning talent have the greatest of all competitive advantages."

Starbucks Coffee Company is known for the benefits package it provides to even its part-time employees across its more than 19,000 retail stores in over 60 countries (Abrahamian, 2013; Associated Press, 2005; S. Kim, 2014). "Since Starbucks was founded four decades ago, how we treat our people has been at the heart of our success," says Corey duBrowa, senior vice president of global communications and international public affairs at Starbucks (personal communication, January 6, 2014). "In fact, for more than 20 years, Starbucks was among the first public companies to offer our partners—that's what we call our employees—comprehensive healthcare coverage and equity in our company."

Reputation, Brands, and Relationships

Strong reputations, brands, and stakeholder relationships are often associated with superior organizational performance (Carroll, 2013; Hutton, Goodman, Alexander, & Genest, 2001; Ledingham, 2003, 2006; Seltzer & Zhang, 2011; Strömbäck & Kiousis, 2011; van Riel & Fombrun, 2007). As a result, organizations are investing more in the communication programs needed to monitor, support, and grow these assets. Of course, reputations, brands, and relationships are built on much more than making promises; they are built on a demonstrated ability to deliver on such promises (i.e., consistency in words and deeds). Therefore, the strategic communication function seeks a seat at the policymaking table so that appropriate promises are made and then kept by the organization. Relevant KPIs include appearances in recognized top reputation or brand lists and reputation, brand, or relationship values calculated by reputable third parties. Other useful metrics may include having stakeholder specific indicators of brand, reputation, or relationship strength (e.g., stakeholder loyalty and the likelihood to recommend the brand). Chapter 9 is dedicated to discussing corporate reputation.

Research and Development

In a knowledge-based economy, the pace of innovation required to remain a successful organization is relentless. Research and development (R&D) is a core driver of an organization's innovation (or lack thereof). The innovations and intellectual property (IP) resulting from R&D and related activities are a key source of competitive advantage. Intellectual property includes patents, trademarks, copyrights, and trade secrets. Research shows that investors and analysts tend to undervalue the long-term financial payoffs from investing in R&D, particularly when information about such R&D investment is limited and murky (Chan et al., 2001; Eberhart et al., 2004; Lev, 2011; Oswald & Zarowin, 2007). This undervaluation is pronounced in industries that may not be automatically associated with innovation, such as oil and gas, metals, and industrials (Amir et al., 2003). Relevant KPIs include tracking and updating stakeholders on the issuance of IP and the income generated from the IP, reputable third party estimates of IP values, and recognized industry awards related to R&D and innovations.

"Disclosures related to not just the number [of patents held], but also the quality of patents held, as well as the licensing income generated, helps to show a company's position within the technology landscape," says James E. Malackowski, chair and CEO of Ocean Tomo, LLC, a merchant banking firm that specializes in intellectual capital equity management (personal communication, April 29, 2014). "Leading innovative firms now also look to R&D activities as a source of IP product development, which allows for the capture and recycling of limited resources."

Environmental, Social, and Governance Performance

Once dismissed as "nice to have" but not "need to have," environmental, social, and governance (ESG) performance is collectively an area that organizations can no longer afford to put on the backburner. Customers, employees, and other stakeholders increasingly choose in part whether to do (or continue doing) business with an organization on the basis of perceptions of the organization's ESG policies and performance. Even financial-minded stakeholders like investors care about ESG policies and performance, if more from a risk management perspective, because poor ESG performers can be greater targets for activism, regulations, and lawsuits. For example, there is some empirical evidence that suggests a positive linkage between ESG disclosures and stock market performance (Clark & Master, 2013; Koehler & Hespenheide, 2013; U.S. SIF Foundation, 2012). Relevant KPIs include appearances on recognized ESG or corporate social responsibility (CSR) indexes and rankings, governance scores computed by reputable third parties, and awards or external recognition related to ESG performance. Chapter 7 and chapter 8 are dedicated to discussing corporate governance and CSR, respectively.

Intangible Assets and Strategic Communication

Developed during an era in which wealth was amassed through the accumulation of physical assets, GAAP accounting standards are largely deficient in informing stakeholders about the performance of intangible assets (Interbrand, 2001; Lev, 2011, 2012b; Lindemann, 2004). With physical assets increasingly commoditized and future value often now created through owning and managing intangible assets, a range of stakeholders have a growing interest in nonfinancial information that sheds light on the performance of these intangibles. From a strategic communication perspective, silence is *not* golden when it comes to intangible assets and nonfinancial information. Organizations that choose to voluntarily share *more* and *better quality* information about themselves are generally rewarded by stakeholders. Conversely, those organizations that are less transparent are likely to face greater caution and higher costs in their dealings with stakeholders (Blankespoor, Miller, & White, 2012; Bushee, Matsumoto & Miller, 2010; Rawlins, 2008, 2009).

The information void resulting from the lack of requirements surrounding the disclosure and reporting of the performance of intangibles and the release of nonfinancial information represents a significant opportunity for strategic communicators to unlock value for organizations and the stakeholders of these organizations. Not only are investors and analysts likely to undervalue companies that are reluctant to share and explain much about the management and performance of their intangibles (e.g., Amir et al., 2003; Eberhart et al., 2004; Edmans, 2011; Lindemann, 2004; Rindova et al., 2010), but nonfinancial information is often easier for customers and employees to comprehend and rally behind than are the numbers on a financial statement. For nonfinancial stakeholders like customers and employees, straightforward metrics about customer loyalty, market share, employee engagement levels, CSR scores, reputation rankings, or new patent issuances may be better received than accounting figures that need to be deciphered.

Strategic communication professionals can play a leading role in engaging with an organization's various stakeholders to determine which categories of intangible assets and types of nonfinancial information are the most valued and assess current stakeholder satisfaction with such information (Rassart & Miller, 2013). Having gathered these opinions, communicators should review the quantity and quality of the nonfinancial information collected and shared by the organization in relation to the priorities expressed by its stakeholders. Once this information is in hand, communicators are in a better position to make a more targeted case to business managers about improving transparency into these key drivers of future success.

The benefits of improving disclosures and dialogue surrounding intangible assets should of course be weighed against the risks, such as additional disclosures potentially putting a company at a competitive disadvantage versus its peers (Amihud & Mendelson, 2003). Further, organizations that decide to become more transparent in the realm of nonfinancial information should be committed to providing regular updates on intangibles and corresponding KPIs through thick and thin (Low & Siesfield, 1998). Said another way, organizations that choose to provide detailed information about intangible assets in good times, only to clamp down on this information flow when times get challenging, damage their relationships with stakeholders. These risks aside, if an organization wants its stakeholders to have a more accurate and holistic view of the health of its operations and future ability to create value, then it will find ways to better communicate the performance of its intangibles. A communicator who is well versed in the language and insights of such intangibles is both critical to and useful for such an organization.

Key Terms

Amortization	Goodwill	Nonfinancial
Balanced scorecard	Human capital	information
Book value	Intangible asset	Physical asset
Capital expenditure	Intellectual property	Research and
Capitalized	Key performance	development
Depreciation	indicator	Selling, general, and
Expensed	Market-to-book	administrative
Financial asset	ratio	expense

Discussion Questions

1. Do you think communication about intangible assets and nonfinancial information will become more or less important to organizations and stakeholders in the future? Why?

2. Out of the various categories of intangible assets (see figure 6.2), which of these categories of intangibles have you used when deciding to begin or maintain a relationship with an organization? Which category of intangibles is generally most important to you?

3. Are you surprised research shows that even financial-oriented stakeholders like professional investors and financial analysts place value on nonfinancial information rather than simply looking at bottom-line accounting reports? Why or why not?

4. Visit the investor relations section of the website of a public company that you are interested in. Pull up the news release for the company's most recent quarterly earnings report. What sort of nonfinancial information on intangibles and associated key performance indicators (KPIs) are included as part of this news release?

5. In this same news release, does the CEO of the company and do any other executives quoted in the earnings news release reference the investment in and performance of the company's intangible assets? If so, which types of intangibles are discussed?

6. Based on your review of this release, how would you rate the effectiveness of the company in communicating the performance of its intangible assets to its stakeholders? How might the company do a better job in conveying this information? Be specific.

PART III

Focal Areas at the Intersection of Business and Communication

CHAPTER 7

Corporate Governance

In spring 2012, ahead of Facebook's planned initial public offering, the social media giant faced increasing public scrutiny over the fact that despite the majority of Facebook users being women, there were no women members of its board of directors (Pesta, 2013).

Even Facebook chief operating officer Sheryl Sandberg, an outspoken advocate for increasing diversity in the C-suite and the boardroom, was not a member of the firm's board. When asked about this issue in 2011, Facebook founder Mark Zuckerberg told Ken Auletta (2011) of *The New Yorker*: "I'm going to find people who are helpful, and I don't particularly care what gender they are or what company they are. I'm not filling the board with check boxes."

Women's issues activists, corporate governance experts, and business journalists seized on the filing of Facebook's IPO prospectus as an opportunity to draw attention to the lack of diversity in corporate boardrooms (Bosker, 2012; Pesta, 2012). Online campaigns by women's rights advocacy groups like Ultraviolet and Face It increased the public pressure on Facebook. Around this same time, a large California pension fund, the California State Teachers' Retirement System (CalSTRS), while owning far less than 1 percent of Facebook's shares outstanding, publicly challenged the company, releasing a letter addressed to Zuckerberg (Letzing & Lublin, 2012).

Soon after Facebook's IPO, in June 2012, the company announced that Sandberg would become Facebook's first female director (Isaac, 2012). While only Facebook knows whether it intended to make this decision after the IPO anyway, the outcry from its current and prospective stakeholders, not just shareholders, certainly seemed to play a role. In March 2013, Facebook named Susan Desmond-Hellmann to its board of directors, marking another step in its board diversification (Isaac, 2013).

Corporate governance—the system of checks and balances that attempts to make corporate boards and management accountable and make them operate in the interest of stakeholders—has become an increasingly salient topic for companies and stakeholders in recent years (Deloitte, 2014). The U.S. SEC (2012c) more formally defines corporate governance as "the framework of rules and practices that reflect and define the responsibilities and the appropriate level of accountability of a company's decision makers—both the directors elected by shareholders and the managers selected by directors" (para. 9). This framework is codified in a firm's corporate charter, bylaws, formal policies, customs, and other processes adopted by the organization.

In the wake of the accounting scandals of the early 2000s (e.g., Enron and Arthur Andersen, WorldCom, Tyco) and the collapse of many Wall Street banks and insurance companies in 2008 (e.g., Bear Stearns, Lehman Brothers, Fannie Mae, Freddie Mac, AIG), followed by the taxpayer-funded bailouts of the banking and insurance sector and the Occupy Wall Street movement of 2012, large professional investors are under growing pressure to take a more active role in managing their investments (Kieffer, 2013). Institutional investors, whether mutual fund managers or pension fund managers, increasingly view governance mechanisms as a way to hold corporate managers and boards more accountable for their actions and performance.

"The financial crisis of 2008 is considered to have been the worst economic crisis since the Great Depression of the 1930s," says Rajeev Kumar, senior managing director of research at Georgeson, a Computershare company and a top provider of strategic shareholder consulting services (personal communication, April 5, 2014). "These institutional investors have taken an increasingly active role in corporate governance instead of merely viewing it as a compliance function. Some of the leading labor and pension funds have pushed for corporate governance reforms, and they have not been shy about using this public forum as a bully pulpit to shame the companies in submission."

Shareholder activism—that is, taking an active role in affecting change at a company—has also proven to be a successful investment strategy. Annual data for 2009–2013 from Georgeson (2013b) and FactSet SharkRepellent (J. Laide, personal communication, June 2, 2014), respectively, show that in the United States alone, on average, a little less than four hundred ninety governance proposals were submitted each year by shareholders and that nearly three hundred seventy activist shareholder campaigns were waged. Even very large, blue-chip companies like Microsoft, Apple, PepsiCo, Procter & Gamble, and Sony have been the subject of activist shareholder demands in recent years. It seems that no company is immune to this groundswell (De La Merced & Creswell, 2013).

Strategic communication professionals working for or advising companies should, at the very least, understand the basics of corporate governance and board-CEO-investor-stakeholder relationships. "Corporate governance deals with the leadership of the company and that is certainly something that anyone in a communication role has to be concerned with too," says James Kristie, editor and associate publisher *Directors & Boards* magazine (personal communication, January 1, 2014). "A company could wake up one morning and find itself under attack from an activist investor who has a strategy or corporate governance dispute, which will generate extensive media scrutiny and perhaps regulatory scrutiny, forcing the communication team to scramble the jets."

Corporations and the Agency Problem

Shareholders are essentially "absentee owners" of a company. While shareholders provide the capital that the organization needs to grow, they are not typically inside the organization on a day-to-day basis to monitor its performance. Under classic agency theory (Fama, 1980; Fama & Jensen, 1983; Jensen & Meckling, 1976; Mizruchi, 1988), the members of board of directors are viewed as "agents" that act on behalf of the "principals"—the shareholders. The board is tasked with advising and overseeing senior management (i.e., the C-suite), which is responsible for the day-to-day performance of the organization. Separate from the board of directors is the executive committee, which consists of a larger group of senior executives drawn from the organization. They typically either hold C-level positions or report to C-level executives.

In an ideal world, the interests of company management, the board of directors, shareholders, and other stakeholders would closely align, but that is not always the case. When the interests of these various groups meaningfully diverge, there is a so-called "agency problem," and the organization and its stakeholders endure "agency costs." Simply stated, management and board members may at times make decisions that enrich and entrench themselves to the detriment of stakeholders and the rest of the organization. Effective corporate governance policies, mechanisms, and practices aim to reduce these conflicts and make boards and managers more responsive to stakeholders. This principal-agent problem is not unique to companies. For example, any elected public official (i.e., agent) could make decisions that protect and advance their own personal interests rather than the interests of their constituents (i.e., principals).

Many boards of directors have traditionally operated under the concept of "shareholder primacy," which means that the interests of shareholders come before—and are more important than—the interests of other stakeholders (Jensen & Chew, 2000; Jensen & Meckling, 1976). Figure 7.1 provides a classic agency theory–based model of the relationships among the company shareholders, the board of directors, the company management, and other stakeholder groups.

While board members do have a fiduciary duty to act in the best interests of an organization, legally they are not obligated to base their decision making first and foremost on how a policy or action would impact shareholders (Adams, Licht, & Sagiv, 2011; Brusch, 2014; Stout, 2012). In fact, a variety of key legal decisions in U.S. courts through the years have sided with corporate boards that have taken into account the interests of a broader range of stakeholders (e.g., employees, customers, local communities, creditors) when making major corporate decisions (Lan & Heracleous, 2010). That being said, "maximizing shareholder value" often remains a top priority for business managers and directors in part because these same individuals own stock in the firm and stand to personally benefit from shareholder-friendly policies and actions (Adams et al., 2011; Brusch, 2014; Stout, 2012; Yang, 2013).

The Proxy Statement and Annual Meeting

Public companies are required to hold an annual meeting to allow shareholders to vote on major corporate matters, such as the election of the board of directors (SEC, 2012c). Other matters that may be voted on include management- or shareholder-submitted proposals, ranging from ratifying the selection of an accounting firm as auditor to approving executive compensation packages. Public companies are required to provide information on company management, board of director nominees, and other matters to be voted on in an important corporate governance document known as

Figure 7.1 Classic agency theory model

a proxy statement. This document is filed with the SEC's EDGAR system under a DEF 14A filing. Proxy statements were traditionally distributed to shareholders via postal mail, but increasingly such statements are distributed electronically, and ballot items are voted on electronically or by phone rather than from the floor of the actual meeting. The term "proxy" comes from the legal right a shareholder has to designate an agent—or proxy—to vote their shares as they specify and to act on their behalf (G. A. Holton, 2006).

Some small shareholders known as "corporate gadflies" have historically attempted to make governance changes at public companies (Marens, 2002; Pound, 1992; Talner, 1983). With limited resources and often minimal stock ownership positions, such investors were generally easy for companies to brush aside. A major change occurred in 1943 when the SEC adopted Rule 14(a)8 (Vogel, 1983). This rule, for the first time, allowed shareholder activists to submit some shareholder proposals for inclusion in the company's proxy materials. While this rule is a welcome tool for shareholder activists, the limitation of such proposals is that they are typically *nonbinding*, meaning that even if a majority of shareholders vote in favor of a proposal, the company doesn't legally have to act on it. Most of the time, such proposals fail to gain serious traction. For example, out of the thousands of shareholder proposals submitted and voted on from 1973–2004, only around 10 percent of these received majority support (Gillan & Starks, 2007).

A historic shift in the relationship between shareholders, corporate boards, and management took place in the mid-1980s, with the founding of the Council of Institutional Investors (CII) by large public pensions funds like the California Public Employees Retirement System (CalPERS). The founding of CII marked the start of public pension funds (and later union pension funds) taking a more active role in their investment portfolios, including submitting shareholder proposals focused on corporate governance issues. Institutional investors, such as large pension funds with considerable resources at their disposal, were much harder for companies to ignore than resource-constrained individual investors. Over the past 20 years, so-called entrepreneurial activists, such as hedge funds and wealthy private investors, have also taken up corporate governance as a key area of focus when they attempt to affect change at companies (Klein & Zur, 2009). Institutional investors have become well versed in running political-style campaigns to draw support for their proposals and ideas (Gillan & Starks, 2007).

Exit, Voice, and Loyalty at Public Companies

Hirschman's (1971) seminal work, "*Exit, Voice, and Loyalty: Responses to Decline in Firms, Organizations, and States*" provides a valuable framework for understanding how shareholders and other stakeholders may interact with a company's management and board of directors. After buying shares in a company, shareholders have three main options for expressing their opinion to company management and the board of directors (Lowenstein, 2009):

1. **Exit**—If a shareholder grows sufficiently dissatisfied with company performance, the shareholder may simply decide to sell the stock, in what has been called "The Wall Street Walk."
2. **Voice**—Alternately, instead of selling the stock, the shareholder may express dissatisfaction either privately or publicly to the company's board and/or management.
3. **Loyalty**—If a shareholder is satisfied with the company's performance, he or she may choose to remain silent, thereby signaling their satisfaction and approval to the company.

To "exhibit voice," a stakeholder may engage in a variety of activities, some of which are only possible if the stakeholder is specifically a shareholder (i.e., owns stock in the company). Such stakeholder activism options include direct private negotiations and requested meetings with company management, public targeting by taking complaints to influential third parties such as the news media, creating and submitting shareholder proposals for inclusion in the company's proxy materials, seeking to effect change through written consent solicitations outside of the annual meeting format, or engaging in a proxy contest (i.e., contested election) to attempt to remove one or more company directors and/or change major corporate policies.

Unlike shareholder proposals, which are typically only advisory and legally *nonbinding*, shareholder votes in proxy contests are *binding* (Ragas, 2010). During a proxy contest, the activist shareholder group pays out of its own pocket to distribute a competing set of proxy materials and an alternate slate of board of director nominees (either a full or a partial slate, depending on the corporate structure and goals of the activist investor) to company shareholders. The two sides then engage in a political-style strategic communication campaign to try and convince shareholders to support their candidate(s) for the board. Such campaigns can cost up to millions of dollars for each side, so typically only a shareholder group with a considerable economic interest in the targeted company engages in such aggressive and costly behavior (Ragas, 2012, 2013b).

Many proxy fights settle before they reach an official shareholder vote, with the two sides making concessions, such as adding one or more of the dissident shareholder's nominees to the board (Ragas, Kim, & Kiousis, 2011). Specialized consulting firms known as proxy advisors play a notable role in influencing the direction of shareholder voting on proxy proposals and proxy contests (Lublin & Grind, 2013). Since professional money managers typically invest in and monitor dozens of different companies, these investors pay firms such as Institutional Shareholder Services Inc. (ISS) and Glass, Lewis & Co. for analysis and advice on how to vote on specific corporate elections and issues. Corporations and activist investors compete for the recommendation of these firms. GMI Ratings, formed through the merger of The Corporate Library, GovernanceMetrics International, and Audit Integrity, is an additional notable player in the corporate governance advisory and ratings category (Daines, Gow, & Larker, 2010).

Another influential category of players on corporate governance matters and proxy contests are known as proxy solicitors. These consultants advise public companies and dissident shareholder groups on everything from making detailed voting projections on contested proxy issues to building support to defeat or pass such ballot items. As the name implies, these firms oversee the process of soliciting votes on contested proxy issues. Within the U.S. stock market, the top proxy solicitation firms include AST Phoenix Advisors, D. F. King & Co., Georgeson, Innisfree M&A Incorporated, MacKenzie Partners, Morrow & Co., and Okapi Partners.

While the number of U.S. proxy fights held annually has retrenched in recent years, this aggressive form of shareholder activism remains active. According to FactSet SharkRepellent data, there were 90 proxy contests held in 2013, compared with a record high of 133 contests held in 2009 (J. Laide, personal communication, June 2, 2014).

Best Practices in Corporate Governance

Corporate governance is a complex and evolving field (Bebchuk & Weisbach, 2010; Daily, Dalton, & Canella, 2003; Monks & Minow, 2011). Seemingly, each proxy season brings a new governance-related topic into the spotlight. Even governance experts do not always agree on what is or is not a so-called "best practice." There is arguably no definitive list of "best practices" in corporate governance. On balance, the empirical evidence indicates that better governance—as defined and measured in quite a variety of ways—does not seem to hurt company financial and stock market performance. However, it does not necessarily lead to company outperformance either. In short, this relationship is complex (Bhagat & Bolton, 2008; Daines et al., 2010; Lev, 2012b). The same goes for the role of shareholder activism in positively contributing to firm performance. Some studies (e.g., Bebchuk, Brav, & Jiang, 2013; Klein & Zur, 2009) find that activism is a driving force behind improved company performance, while others find the impact is inconsistent (e.g., Gillan & Starks, 1998, 2007).

This mixed empirical evidence does not invalidate the need for companies to improve their governance mechanisms and better communicate the reasoning behind such mechanisms and policies. Companies that are perceived to have mediocre to poor corporate governance could face greater regulatory and governmental scrutiny, potentially embarrassing and costly stakeholder activism that diverts management and the board's focus, and diminished overall reputations with current and prospective stakeholders (Reputation Institute, 2013a, 2013b).

Communication is key in engendering greater understanding for governance policies and positions says Kevin Kelly, managing director with Morrow & Co., LLC, a proxy advisory and solicitation services firm (personal communication, January 14, 2014). "There is no one-size-fits-all when it comes to corporate governance," Kelly says. "Each company must determine what is in its best interest and adopt corporate governance policies accordingly. Corporate governance policies should suit the company, which in turn leads to the message. However, shareholders have the right to submit shareholder proposals to issuers, and these can have a significant impact on how the engagement proceeds."

The following corporate governance areas have received noteworthy attention in recent years (Deloitte, 2013, 2014; Georgeson, 2011, 2012, 2013a; Rassart & Miller, 2013).

Board Independence and Accountability

Securities laws and exchange requirements now mandate that the majority of a company's board members be independent directors, meaning they are not employees or consultants of the company and that they do not have other material business relationships with the company. To improve accountability, more companies have moved to declassify their board, meaning that all directors come up for election each year rather than over a staggered, multiyear period. At some companies, a director must offer his or her resignation if the majority of shareholders don't vote in favor of the individual—even if the nominee runs unopposed.

Board Diversity

In addition to the push for more independent, outside directors in the boardroom, stakeholders and governance experts are also pushing for more diversity in the boardroom. This includes appointing more women directors, as was the case with Facebook at the start of this chapter, as well as ensuring greater director diversity in terms of race, nationality, background, and experience. Interestingly, research shows that companies with women board members outperform all-male boards (Carter & Wagner, 2011; Joy, Carter, Wagner, & Narayanan, 2007).

Board and Executive Compensation

In the wake of the passage of the Dodd-Frank Wall Street Reform and Consumer Protection Act and the say-on-pay advisory voting requirement, companies are tightening the linkage between compensation and performance. This includes requiring directors and executives to maintain minimum stock ownership levels, making performance-based equity grants, eliminating the accelerated vesting of stock, reducing "golden parachute" packages for executives following takeovers, and implementing stronger compensation "clawback" provisions in employment contracts (Joshi, 2013; T. Spangler, 2013).

CEO and Chair Duality

In part because of shareholder pressure, a growing number of companies have separated the CEO and chair of the board positions. The idea behind removing this duality is that it eliminates the risk of placing too much power in the hands of one individual. An independent chair may provide better oversight of management. Research shows that companies with an independent chair do *not* significantly outperform companies in which these positions are held by the same individual (Krause & Semadeni, 2013; Lublin, 2013). The move toward lead directors at many companies helps address this duality.

Shareholder Voting Rights

In recent years, there has been a move toward shareholders having stronger voting rights. This includes eliminating dual class stock (e.g., Class A and Class B shares) with special voting power, reducing or eliminating supermajority voting provisions, removing antitakeover provisions known as "poison pills," implementing cumulative voting in director elections (i.e., allowing shareholders to pool their votes for a single board nominee), and giving shareholders the right to act by written consent or call special meetings.

Dodd-Frank and Executive Compensation

Following the taxpayer-funded bailouts of the Wall Street banks and the Detroit automakers, the U.S. Congress signed into law the Dodd-Frank Act in July 2010. This financial reform legislation puts into place dozens of new financial regulations designed to prevent another financial crisis and to better protect the investing public. As part of this act, public companies are required both to disclose additional information in their proxy statements and to provide shareholders with an advisory vote (i.e., a nonbinding vote)—typically held annually—on executive compensation packages. This advisory vote has become known as a say-on-pay vote. As witnessed by the 2011–2012 Occupy Wall Street protests over income inequality, the disparity in executive compensation (i.e., "the 1 percent") relative to average workers (i.e., "the 99 percent") was already a contentious issue. The mandatory say-on-pay vote held each proxy season has further thrust executive compensation practices into the media and public spotlights (AFL-CIO, 2011).

In the 1950s, the typical CEO of a large U.S. company received a pay package that was 20× the average rank-and-file worker's pay (E. B. Smith & Kuntz, 2013). By 1980, that ratio had risen to 42-to-1, and by 2000, it had expanded to 120-to-1. As of 2013, this ratio stood at 204-to-1 (E. B. Smith & Kuntz, 2013). The average total compensation package for the CEO of a large U.S. company is a little more than $11 million per year (Francis & Lublin, 2014). This total includes salary, an annual bonus, and equity grants (i.e., stock options and restricted stock awards), with such grants representing the largest percentage of total compensation (Francis & Lublin, 2014). Some companies specifically set a limit on executive compensation relative to the average or median pay level of its workers. Whole Foods Market Inc., for example, sets a salary cap for top executives of no more than 19× the company's average annual wage—not including stock options or pension benefits (Ackerman, 2013; Brancaccio, 2012). Other companies like Costco don't set official caps but instead set average worker pay at compensation levels that are significantly higher than their peers, thus resulting in smaller relative pay gaps between executives and rank-and-file workers.

Since the say-on-pay requirement went into effect in 2011, shareholders have voted in favor of compensation packages at the vast majority of U.S. companies (A. Brown, 2013). In fact, at approximately seven out of ten U.S. companies, executive pay packages receive favorable votes of 90 percent or more (Georgeson, 2012). However, opposition votes of even 20–25 percent can serve as a source of embarrassment and future stakeholder scrutiny for a company, its management, and board (Thurm, 2013). Not surprisingly, companies with poor shareholder returns and high CEO pay packages are significantly more likely to receive low say-on-pay support from shareholders (A. Brown, 2013). Companies increasingly design compensation packages that more closely align pay with long-term company performance (Georgeson, 2013b). Strategic communication and investor relations professionals are tasked with both clearly communicating such compensation details and providing reasoning to stakeholders in the proxy statement and through other materials.

Even public companies with strong financial and stock market performance may be at risk of shareholders voting against executive pay packages if shareholders feel the compensation is excessive. For example, at Chipotle Mexican Grill Inc.'s 2014 annual meeting, nearly eight out of ten shareholders voted against the fast-casual restaurant company's executive pay package (Jargon, 2014). In 2013, Chipotle's two co-CEOs were awarded total compensation of nearly $50 million (Jargon, 2014). From 2010–2014, Chipotle shareholders were richly rewarded as well, with the company's stock price increasing by more than 550 percent (Levine-Weinberg, 2014).

Corporate Governance and Strategic Communication

Corporate governance and stakeholder activism are likely to remain pressing topics on the corporate agenda for the foreseeable future. A global research study conducted by Deloitte (2013) finds that three out of four directors surveyed expect scrutiny by shareholders to increase in the years ahead. As a result, the majority (64 percent) of these directors expect shareholder engagement between the board and investors to increase over the coming years (Deloitte, 2013). While shareholder relationships are important, they are far from the only stakeholders concerned with effective corporate governance. Employees, customers, regulators, and suppliers are increasingly interested in the corporate character, practices, and leadership of the organizations they choose to support. Accountability, engagement, and transparency are critical to building and sustaining strong organizational-public relationships (Arthur W. Page Society, 2013a, 2013b).

According to Roger Bolton, president of the Arthur W. Page Society, enterprises, like people, have character (personal communication, January 12, 2014). "The challenge for companies wishing to be trusted is to build a corporate character that is worthy of trust," Bolton says. "Trusted organizations carefully balance the needs of all stakeholders, making responsible choices aligned with their mission and values. They listen to and consider others' points of view and are willing to change their own policies when appropriate."

Such trust takes time to build. Corporate governance expert Nell Minow says that companies should try to make friends with shareholders and other stakeholders *before* they need their support on a governance issue (personal communication, October 10, 2013). "Directors should meet with large shareholders and respond to questions at annual meetings," says Minow, a board member at GMI Ratings and cofounder of The Corporate Library. "And companies should be transparent and accessible in their financial reports and compensation disclosure, including a clear statement of how compensation is tied to the achievement of specific goals leading to sustainable long-term growth."

In today's business environment, ignoring activist shareholders is not an option for the management teams and boards of directors of publicly held companies says Rajeev Kumar, senior managing director of research at Georgeson, a Computershare company and a leading provider of proxy solicitation and strategic shareholder consulting services (personal communication, April 5, 2014). "If an activist shareholder reaches out to the company, it is better to engage than to ignore the shareholder," Kumar says. "Ignoring the shareholder will not make the problem go away; it would only make it worse by antagonizing the shareholder."

Strategic communicators who understand at least the basics of corporate governance and trending issues like executive compensation are better positioned to contribute to policymaking discussions within the organization on governance and stakeholder activism. Such professionals are better equipped to monitor and listen to the governance-related concerns of stakeholders, accurately convey these issues to both business managers and potentially the board of directors, and explain and contextualize the corporate governance policies of the organization's management and board to its internal and external stakeholders.

In practice, corporate governance is a particularly tricky area for strategic communication professionals because the communication function does not necessarily have a direct hand or voice in governance decisions like executive compensation, board diversity, or shareholder rights. Strategic communicators should be aware that providing counsel on governance policies and communication could be a sensitive area for an organization's management and board members because talk of performance and accountability could hit close to home in some organizations.

But a strategic communicator can add value in this area by (1) staying current and educated on trends in good governance and stakeholder activism, to know whether an organization is in-line or out-of-line with a specific governance practice (and vulnerable to activists), (2) making sure there is a program in place to monitor and listen to the governance concerns of a range of stakeholders (not just shareholders) while relaying these priorities to business managers, and (3) encouraging the organization to release more timely and accessible information on governance topics that stakeholders indicate are most important to them. While potentially uncomfortable at times, shining more light into the boardroom and C-suite should ultimately benefit both the organization and its stakeholders in collectively creating long-term shared value.

Key Terms

Agency problem	Corporate governance	Majority voting
Agency theory	Cumulative voting	Poison pill
Board of directors	Dodd-Frank Act	Proxy contest
Chair	of 2010	Proxy statement
Chief executive officer	Dual class stock	Rule 14(a)8
Chief financial officer	Executive committee	Say on frequency
Chief operating officer	Exit, voice, and loyalty	Say on pay
Classified board	Fiduciary obligation	Shareholder activism
Clawback provision	Independent director	Shareholder primacy
Corporate gadfly	Lead director	Shareholder proposal

Discussion Questions

1. Visit the corporate governance section of the website of a public company that is of interest to you. This section may be found under the investor relations section of the site. What sort of company information is included under this section of the site?

2. What did you think of the presentation of the information found under the corporate governance section of this company's website? How would you improve it? Is there any information that you would add and want to learn about if you were a stakeholder?

3. Would you choose to work for a company that has "poor" corporate governance practices according to the list of current governance trends and priorities reviewed in this chapter? What about choosing to buy from such a company? Please explain your reasoning.

4. Do you think there are instances in which shareholder activism is actually detrimental to the long-term value of a company and its other shareholders? Can you think of any examples from the news in which a shareholder activist's demands harmed other stakeholders?

5. Following classic agency theory, the board of directors (i.e., agents) makes decisions first and foremost that benefit the organization's shareholders (i.e., agents). Do you agree with the shareholder primacy perspective embraced by this theory? Why or why not?

6. Executive compensation remains a hot-button issue in the boardroom and on Main Street. Do you think companies should place limits on the amount of executive compensation relative to the median or average pay of the organization's employees? Why or why not?

CHAPTER 8

Corporate Social Responsibility

Corporate social responsibility (CSR) is hardly a new concept (Rawlins, 2005). Over a century ago, industrial magnate Andrew Carnegie (1901) wrote "The Gospel of Wealth," in which he implored businesspeople to contribute to the public good. More than 60 years ago, corporate communication pioneer Arthur W. Page advised AT&T, then one of the world's largest companies, to run its business not only for its shareholders but also for the benefit of the public (Jones & Kostyak, 2011). A half century ago, GOLIN founder Al Golin encouraged McDonald's CEO Ray Kroc to give back to the communities that contributed to the company's success. As a result of that charge, Ronald McDonald House was formed, and houses have since been established around the world (Golin, 2006). More recently, Whole Foods Market founder John Mackey and his coauthor Rajendra Sisodia (2013) have espoused the virtues of "conscious capitalism." What is different about decades past and today is that caring for society and not just profits is no longer the exception but the rule for successful, enduring corporations and business managers.

Global survey research by Cone Communications and Echo Research (2013) finds that only 6 percent of consumers today believe the singular purpose of business is to make money for shareholders. Nine in ten consumers want companies to go beyond the minimum standards required by law to operate responsibly, and a clear majority expect companies to play more of a role in the community than to simply donate time and money (Cone Communications & Echo Research, 2013). Stakeholder perceptions of a company's CSR performance have emerged as one of the most important drivers of a company's overall reputation (Carroll, 2013; Reputation Institute, 2013a, 2013b; van Riel & Fombrun, 2007). "Profit with purpose" is increasingly on the lips of not just social responsibility and sustainability advocates but business managers and the C-suite as well.

According to corporate communication scholars Timothy Coombs and Sherry Holladay (2012), corporate social responsibility, also known as simply "social responsibility," is "the voluntary actions that a corporation implements as it pursues its mission and fulfills its perceived obligations to stakeholders, including employees, communities, the environment, and society as a whole" (p. 8). This definition embraces the notion of an organization measuring its performance using a "triple bottom-line" approach—that is, concern for people, the planet, and profits. Sustainability is often viewed as an extension of social responsibility and understood as broader than simply concern for the environment (Ahern & Bortree, 2012). For example, the Global Reporting Initiative (GRI), a leader in triple bottom-line reporting standards, defines sustainability for organizations as covering "the four key areas of [organizational] performance and impacts: economic, environmental, social and governance" (2013, para. 3). Other related terms that emerge in social responsibility and/or sustainability discussions include the concepts of environmental, social, and governance (ESG) performance (Dowse, 2012; Kiernan, 2007; Koehler & Hespenheide, 2013; U.S. SIF Foundation, 2012) and corporate social performance (CSP) (Margolis, Elfenbein, & Walsh, 2009; Peloza, 2009).

The strategic communication function has often been described as the ethical and social conscience of an organization (Bowen, 2004, 2005, 2008). Strategic communication professionals are frequently on the front lines of helping to create and implement CSR programs and initiatives that align with the organization's character, mission, and values (Arthur W. Page Society, 2012, 2013a, 2013b); gain internal and external support from stakeholders for such efforts; communicate the value of these efforts internally and externally (Servaes & Tamayo, 2013); and evaluate the success of such programs. It is critical, therefore, for communicators and those in related areas to have a good understanding of this fast-moving and complex field.

Shareholder Theory versus Stakeholder Theory

There are at least two major theoretical perspectives that examine the role of business in society. Nobel Prize-winning economist Milton Friedman (1965, 1970) and others (e.g., Altman & Berman, 2011; Machan, 2011) assert that business creates the most value for society by concentrating on maximizing profits for shareholders, while conforming to the basic rules of society. According to shareholder theorists, this focus on single bottom-line profit creates value through the making of products and services that satisfy customers and fulfill market demand. This process creates jobs for employees and profits for investors, the so-called "owners of the business," to do with as they so please (Altman & Berman, 2011). The free market-centric shareholder perspective is summarized in Friedman's (1970) aptly titled essay in *The New York Times Magazine*: "The Social Responsibility of Business Is to Increase Its Profits."

Embedded in shareholder theory is the idea of shareholder primacy (Jensen & Chew, 2000; Jensen & Meckling, 1976)—that a corporate executive acts as an "agent" or "employee" of shareholders, the "principals" or "employers" of the business and its management (Friedman, 1965, 1970). Friedman argues that it is *not* inappropriate for business to engage in social responsibility initiatives if these actions help improve the long-term financial performance of the organization (Friedman, Mackey, & Rodgers, 2005). Such a business would then be engaging in social responsibility to advance its own enlightened self-interest. As Adam Smith (2004) wrote in *The Wealth of Nations* more than 200 years ago: "By pursuing his own interest [an individual]

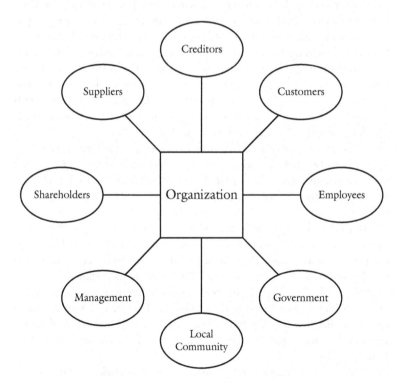

Figure 8.1 Stakeholder theory model

frequently promotes that of the society more effectually than when he really intends to promote it" (p. 264). In short, shareholder theorists do not believe that corporations have a moral obligation to CSR but believe that corporations may engage in such activities if they are found to benefit shareholders. On the opposite end of the social responsibility spectrum is stakeholder theory. The work of business ethicist R. Edward Freeman (2010) and others formally introduced the concept of stakeholders—those groups and individuals that have a shared interest or "stake" in the performance of an organization. According to stakeholder theorists, far more than satisfying shareholders is critical to the success of an organization; customers, employees, suppliers, communities and other stakeholder groups are also all rightful "owners" of a business (Freeman, Harrison, Wicks, Parmar, & de Colle, 2010). As such, these groups deserve a meaningful voice in firm decisions. Figure 8.1 outlines the stakeholder theory approach to managing an organization.

While, practically speaking, organizations must prioritize the weight they give various stakeholder interests, depending on the situation (Rawlins, 2006b), stakeholder theorists believe that business managers should seek to balance the interest of all stakeholders when developing firm strategy and making corporate decisions (Freeman, Harrison, & Wicks, 2007). Simply privileging shareholders and focusing on the bottom line at the expense of other stakeholders is unacceptable; strong business ethics are paramount. Under stakeholder theory, business managers have a moral obligation to create value for *all* stakeholders, while engaging in socially responsible behavior (Rawlins, 2005). "Profit with purpose" is the mantra. According to R. C. Solomon (1992), "business ethics, rightly conceived, is just good business" (p. 21).

The work of Freeman (2010) and others popularized the stakeholder approach to business in society, but some businesses have long operated under such principles. For example, Robert Wood Johnson, former chair of Johnson & Johnson (J&J), crafted J&J's corporate credo 70 years ago, long before the term CSR had been coined (Johnson & Johnson Services Inc., 2013). In the credo, Johnson outlined that the firm's first responsibility was to the doctors, nurses, and patients that use its products; its second responsibility was to its employees; its third responsibility was to the communities in which it operates; and its fourth responsibility was to its stockholders.

Willard "Bill" D. Nielsen, the retired former corporate vice president of public affairs and corporate communications for Johnson & Johnson, says he came to realize that the J&J credo "wasn't just a set of principles to which we subscribed, it was a statement of who we were" (personal communication, June 5, 2014).

"I believe the genius of the Johnson & Johnson credo is that it translates performance factors critical for business success into responsibilities the corporation accepts for its stakeholder groups—consumers, employees, communities and stockholders," says Nielsen, who serves on the board of trustees of the Robert Wood Johnson Foundation and is a former two-term president of the Arthur W. Page Society. "It commits the corporation to behavior that is always consistent with these responsibilities and thereby establishes its moral and ethical imperatives" (W. Nielsen, personal communication, June 5, 2014).

Costco Wholesale Corporation, the second largest retailer in the United States behind Walmart, espouses a similar approach to stakeholder relationships and generates impressive long-term financial results (Stone, 2013). For example, for the ten-year period that ended in 2013, Costco's share price rose approximately 280 percent, far outpacing the 100 percent gain of the Standard & Poor's 500, an index of five hundred large, widely held public companies, over this same period. This stock market performance has not come at the expense of employees because Costco commits to paying its employees living wages and has never had significant labor troubles in its 30 year history (Stone, 2013). As Costco CEO Craig Jelinek told *Bloomberg Businessweek* magazine: "I just think people need to make a living wage with health benefits. It also puts more money back into the economy and creates a healthier country. It's really that simple" (Stone, 2013, para. 4).

In Costco's (2010, para. 3) code of ethics, Costco describes its business priorities as follows:

1. Obey the law.
2. Take care of our members.
3. Take care of our employees.
4. Respect our suppliers.

If we do these four things throughout our organization, then we will achieve our ultimate goal, which is to:

5. Reward our shareholders.

Regardless of the corporate code or credo, companies likely still need to produce high quality products or services that customers actually want or need to remain successful. "In the final analysis, will Adam Smith be right about the metrics of self-interest and the good of society? Or will we simply be forced by circumstances to greenwash the record clean?" asks Arthur Lubow, president and creative director of AD Lubow LLC, an advertising agency that specializes in content creation for corporate responsibility, social change and the public good (personal communication, March 22, 2014). "The answer is probably 'yes and no.' In the meantime, let's all of us in business try to do well by doing what the world will always want: something good."

Doing Well by Doing Good: Empirical Evidence

A critical question for strategic communicators, business managers, and other financial-oriented stakeholders to ask is: does being a good corporate citizen result in improved financial performance? In other words, is there empirical evidence behind the claim of "doing well by doing good?" Several extensive reviews (Aguinis & Glavas, 2012; Margolis, Elfenbein, & Walsh, 2009; Peloza, 2009) of dozens of academic studies into this question conclude that, yes, there is a small but statistically significant, positive relationship between CSR actions/policies and firm financial performance. At the very least, CSR does not seem to hurt financial returns.

This is an important conclusion as it suggests that advocates of both stakeholder theory and shareholder theory should support at least some CSR efforts, even if they come at this conclusion from different business philosophies. In the case of stakeholder theorists, behaving ethically and responsibly with all stakeholders is simply the "right thing" for businesses to do, and a better way of managing a business and its web of relationships. On the other hand, shareholder theorists can get behind "investing" in CSR if they believe such behaviors will lead to superior financial returns for the company's stockholders. Viewed in this light, it is hard to see how business managers, regardless of their philosophical orientation, cannot afford to support sustainable business practices that seek to reward many different stakeholder groups.

Starbucks Coffee Company is a good case in point of how a stakeholder theorist approach to business can richly reward both shareholders and other stakeholder groups, such as customers, employees, and suppliers. Starbucks CEO Howard Schultz and his managers drive organizational performance through what the company calls "the lens of humanity" (Starbucks Coffee Company, 2014). In recent years, Starbucks has consistently posted record financial results. From the depths of the financial crisis in the fall of 2008 through the end of 2013, Starbucks' stock price rose roughly 600 percent, far outpacing the 150 percent gain of the NASDAQ composite, the stock exchange where Starbucks shares are listed, during this same period.

These financial and stock market gains do not seem to have come at the expense of other stakeholders. Starbucks has maintained a strong reputation. The company is generally credited as being a responsible corporate citizen (D. A. Kaplan, 2011). New CSR initiatives in recent years have included a 2011 pledge led by Schultz and signed by more than 100 CEOs to halt all U.S. political contributions until politicians presented more bipartisan solutions;

Create Jobs for USA, a 2012 program that helped customers make donations to fund loans for small businesses and reduce unemployment; Come Together, a nationwide petition that customers signed urging the U.S. government to reopen during the 2013 federal government shutdown; and a commitment by Starbucks to hire 10,000 veteran and military spouses by the end of 2018 as a way to help service members and their families transition back to civilian life (Starbucks Coffee Company, 2014).

"As we continue on our journey to build one of the world's most enduring and admired brands, we are committed to leading through the lens of humanity and finding new and world-changing ways to use Starbucks' global scale for good," says Corey duBrowa, senior vice president of global communications and international public affairs at Starbucks (personal communication, January 6, 2014).

Most large businesses are now quantifying the direct financial benefits of CSR initiatives, particularly the cost savings generated from operating organizations more sustainably. "Corporate responsibility, a core pillar of a strong corporate reputation, can have a meaningful impact on the bottom line," says Kathryn Beiser, executive vice president of corporate communications for Hilton Worldwide, the global hospitality company with brands that range from Hampton Inn to the Waldorf Astoria (personal communication, January 28, 2014). Hilton Worldwide, for example, estimates that it saved $253 million dollars between 2009 and 2012 just through its sustainability efforts to reduce energy use, carbon output, waste output, and water use.

CSR and Triple Bottom-Line Reporting

There is no definitive list of what does or does not qualify as CSR and embody a triple bottom-line approach to business (Aguinis & Glavas, 2012; Cone Communications & Echo Research, 2013; Coombs & Holladay, 2012; IRRC Institute & Sustainable Investment Institute, 2013; U.S. SIF Foundation, 2012). As such, CSR includes, but is not limited to, issues and areas such as climate change and environmental management (e.g., sustainable buildings, factories, products and business practices); product or service quality and safety for consumers; employee health, safety, advancement, diversity, and volunteering opportunities; ethical and diverse supply chains with suppliers that respect human rights and have fair labor practices; organizational ethics and governance; sustainable and responsible investing; community development and empowerment; and traditional philanthropic and charitable contributions and initiatives.

Given the diversity in issues and topics that may be considered part of CSR, it is not surprising that communicating with stakeholders about CSR poses challenges. By some estimates, there are more than 1,200 different CSR and sustainability metrics that an organization may track (Dowse, 2012). All but one member of the S&P 500 index, made up of the largest publicly traded companies in the United States, made at least one sustainability-related disclosure in 2012, with environmental management being the most common type of such disclosure (IRRC Institute & Sustainable Investment Institute, 2013). A little more than half of S&P 500 companies now issue a separate annual CSR, sustainability, or citizenship report (Clark & Master, 2013).

To help bring greater consistency, credibility, and transparency to this process, a growing number of companies have chosen to adopt the global sustainability reporting frameworks designed by various nonprofit bodies that specialize in this area (Clark & Master, 2013). Similar in many ways to how financial accounting standards aid in the interpretation of financial statements across companies and industries, sustainability frameworks help harmonize sustainability reporting disclosures regardless of organization size, type, industry, or geography.

The leading sustainability reporting frameworks include the Global Reporting Initiative (GRI), the Carbon Disclosure Project (CDP), the Dow Jones Sustainability Index (DJSI), the United Nations Global Compact, and Ceres (Davies, 2013). As of August 2014, nearly 16,000 GRI reports for more than 6,500 organizations from around the world were searchable in the GRI Sustainability Disclosure database (database.globalreporting.org/search). The United Nations Global Compact also offers a searchable database (unglobalcompact.org/participants/search).

Most companies still choose to produce both an annual report focused on financial reporting and a separate CSR, sustainability, or citizenship report. There is a move afoot, however, toward integrated reporting in which financial and sustainability reporting will be more closely aligned and will ultimately be one and the same (Eccles & Kruz, 2010). A small number of U.S. companies have made this move to an integrated "one report" model that combines financial and sustainability reporting into one annual document intended for all stakeholders. These pioneering companies include Dow Chemical, Eaton, Ingersoll Rand, Clorox, Pfizer, American Electric Power, and Southwest Airlines (IRRC Institute & Sustainable Investment Institute, 2013).

Discount carrier Southwest Airlines has produced an integrated annual report with financial and nonfinancial social and environmental disclosures since 2009. "At Southwest Airlines, we are known as a champion for both our employees and our customers, making decisions that promote job security as well as one that allows a family to check bags for free," says Ginger Hardage, senior vice president of culture and communications for Southwest Airlines (personal communication, September 30, 2013). "We believe you cannot just focus on the bottom line—you must focus on the triple bottom line, which is to say that Performance, People and Planet are all part of the equation when making decisions."

CSR and Sustainability Rankings

There are countless rankings released each year by media organizations, research providers, and other entities in the areas of CSR, sustainability, and corporate citizenship. Stakeholders, ranging from customers to employees, monitor such lists for both signs of how a company is performing relative to its peers and claims the company may be making about its CSR performance. Companies actively try to improve their standing in such rankings, particularly on those lists and ratings systems that are objective and credible, are more methodologically sound, and have more influence with current and prospective stakeholders (Thomas & Corrigan, 2013). Strategic communication professionals are often tasked with helping prepare and submit the information required for consideration in such rankings. Research firm SustainAbility estimates there are more than 100 rankings and ratings dedicated to CSR (Sadowski, Whitaker, & Buckingham, 2010).

Some CSR and sustainability rankings may carry more weight within a specific industry or within a specific company, depending on how CSR is defined and prioritized by the industry and the organization. This being said, five of the major annual gauges of CSR and sustainability are as follows:

- *Newsweek* magazine's Green Rankings
- RobecoSAM Dow Jones Sustainability indices
- *Corporate Responsibility* magazine's (CR's) 100 Best Corporate Citizens
- Carbon Disclosure Project (CDP) Leadership Index
- FTSE4Good Index Series

Two other annual lists that track CSR ratings and receive attention beyond the sustainability field include the Best Global Green Brands rankings, developed by branding consultancy Interbrand and The CSR RepTrak® 100 rankings developed by Reputation Institute, a top reputation research and consulting firm.

Third-Party Monitoring and Verification of CSR Performance

With trust in corporations still on shaky footing following several waves of corporate misdeeds and financial issues, it is not surprising that public confidence in companies "doing the right thing" remains muted. A global survey by Reputation Institute (2013c) finds that nearly three out of four consumers are willing to recommend companies that are perceived as delivering on CSR. Only 5 percent of companies are seen, however, as delivering on those promises (Reputation Institute, 2013c). In a marketplace increasingly crowded with social responsibility claims, not to mention outright "greenwashing," greater skepticism among stakeholders is inevitable (Ahern & Bortree, 2012).

Seeking to build greater credibility and improve their CSR performance, corporations are increasingly partnering with nongovernmental organizations (NGOs) and other independent third parties to provide monitoring, verification, and certification of various CSR and sustainability activities. The growing number of partnerships between NGOs and companies go far beyond traditional cause marketing alliances in which companies dedicate a portion of product sales to a cause and an organization. It is one thing for a company to say on its own that it is a responsible steward of the environment or that it has ethical supply chains; it is more credible if a third party such as an NGO collaborates with the company on such practices and verifies its performance (Ahern & Bortree, 2012; Carroll, 2010; Doh, Howton, Howton, & Siegel, 2010; Rindova et al., 2005).

McDonald's, for example, in 2013 partnered with the Alliance for a Healthier Generation, an NGO founded by the Clinton Foundation and the American Heart Association, to help reduce childhood obesity. As part of this global partnership, McDonald's announced that it would voluntarily commit to providing its customers with more access to healthier choices, including fruits and vegetables (Jargon, 2013). In a separate announcement in 2013, McDonald's USA announced that all of the coffees used in its espresso drinks were 100 percent Rainforest Alliance certified (C. Brown, 2013). This certification means that the coffee beans are grown on farms that must meet Rainforest Alliance's social and environmental standards. This same year, McDonald's USA announced that all fish sold in its restaurants had earned certification as sustainable from the Marine Stewardship Council (Brandau, 2013).

Facing criticism over labor practices in its supply chain, in early 2012 Apple become the first technology company to join the Fair Labor Association (FLA). As part of this new relationship with the FLA, Apple invited the nonprofit global monitoring group to conduct inspections of its suppliers' factories (Wingfield, 2012). While the initial FLA inspections of Apple supplier Foxconn revealed some violations of labor laws and regulations, subsequent inspections by FLA identified progress in the work conditions in these factories (FLA, 2013). Inspections alone likely will not fully satisfy critics of Apple's supply chain partners (Greenhouse, 2012), but by voluntarily opening its supply chain to a third party and making a greater effort at transparency, Apple's CSR and sustainability claims become more credible.

Linking CSR and Business Performance

There is growing acceptance among organizational leadership around the world of "doing well by doing good." CSR and sustainability initiatives that do not seem to drive—or at least align with—business objectives can face an uphill struggle for organizational resources and support. Although business managers and boards of directors increasingly acknowledge the value of adopting a stakeholder perspective, financial returns will always remain an important consideration (Aguinas & Glavas, 2012; Coombs & Holladay, 2012; Friedman et al., 2005; Ragas & Roberts, 2009).

For example, consumer packaged goods giant Unilever is widely lauded for its commitment to putting sustainability at the very core of its business. This commitment is summed up in the "Sustainable Living Plan" manifesto that it released to stakeholders in 2010. This approach seems to have helped Unilever outperform its competitors in terms of financial and stock market performance in recent years. As Unilever CEO Paul Polman explained to *Fortune* magazine (Gunther, 2013, para. 4): "Sustainable solutions—it drives our top line, it drives cost out, it motivates our employees, it links us with retailers." Polman told prospective Unilever shareholders (Gunther, 2013, para. 1): "If you buy into this long-term value model, which is equitable, which is shared, which is sustainable, then come and invest with us." By the same token, he acknowledges that "the moment Unilever underperforms, the guns will come out" (Gunther, 2013, para. 19).

The guns did come out for PepsiCo and a signature community-engagement program it had devised. In 2010, for the first time in two decades, PepsiCo decided to withdraw from buying a television commercial in the Super Bowl (Esterl & Bauerlein, 2011). Instead, PepsiCo placed these funds in an innovative $20 million dollar community-engagement and social impact program called the "Pepsi Refresh Project" in which consumers submitted their ideas and competed for votes to win grants (Preston, 2011). More than 120,000 ideas were submitted and the project received 80 million online votes. Grants funded ranged from new uniforms for a high school band to opening new playgrounds. Although PepsiCo executives argued that the Refresh Project improved brand health (Preston, 2011), Pepsi slipped to third in U.S. soda sales, behind Coke and Diet Coke (Esterl & Bauerlein, 2011). In turn, PepsiCo decided to ramp up its advertising spending and discontinue the Refresh Project. Business managers care about contributing to the public good but also want to see a clear business case for such actions.

CSR and Strategic Communication

The majority of Millennials—those born between 1979 and 2001—feel personally responsible for making a difference in the world and believe companies have a responsibility to contribute to the public good as well (Cone Inc. & AMP Agency, 2006). This community-minded, social media-empowered generation (Achieve, 2013) represents companies' future stakeholders, whether as consumers, employees, investors, or even regulators. As such, the expectations for CSR and sustainable business practices are likely to only increase in the years ahead (Cone Communications & Echo Research, 2013). The gap between the public's desire to support socially responsible organizations and the perception that many companies are *not* doing enough in this regard (Reputation Institute, 2013c) represents both a major opportunity and a challenge for business managers and strategic communication professionals.

Strategic communication professionals, whether working internally within an organization or serving as outside advisers, can play a critical role in advocating for, implementing, and communicating policy decisions and initiatives that increase an organization's triple bottom-line impact. First, as the eyes and ears of an organization, strategic communicators can take an important role in inventorying the CSR priorities of the various stakeholder groups. Next, after assessing which priorities link with organizational business objectives (Chin, Hambrick, & Trevino, 2013) and are in keeping with organizational character (Arthur W. Page Society, 2012, 2013b, 2013d), these top priorities should be shared with business managers so that well-informed decisions may be made. Upon implementation of such policies, to realize full value, strategic communicators can help communicate the rationale and benefits of such initiatives to stakeholders (Servaes & Tamayo, 2013). Finally, stakeholder reactions and feedback should be monitored so as to inform future business strategy.

Strategic communicators can and should serve as a bridge between the organization and its stakeholders, with an eye on driving mutual understanding and support on CSR policies. This may mean having difficult discussions with management to ensure that all stakeholder viewpoints, rather than an investor-dominated mindset, are represented and considered. At other times, this may mean having difficult discussions with stakeholder groups over why a proposed policy or concern does not align with the character, mission, and values of the organization. Maintaining harmony among all stakeholders is often easier said than done, but doing so is more difficult without open lines of communication. Strategic communicators can provide the glue that helps bind these organization-stakeholder relationships together through thick and thin.

Former Coca-Cola CEO Neville Isdell and World Wildlife Fund president and CEO Carter Roberts have argued that CSR is not enough anymore and that the socially responsible corporation (SRC) is the new CSR. In the words of Isdell and Roberts (2013): "smart companies are shifting to SRC and building sustainability into the very core of their business models" (para. 6). Realizing this vision will require strategic communication professionals who not only are proficient in traditional communication skillsets but are also savvy about the forces impacting how the business makes and loses money and the role of sustainable business practices in pulling these levers. Strategic communication professionals that push and challenge themselves in this regard are uniquely positioned to lead this transformation from CSR to SRC in the years ahead.

Key Terms

Andrew Carnegie
Cause marketing
Corporate social
 responsibility
Environmental, social,
 and governance
 (ESG)
R. Edward Freeman
Milton Friedman
Global Reporting
 Initiative (GRI)

Al Golin
Greenwashing
Integrated reporting
Nongovernmental
 organization (NGO)
Shareholder primacy
Shareholder theory
Adam Smith
Socially responsible
 company (SRC)
Stakeholder

Stakeholder theory
Sustainability
Sustainability reporting
 frameworks
Third-party endorsement
Triple bottom line

Discussion Questions

1. Where do you come down in the debate over the role and responsibilities of business in society today? Do you agree more with shareholder theory or stakeholder theory? Why?

2. In your own experience, what impact, if any, do evaluations of a company's contribution to society and the environment play in your decision to support that company, whether as a customer, an employee, an investor, or in some other role? Explain.

3. Visit the corporate social responsibility, sustainability, or corporate citizenship section of the website of a public company that you are interested in. How does this company say it improves the environment? How does it say it improves society and the community?

4. For this same company, does this section of the website discuss awards, recognition, certifications, and related endorsements that the company has received

from third parties, such as NGOs and other nonprofit entities, for its CSR efforts? What is notable?

5. In general, what did you think of the presentation of the information found under the CSR, sustainability, or citizenship section of this company's website? Was there any information that you thought was missing? How would you improve this reporting?

6. Do you think CSR, sustainability, and corporate citizenship will remain an important area of focus for organizations and stakeholders in the years ahead? Does this area deserve the amount of attention that it has received over the past decade? Why or why not?

CHAPTER 9

Corporate Reputation

While reputation has always been talked about as a valuable asset, it hasn't always been treated as one by businesspeople and the organizations they help run. Widespread support across the corporate world for the idea that reputation is an invaluable source of competitive advantage and should be treated as such has only emerged over the past 20 years or so (Barnett & Pollock, 2012; Bauer, 2010; Carroll, 2013; Fombrun & Shanley, 1990; Hutton, Goodman, Alexander, & Genest, 2001; Ragas, 2013a, 2013c).

Corporate titans didn't always seek out public approval or concern themselves with how they were perceived by nonbusiness elites. A century ago, railroad magnate William Henry Vanderbilt infamously said: "the public be damned . . . I don't take any stock in this silly nonsense about working for anybody but our own" (E. S. Watson, 1936, p. 7). To say Vanderbilt didn't much care about public opinion of himself or his organization's reputation would be an understatement.

Contemporary business takes a much different view of securing public approval and building and protecting corporate reputations. Warren Buffett, one of the world's richest people and the CEO of Berkshire Hathaway Inc., a multinational conglomerate that owns everything from GEICO to Dairy Queen, is known for saying: "Lose money for the firm and I will be understanding; lose a shred of reputation for the firm, and I will be ruthless" (Sorkin, 2011, para. 3). Said another way, one's reputation in the marketplace is a precious and irreplaceable commodity.

We have more recently witnessed significant changes that have made building and protecting reputations more important for organizations than ever before (Doorley & Garcia, 2011; Goodman & Hirsch, 2010). Globalization has drastically lowered costs and expanded the number of choices available to stakeholders. Major innovations like the Web have given stakeholders much more effective ways to communicate, organize, and express their views on companies. Nongovernmental organizations (NGOs) and governmental regulatory bodies have gained more influence and support. Society, in general, simply expects more from business.

According to Kathryn Beiser, executive vice president of corporate communications for Hilton Worldwide, a strong corporate reputation is critical to ensuring a firm's permission to operate (personal communication, January 28, 2014). "We live in a highly connected world with numerous stakeholders—from employees and customers, to governments and NGOs, to investors and business partners—all of whom have different needs and expectations for our company," Beiser says. "If we don't live up to their expectations, our ability to be successful is impaired. Managing these relationships holistically and through the lens of maintaining a strong corporate reputation helps ensure we do the right thing for both our company and our stakeholders, resulting in shared value and mutual success."

Corporations remain powerful forces, of course, but today they need society's approval and support if they hope to survive and thrive. Prospective and current stakeholders gravitate toward—and continue to maintain relationships with—those organizations that have the best reputations.

Benefits of a Strong Corporate Reputation

The C-suite and the boardroom have become believers in amassing and protecting reputational capital. A national survey conducted on behalf of the Public Relations Society of America (PRSA) found that respondents were nearly unanimous (97 percent) in their belief that it is important for CEOs to have an understanding of corporate reputation management (PRSA, 2011). A similar number (98 percent) believe that executives at any level of an organization should have knowledge of how reputations are built and protected. However, those surveyed felt that only about four out of ten (41 percent) of their recent hires were extremely strong in building and protecting the organization's reputation (PRSA, 2011).

The shift in C-level support toward reputation management is at least partly due to an explosion in empirical evidence demonstrating that organizational reputation is an *intangible* asset that yields very *tangible* financial performance improvements. A survey by Reputation Institute (2013a) of business professionals in 25 countries found that a majority of respondents believe that reputation drives customer retention (68 percent) and influences sales (53 percent). A majority of these professionals (56 percent) also say that reputation is already a high priority among executive management and the board of directors, with six in ten (63 percent) indicting they expect reputation to become an even greater corporate priority within the next 2–3 years.

Cees van Riel and Charles Fombrun (2007), the founders of Reputation Institute and pioneers in reputation research, describe a positive corporate reputation as being like a high-powered magnet that attracts stakeholders and resources toward it. A review of the academic and industry research on organizational reputation finds that the positive outcomes of a strong reputation may include improved customer retention, growth in sales, increases in market share, reductions in costs associated with hiring/retention, less regulation, more favorable analyst opinions, better media coverage, a higher stock price, and improvements in profitability (e.g., Carroll, 2011, 2013; Carroll & McCombs, 2003; Doorley & Garcia, 2011; Fombrun & Shanley, 2004; Harris Interactive, 2013; van Riel & Fombrun, 2007; Ragas, 2013a; Roberts & Dowling, 2002; Reputation Institute, 2013b; Rindova, Williamson, Petkova, & Sever, 2005). While a strong reputation doesn't guarantee future business success, it is certainly a notable contributing factor.

Defining Corporate Reputation

An organization's reputation establishes expectations of future performance and perceptions of its previous performance set the foundation for these baseline expectations (Doorley & Garcia, 2011). High levels of admiration, trust, esteem, and good feelings (i.e., emotions) are at the core of strong reputations. Corporate reputation is an overall assessment of an organization by its stakeholders using a company's various dimensions as the evaluative criteria (Ragas, 2013a). These rational company dimensions serve as the measuring sticks that stakeholders use to assess a company and form an impression of it (Reputation Institute, 2013b). Such dimensions include company products and services, innovation, workplace environment, corporate governance, corporate citizenship and social responsibility, leadership and vision, and financial performance (Carroll, 2011; Harris Interactive, 2013; Reputation Institute, 2013b).

Different types of stakeholder groups tend to weigh these various company dimensions more or less when forming their overall impressions of a company (van Riel & Fombrun, 2007). For example, a growing body of research shows that investors and financial-oriented stakeholders typically place the most weight on perceptions of company financial performance and company leadership in shaping overall corporate reputation (Fombrun, 1996; Fombrun & van Riel, 2004; Fombrun & Shanley, 1990). Consumers, however, tend to weigh perceptions of the company's products and services, governance, and citizenship more heavily.

Anthony Johndrow, managing partner for North America with Reputation Institute, says that all stakeholders do have at least one thing in common—their behavior toward companies is based on the strength of the emotional connection they have with them (personal communication, February 2, 2014). "What drives that emotional connection does tend to vary among stakeholders," Johndrow says. "For example, the combination of product perceptions and governance (fairness/ethics) is powerful with consumers, but investors tend to pay close attention to aspects of leadership and financial performance." These fluctuations in the importance that various stakeholder groups assign to specific dimensions of corporate reputation mean that a company must strive to be well regarded across *all* of these major dimensions if it wants to be held in high esteem by stakeholders overall.

Another way to think of corporate reputation is as an *attitude* toward a company (Meijer & Kleinnijenhuis, 2006). Attitudes gauge how positively/negatively, favorably/unfavorably, good/bad and strongly/weakly people feel toward something (Fabrigar, Krosnick, & MacDougall, 2005). Political communication professionals, policymakers, and the news media are acutely aware of the public's attitude toward elected officials, which are frequently measured as approval ratings. Researchers track and study attitudes because they may be predictive of people's behaviors (Fazio & Roskos-Ewoldsen, 2005); in the case of politics and public approval, attitudes often predict how and whether the public will vote on a candidate or issue. The corporate sector is not all that different. Someone's attitude (i.e., reputation) toward a firm often predicts whether they will "vote" for or against choosing to do business with a company, whether that is as a new customer, as a potential investor, as a prospective employee, as a supplier to that business, or through some other possible stakeholder action (Meijer & Kleinnijenhuis, 2006).

Measuring Corporate Reputation

There are several widely followed and accepted annual measures of corporate reputation. Companies actively gauge their reputational performance on the basis of these lists and look to move up the rankings each year. The major annual gauges of corporate reputation in the United States are as follows:

- *Fortune* magazine's Most Admired Companies
- Harris Interactive's Reputation Quotient® (RQ®)
- Reputation Institute's RepTrak®

In addition to these three major annual studies of reputation, each year, global public relations firm Edelman releases the Edelman Trust Barometer.

While this barometer does not directly assess the reputations of specific companies, trust is widely viewed as being at the core of reputation. Started in 2000, the Trust Barometer provides valuable longitudinal data on trust perceptions, by country, on institutions, informational sources, and sectors.

Launched in 1982, *Fortune* magazine's Most Admired Companies list is the longest-running annual report card on corporate reputations. This list has played an influential role in popularizing the concept of reputation among the C-suite and financial stakeholders. A limitation of the Most Admired Companies list is that it is based on a survey of financial stakeholders (i.e., financial analysts, investors, managers, directors) rather than the general public, so there is a financial bias to these rankings (Roberts & Dowling, 2002; van Riel & Fombrun, 2007). This bias doesn't invalidate these rankings, and they continue to be tracked by managers and the press. It is important, however, to understand the underlying source of the collective perceptions for this list.

The Harris Interactive Reputation Quotient® (RQ®) and Reputation Institute RepTrak® reputation measures use more sophisticated methodologies to survey the general public. In collaboration with Harris Interactive and scholar Charles Fombrun, the Harris RQ® first launched in 1999. It evaluates companies' reputations by asking respondents to rate companies on 20 items

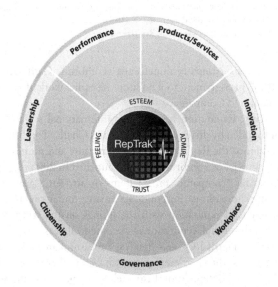

Figure 9.1   Reputation Institute's RepTrak® scorecard
Source: Reputation Institute.

Table 9.1 The world's most reputable companies for 2014

Rank	Company	RepTrak Pulse Score
1	The Walt Disney Company	77.3
1	Google	77.3
3	BMW	77.2
3	Rolex	77.2
5	Sony	75.9
6	Canon	75.7
7	Apple	75.6
8	Daimler (Mercedes-Benz)	75.4
9	LEGO Group	75.1
10	Microsoft	75.0
10	Samsung Electronics	75.0
12	Volkswagen	74.9
12	Intel	74.9
14	Adidas Group	74.5
15	Michelin	74.2
16	Johnson & Johnson	73.8
16	Nestle	73.7
18	Philips Electronics	73.5
19	Rolls-Royce Aerospace	73.2
20	Nike	73.0

Note: Pulse scores are based on questions measuring trust, admiration, & respect; good feeling; and overall esteem (captured in the Pulse score on a 0–100 scale).
Source: Reputation Institute (2014) Globak RepTrak® 100.

grouped around six company dimensions (Fombrun, Gardberg, & Sever, 2000). The RQ® measurement tool built on the earlier work of *Fortune* magazine's Most Admired Companies.

More recently, Reputation Institute, an international research and consulting firm founded by distinguished academics Charles Fombrun and Cees van Riel, developed the RepTrak® system to measure and monitor corporate reputations (van Riel & Fombrun, 2007). Launched in 2005, RepTrak® asks respondents to rate companies on 23 items or attributes grouped around seven company dimensions. Respondents answer four items to provide an overall assessment of reputation with the ratings on the seven dimensions used to explain this overall reputational assessment. Released with much fanfare each year, the Harris RQ® and RepTrak® measures are widely tracked by corporate managers, the news media, investors, and other stakeholders.

Figure 9.1 provides Reputation Institute's RepTrak® scorecard, while table 9.1 provides a list of the world's top 20 most reputable companies for 2014 according to RepTrak® data.

Influences on Corporate Reputation

There are a variety of ways that people may learn about a company and form their perceptions of it (Fombrun, 1996). An individual may form their impression on the basis of firsthand personal experience with a company, such as buying its products and services or working for or with the company. Another way someone may learn about a company is from hearing what their friends, neighbors, or relatives have to say about their experiences with a company. This may include going online and reading reviews or online discussions about a business. People may also learn about a company from the information the company shares through its website and social media, its advertising campaigns, and other company-controlled channels.

An individual may learn about a company from what third-party mass media sources have to say about the organization. This could include everything from viewing traditional news reports in newspapers, on television, or on news websites to reading, watching, or listening to the reports and commentary of bloggers and other online influencers. Additional specialized sources that some individuals may encounter include industry and investment analyst reports, audit reports issued by accountants, and informational materials prepared by activist and advocacy groups, nongovernmental organizations (NGOs), or regulatory and governmental agencies and officials.

Bromley (2000) outlines three levels of information processing that influence the formation of people's opinions of a company's reputation. These three levels are:

1. **Information processing at a primary level** (based on personal experience(s) with the company in question),
2. **Information processing at a secondary level** (based on what friends, family, and relatives, whether online or offline, have to say about the company), and
3. **Information processing at a tertiary level** (based on mass media information, including news reports, paid advertising, and owned or earned public relations messages).

Corporate reputation research generally finds that personal experience (i.e., the primary level) has the greatest impact on reputation formation (van Riel & Fombrun, 2007). However, the public likely has direct experience with only a limited number of companies and, even for those companies with which we have direct experience, that experience may be narrow or dated. Therefore, people often turn to their colleagues, friends, and family (i.e., the secondary level) as a source for insights into many companies. Finally, there is little escaping the ubiquitous nature of the mass media (i.e., the tertiary level) today. In many cases, stakeholders are likely to be exposed either intentionally or incidentally to a mix of company-controlled traditional or online messages and news media reports about the organization (Blankespoor, Miller, & White, 2012; Bushee, Core, Guary, & Hamm, 2010; Carroll, 2011; Ragas, 2013a, 2013c, 2014).

Research based on theories that integrate mass and interpersonal communication, such as the diffusion of innovations (Rogers, 2003) and the multiple-step flow (Katz & Lazarsfeld, 1955) generally find that, in the presence of both, interpersonal communication exerts the stronger influence on attitudes and behaviors. There are many times in which a prospective stakeholder has had minimal or no direct experience with a company and/or an individual's circle of interpersonal sources has limited knowledge of the company as well. As shown by media system dependency theory (Ball-Rokeach, 1985; Ball-Rokeach & DeFleur, 1976), in these situations, prospective stakeholders are more reliant on the mass media, such as news reports and a company's own corporate communication messages, to shape their perceptions of the organization (Einwiller, Carroll, & Korn, 2010). This heightened need for orientation (Weaver, 1980) results in mass media presentations of a company playing a stronger agenda-setting role (Carroll & McCombs, 2003; McCombs & Shaw, 1972) in how the company is perceived.

Research finds that, at least with financial stakeholders, information provided directly by companies weighs more heavily in decision making than information provided by third-party sources (Duckworth, Golz, & Trayner, 2009; Golz, Zivin, & Spero, 2012). Among third-party sources, financial stakeholders place the most importance on analyst research, followed by real-time subscription information services, like Bloomberg and Thomson Reuters, and primary market research. Traditional business media in print, online, and digital/social media are perceived as having the least influence on stakeholder decision making. Research also finds that information provided by organizations directly to stakeholders is having a growing influence in public affairs and political communication as well (e.g., Kiousis & Stromback, 2010).

Confluence of Words and Deeds

There is little doubt that the image a company projects of itself through advertising, earned media coverage, and company-controlled media channels has an effect on how a company is perceived by its stakeholders. A variety of studies show that companies that devote more resources to external communication efforts tend to score more highly in corporate reputation rankings (Harris Interactive, 2009; Hutton et al., 2001; Y. Kim, 2000, 2001).

However, if the projected image and underlying behaviors of an organization are disjointed and not in alignment, then the organization is at an elevated risk of eventually suffering a major reputational decline. "Communicators today are the keepers of a company's values. But values must be more than words. They must be manifest in actions that generate credibility and drive trust," says Wendi Strong, chief communications officer for USAA, a leading diversified financial services company with a vaunted corporate reputation (personal communication, February 15, 2014). "At its core, reputation is trust. A communicator's job is to foster trust between a company and its stakeholders. That means ensuring your organization is trustworthy—in other words, willing and able to keep its promises."

Public relations pioneer Arthur W. Page, the first communication executive to serve as a director of a major corporation (AT&T), argued passionately throughout his career that what a company *does* is more important that what it *says*. Strong reputations are built on business managers and employees demonstrating a commitment to the organization's stated mission and vision through policies and actions that are consistent with these values (Arthur W. Page Society, 2012, 2013a, 2013b, 2013c). In the words of Page some 60 years ago, decades before the field of reputation management had been created (Jones & Kostyak, 2011):

I am not belittling the influence or the importance of the public relations officer, but the major part of public relations is, and must be, conducted by the line organization. A company's reputation is chiefly dependent on what it does and in a lesser degree on what is says and this lesser degree becomes very small indeed if what it says and what it does do not jibe. (p. 214)

"Actions often speaking louder than words" is particularly the case in the new business environment, in which the "truth" often bubbles to the surface, courtesy of the Web and social media, whether an organization likes it or not (Arthur W. Page Society, 2007, 2012; Ragas, 2013a).

One of the stated principles of the Arthur W. Page Society (2013a, para. 3), which grew out of the writings of Page, is "*Prove it with action*. Public perception of an organization is determined 90 percent by what it does and 10 percent by what it says." While the exact ratio is debatable and may shift depending up the situation, this idea is very powerful. The strategic communication function is most effective at reputation management when the communication is grounded in and supported by a company's actual behaviors and policies. It is not just the "words" but also the "deeds" that show that the company believes in what it says and that the company behaves accordingly. Much of what the news media and other opinion leaders report and comment on about organizations are based at least partially on what an organization has or has *not* done with its various policies and decisions, not just what it says or how it says it (Deephouse, 2000).

For example, multinational energy giant BP PLC carefully cultivated its image as that of a progressive, environmentally friendly corporate citizen, removing "petroleum" from its name; developing a modern, bright green logo; and spending millions on a "Beyond Petroleum" ad campaign (G. Solomon, 2008). BP did, in fact, become the world leader in solar energy. This investment was undone, however, by a series of environmental problems, starting with the deadly Texas City refinery explosion in 2005 and the oil spills at Prudhoe Bay and the Alaska pipeline in 2006 and capped by the epic 2010 Deepwater Horizon explosion and oil spill in the Gulf of Mexico (Rudolf, 2010). Perceptions that BP did not take all possible safety precautions and might not have been fully forthcoming in the immediate aftermath of the Gulf spill will likely hang over the company for many years to come. Harris Reputation Quotient® data (Harris Interactive, 2013) reveal that BP's reputation is on the mend, thanks in part to aggressive reinvestment in the Gulf Coast and a campaign to communicate these actions, but BP's reputation still lags its peers.

Managing Corporate Reputation

There is much talk about "managing corporate reputation," as this chapter demonstrates, but what does that really mean and how does a company accomplish that, particularly from the perspective of a strategic communicator? First, it is important to pinpoint where a company is in its corporate lifecycle because this affects both where the company is in the reputation management process and what type of strategic communication efforts and activities are most important. According to Barnett and Pollock (2012), the process generally entails three stages:

1. **Attention generation**, in which the new firm develops a public profile
2. **Uncertainty reduction**, in which the maturing firm explains its mission—and, if necessary, that of its industry—to stakeholders via its strategic communication
3. **Evaluation**, in which the maturing or mature firm demonstrates the competence with which it fulfills its mission

In the first stage, a company is most interested in raising its public profile and becoming known. A baseline level of visibility is necessary for the public to even become aware of a company and for the company to establish the basis for a reputation (Carroll & McCombs, 2003; Fombrun & van Riel, 2004). At such an early stage, strategic communication is often focused on raising top-of-mind awareness of the company and getting the organization into the "consideration set" of prospective stakeholders (Carroll, 2011). A larger and more mature company is generally less concerned with the amount of raw attention it receives relative to competitors. It may, in fact, want to limit the amount of attention at times (Ragas, 2014a).

At the second stage, the company begins explaining in more detail its business and mission, how it is positioned in relation to the industry and sector with which it competes, and how it positively impacts society (i.e., the corporate narrative). Instead of focusing on the raw amount of attention that may be generated about the firm, strategic communication starts focusing more on articulating the various dimensions that make up the business: company products and services, innovation, workplace environment, corporate governance, corporate citizenship and social responsibility, corporate leadership and vision, and financial performance. Prospective stakeholders must feel there is not a high level of risk in initiating a relationship with the company. Uncertainty can be reduced through strategic communication and action that provides prospective stakeholders with a more detailed understanding of the firm's dimensions.

At the third stage, strategic communicators are concerned with both attracting new stakeholders and maintaining and strengthening existing stakeholder relationships. Because different stakeholder groups place more or less weight on particular company dimensions when evaluating and deciding whether to support an organization, it is important for strategic communication efforts to be in sync with this reality. Competence is demonstrated for investors largely through strong financial performance and company leadership, whereas consumers determine competence more through evaluating company products and services and corporate social responsibility (Fombrun, 1996; Fombrun & van Riel, 2004; Fombrun & Shanley, 1990; van Riel & Fombrun, 2007). While a company should strive to be viewed favorably and excel in each of these various company dimensions, it should at the very least emphasize and explain the dimensions that resonate the most when messaging to and with particular stakeholder groups.

The whole idea of managing corporate reputation is particularly complex because the intangible asset in question—corporate reputation—is not solely "owned" by the company, but rather is "co-owned" between the company and its stakeholders (Barnett & Pollock, 2012). Corporate reputation is a collective assessment in the minds of prospective and current stakeholders that is *earned*, rather than an asset that may be *purchased* and stored away.

"Reputations are earned, not created. They can evolve. They can be burnished. They absolutely must be protected," says Steve Doyal, senior vice president of public affairs and communications for Hallmark Cards Inc. (personal communication, January 27, 2014). "And, sadly, [reputations] can be damaged by real or perceived missteps. Hallmark enjoys a good reputation, based on years of adherence to a core set of beliefs and values that genuinely guide our decisions and actions."

To revisit Harold Burson's evolution of communication in the first chapter, strategic communication has a greater impact on corporate reputation when communicators are consulted on not just "what to say" but on "what to do." What the organization *does say* should be consistent with its corporate character and values (Arthur W. Page Society, 2012, 2013b, 2013c; Christian, 1997).

According to Rod Cartwright, global partner and director of the global corporate and public affairs practice at Ketchum, the need to align words and deeds has only become more pressing in the era of radical transparency (personal communication, January 17, 2014). "With this alignment becoming ever-more pivotal for brands and corporations, the communication function will see itself supporting not only 'downstream' engagement—once business decisions have been taken—but rather informing those business decisions in the first place and the actions that stem from them," Cartwright says.

The rise and acceptance of corporate reputation among modern business leaders like Warren Buffett has been a boon to the growth and stature of the strategic communication function in many organizations. Research by the Strategic Communications and Public Relations Center at the University of Southern California finds that influence on corporate reputation is the number one way that strategic communication professionals now gauge the success of their efforts (Swerling et al., 2012). Times change, and a business and its managers either adapt to changing stakeholder demands or ultimately fade away. Even William Henry Vanderbilt would likely agree with this statement. In fact, if placed in a time machine, the Vanderbilt of today might sing a different tune about the importance of maintaining public approval. In a hyperconnected, stakeholder-empowered world, reputation is not everything; it is often the *only* thing.

Key Terms

Agenda-setting theory	*Fortune* magazine's	Reputation Institute
Warren Buffett	Most Admired	Reputation management
Corporate reputation	Companies	Reputation Quotient®
Diffusion of innovation	Harris Interactive	(RQ®)
theory	Multiple-step flow theory	Trust Barometer
Charles Fombrun	RepTrak®	Cees van Riel

Discussion Questions

1. Choose three different companies in the same industry. How did you learn about them: first-hand experience, friends and family, company communication, news reports, or some other way?

2. For these same three companies, which of these above identified factors do you feel had the greatest impact on your perception of each company's reputation? Why?

3. From your own experience, what have you noticed are the benefits of a company having a strong reputation? What is the downside of a mediocre or even poor reputation?

4. Review the most recent Reputation Institute RepTrak® rankings as provided in table 9.1. Which companies did you expect to rank higher on these lists? Which companies did you expect to rank lower? Why?

5. Do you think that a corporate reputation can be "managed"? Why or why not?

6. Why do you think the strategic communication function is often assigned the primary responsibility over corporate reputation management? Is this a good or bad idea?

PART IV

Demonstrating and Improving the Business Value of Communication

CHAPTER 10

Research, Measurement, and Evaluation

Two well-known phrases among business managers are "you cannot manage what you cannot measure" and "what gets measured gets done" (see House & Price, 1991, p. 92). Unfortunately, strategic communication has traditionally lagged as a field when it comes to research, measurement, and evaluation. In fact, communicators have even been known to say: "I know I wasted half of my communication budget. I just don't know which half." This is now changing.

After years of "talking the talk" about the importance of research, measurement, and evaluation, more strategic communication professionals are now "walking the walk" as well (Motley, 2014; NASDAQ OMX & Lawrence Ragan Communications Inc., 2013; "Study Shows PR Pros Making Progress in Following the Barcelona Principles," 2013; T. Watson, 2012; Weiner, 2012). In 2010, representatives from the world's top communication associations came together in Barcelona, Spain, to adopt the Barcelona Declaration of Measurement Principles (International Association for the Measurement and Evaluation of Communication, 2010; Manning & Rockland, 2011). A national survey of the profession conducted by the Strategic Communication and Public Relations Center at the University of Southern California Annenberg School for Communication and Journalism found that U.S. companies in recent years more than *doubled* (i.e., from 4 percent to 9 percent) the percentage of their communication budgets dedicated to measurement (Swerling et al., 2012).

Our own survey of senior communication professionals (see chapter 1 for a more detailed discussion) revealed that linking strategic communication's contribution to organizational strategy was a top priority. Respondents rated "communication's contribution to company strategy" behind only "financial statement basics" and a "financial terminology primer" as the most important components of a business education for strategic communication professionals. As the field matures, communicators at all levels of the organization—and not just those working in research—are increasingly expected to demonstrate how communication campaigns and programs contribute to the success of organizational strategies, goals, and objectives.

"While we may not all be experts in the nuts and bolts of research and analytics, all strategic communicators can and should conceptually understand why we engage in research, measurement and evaluation as part of our campaigns and programs," says David Rockland, partner and managing director, global research at Ketchum. "PR practitioners often cry out that they lack a seat at the big table, the adults table, the C-suite table. Obviously, if we measure our results in terms of how what we do drives the objectives of the business or the organization we are working for, PR wouldn't worry so much about getting a seat at the right tables." Rockland adds that measurement is not about just proving "the value of what we have done" but in improving the *performance* of strategic communication campaigns and programs.

With this in mind, every strategic communicator, regardless of their position or years of experience within the field, should understand at least the basics of communication research methods, measurement, and evaluation. Strategic communication professionals with even base knowledge in this area are better positioned to set clear goals and objectives—the starting point for effective measurement and evaluation. Further, those professionals are then better prepared to screen and hire research specialists and assess the quality of their recommendations. Such communicators can also converse more confidently and effectively about research with other departments, such as marketing. Finally, research-savvy communicators are better able to use metrics and analytics to demonstrate and improve performance, which can in turn lead to larger budgets and more support.

Research Methods

Communication research is conducted for many different reasons. *Basic* research is research conducted by scholars for academic purposes with a primary goal of building theory and contributing to the general body of knowledge (Wimmer & Dominick, 2014). *Applied* research is research conducted by or on behalf of organizations, such as businesses, to address organization-specific problems or opportunities (Wimmer & Dominick, 2014). Such research is frequently kept private and not released beyond the organization or its partners. Communication measurement and evaluation research frequently falls into this latter category.

Whether conducting basic or applied research, researchers have a wide array of methods, techniques, and tools at their disposal. Strategic communication research often draws from the research traditions found in the social sciences, particularly mass communication, which emerged as a scientific field of study following World War II (Bryant & Cummins, 2007; Bryant, Thompson, & Finklea, 2013; Rogers, 1997). There are two broad categories of research methods for conducting measurement and evaluation: qualitative research methods and quantitative research methods. Each general approach has its own strengths and weaknesses.

Qualitative research methods consist of collecting open-ended information without preset response categories (Wimmer & Dominick, 2014). This approach yields nonnumeric textual or image-based data, which are also known as "soft data" (Creswell & Creswell, 2005; Lindenmann, 2003, 2006). Qualitative methods tend to rely on relatively small samples to uncover deep, rich insights (i.e., focus on *qualities*) into whatever is being studied (Babbie, 2013). Focus groups, depth interviews, ethnographies, case studies, and historical analyses are typically considered qualitative research techniques. Quantitative research seeks to generalize the closed-ended information (i.e., focus on *quantities*) collected from random samples to larger populations through the use of statistics (Lindenmann, 2003, 2006; Wimmer & Dominick, 2014). Quantitative methods yield numeric data, therefore this information is often known as "hard data" (Babbie, 2013). Examples of quantitative research techniques include field or laboratory experiments, survey research, and some content analyses.

Qualitative research is often exploratory in nature and best at providing *depth* of knowledge (i.e., answering the "why" and "how" questions), whereas quantitative research tends to be descriptive or explanatory and best at providing *breadth* of knowledge (i.e., answering the "what," "where," and "when" questions). Quantitative and qualitative techniques often complement and offset the weaknesses of one another. Many communication measurement experts (see Lindenmann, 2003, 2006; Michaelson & Stacks, 2014; Ruler, Vercic, & Vercic, 2008; Stacks, 2010; T. Watson & Noble, 2007) recommend that organizations collect both quantitative and qualitative data to more fully measure and evaluate the effectiveness of communication campaigns and programs. The use of both quantitative and qualitative methods is known as mixed-methods research (Molina-Azorin, 2010; Pasadeos, Lamme, Gower, & Tian, 2011; Ragas & Laskin, 2014; Tashakkori & Teddlie, 2010). There, of course, may be resource or time constraints that limit a communicator or organization to relying on just one research method (Bryman, 2007).

The Barcelona Principles and Developing Standards

While strategic communication professionals and academics have long talked about the importance of measurement and evaluation, until fairly recently the field lacked agreed upon general research principles (Michaelson & Stacks, 2014), standards (Michaelson & Stacks, 2011), or best practices (Michaelson & Macleod, 2007). A positive change came in 2010 when representatives of many top communication associations from around the world met in Barcelona, Spain, to adopt the Barcelona Declaration of Measurement Principles. The International Association for the Measurement and Evaluation of Communication (AMEC), an organization that played a lead role in the Barcelona Principles, continues to hold annual European summits that bring together communication research experts to advance this work.

The Barcelona Principles (AMEC, 2010, para. 3) are as follows:

- Principle 1. Importance of goal setting and measurement
- Principle 2. Measuring the effect on outcomes is preferred to measuring outputs
- Principle 3. The effect on business results can and should be measured where possible
- Principle 4. Media measurement requires quantity and quality
- Principle 5. Advertising Value Equivalents (AVEs) are not the value of public relations
- Principle 6. Social media can and should be measured
- Principle 7. Transparency and replicability are paramount to sound measurement

While two of the Barcelona Principles—Principles 1 and 2—are explored more in depth later in this chapter, all seven are equally important. To learn more about each of the principles, visit the website of AMEC and search for the principles: http://amecorg.com

In addition to the efforts of AMEC, the Measurement Commission of the Institute for Public Relations (IPR), a nonprofit research foundation dedicated to the science beneath the art of public relations, has long worked to develop and promote standards and best practices for research, measurement, and analytics. This includes IPR working with AMEC and four other industry associations to form the Coalition for Public Relations Research Standards. In 2013, this coalition announced that four major corporations (General Electric, McDonald's USA, General Motors, and Southwest Airlines) had adopted a preliminary set of voluntary standards for research and measurement (Institute for Public Relations [IPR], 2013). More than 60 organizations have pledged their support for these voluntary standards (IPR, 2014). These standards are now being field tested and validated by these organizations and their vendors (Global Alliance for Public Relations and Communication Management, 2013). For more on these standards, visit the IPR website: http://www.instituteforpr.org/researchstandards

"Such standards are not intended to hinder innovation, but rather encourage more of it," says Frank Ovaitt, president and CEO of the Institute for Public Relations (personal communication, April 25, 2014). "This broad platform of standards is applicable to many areas of the practice, from media relations to corporate communication. By having a shared foundation, researchers and professionals will be better positioned to focus more of their energy and efforts on generating insights from research."

This broad platform of standards includes standards specifically about the measurement and evaluation of social media content. This work has been led by a group called The Social Media Measurement Conclave. The Conclave, comprising representatives from corporations, agencies, academia, and industry groups (including AMEC and IPR), first met in 2011 to establish standard definitions and best practices for social media measurement (Paine, 2011b). After several years of work, in June 2013 The Conclave published a complete set of social media measurement standards (The Social Media Measurement Conclave, 2013). The full set of standards is available on The Conclave's website: http://www.smmstandards.com

"The Conclave's standards provide definitions and best practices for the most frequently debated numbers in social media—reach, impressions, influence, sentiment and ROI," says communication measurement expert Katie Delahaye Paine, publisher and CEO of Paine Publishing, and the organizer of the first meeting of The Conclave. "Even more importantly, they frame the issue of measurement standards around the most fundamental tenet of measurement, which is that what metrics you use should always be based on the goals for your program." According to Paine: "If more organizations measure the impact of their communication programs on business, rather than chase meaningless big numbers, the entire profession wins."

After years of talking about the value of research, measurement, and evaluation, more leading players are now heeding this advice and taking action. Standards are important because they ensure that communication professionals all talk the same language and have similar expectations when it comes to research, measurement, and evaluation. Standards help put the field "on the same page," thereby limiting uneven research quality, inconsistency in the comparisons of results across campaigns and programs, and confusion among clients and research partners over measures, metrics, and terms (IPR, 2013; Michaelson & Stacks, 2011). The good news is these efforts help raise the performance of the field. The bad news is perhaps that all communication professionals—not just those working in research and analytics—need to do a better job of demonstrating the contribution of communication to organizational strategy.

"Sometimes I still hear public relations professionals say that they entered the field because they are 'bad at math'," says Joe Cohen, senior vice president of MWW, a top independent public relations agency, and 2014 chair of the Public Relations Society of America (PRSA). "This may be one of the most damaging and reckless comments a PR professional can make and an instant credibility-killer. Being able to read and leverage data to inform strategic communications decisions is becoming a critical competency. Just like a CEO or a CMO [chief marketing officer], a good PR professional should be obsessed with analytics and always be looking for opportunities to quantify the results of their work and demonstrate how it ladders back to larger business goals" (personal communication, January 7, 2014).

Goal and Objective Setting

At its most basic level, strategy refers to an organization's overall plan (Smith, 2012). In a corporate context, the policy level decisions that a company makes about its business goals are at the heart of corporate strategy (Botan, 2006). Strategic communication is not unlike any other department or adviser to a company in that it attempts to support and advance the business strategy, goals, and objectives of the organization or client (Grondstedt, 1997; Pieczka, 2000). Strategic communicators are best positioned to contribute to organizational success when communication campaign or program goals and strategies clearly connect back with the larger business strategy and goals (Anderson, Hadley, Rockland, & Weiner, 2009; Pieczka, 2000).

"It's hard to imagine an organization being successful without communications leading the pursuit of all their business objectives," says Gary McCormick, director of partnership development for HGTV, a Scripps Networks company, and a former chair and CEO of the Public Relations Society of America (PRSA). "Just like in sports, if the entire team doesn't know the play, it's going to be hard to have any forward progress much less win any games" (personal communication, August 28, 2013).

Not surprisingly, the first of the Barcelona Principles stresses "the importance of goal setting and measurement" (AMEC, 2010, para. 3). The establishment of clear campaign or program goals and objectives are at the very core of successful strategic communication measurement and evaluation (Anderson et al., 2009; Lindenmann, 2003, 2006). It is difficult to know whether a campaign or program was successful if the campaign

Table 10.1 Allstate corporate responsibility objectives

Business Practices

- Earn a spot on The DiversityInc Top 50 Companies for Diversity® list on an annual basis. DiversityInc's Top 50 measures four key areas: CEO Commitment, Human Capital, Corporate and Organizational Communications, and Supplier Diversity.
- Achieve 9% of Allstate's total procurement spend with businesses owned by minorities, women, veterans and members of the lesbian, gay, bisexual and transgender community by 2015.

Environment

- Reduce energy use by 20% by 2020 for Allstate-owned facilities (2007 baseline).
- Maintain or reduce Allstate's carbon footprint on an annual basis (2007 baseline).
- Focus on the sustainability of our real estate by ensuring that many major office renovations and most new construction projects are Leadership in Energy and Environmental Design (LEED) certified by the U.S. Green Building Council.
- Maintain or exceed the paper-reduction levels established in 2010.
- Reduce paper delivery to customers by 20% by 2013 (2009 baseline).

Social Impact

- Contribute to reducing teen driving fatalities by 50% and create the safest generation of teen drivers by 2015.
- Reach 500,000 survivors of domestic violence with Allstate Foundation–funded financial empowerment services by 2015.

Source: Allstate

or program did not clearly state up front where it was trying to go and what it intended to accomplish (Bissland, 1990). Once this has been done, those involved in the campaign or program can decide which research techniques and metrics are appropriate for actually measuring and evaluating performance.

Most communication measurement and research experts (e.g., Anderson et al., 2009; Smith, 2012) define a goal as a general statement rooted in the organization's mission, vision, and character that states what the organization intends to achieve. A goal tells stakeholders "*where* the organization is trying to go." An objective, on the other hand, emerges from a goal and is a specific statement presented in clear, measurable, realistic, and time-bounded terms. In essence, an objective tells stakeholders "how we'll know *if* and *when* we've gotten there." A well-written objective should be (1) rooted in a goal, (2) focused on a specific target stakeholder group, (3) measurable (i.e., quantifiable numbers or percentages), (4) time definite, (5) singular (i.e., tries to avoid using "and" or "also"), (6) explicit and clearly defined, and (7) challenging, but attainable.

See table 10.1 for an example of a clear set of multiyear objectives developed by Allstate Insurance Company for its public social responsibility program and shared each year in its corporate responsibility report. According to Vicky Dinges, vice president of public social responsibility and enterprise communication for Allstate Insurance Company, Allstate's corporate responsibility goals are integrated with the firm's business goals, thereby helping her team better focus its investments and increase the impact of its programs. Dinges emphasizes that the success of Allstate's CSR does not matter "if our results take place in a vacuum" (personal communication, December 10, 2013).

"Transparency—regarding our goals, achievements and challenges—is crucial. Several years ago, we established a set of Key Performance Indicators that reflect our priorities and track our progress," Dinges says (V. Dinges, personal communication, December 10, 2013). "Each year, we inspire our colleagues to set higher goals and hold ourselves accountable by publishing results in our annual corporate responsibility report. Striving for complete transparency is the right thing to do for Allstate and our stakeholders. It's helped us improve operational efficiency and reduce cost, and elevated the engagement of our people across all of our efforts." Dinges adds: "Best of all, our commitment to evaluation makes continual improvement a reality for Allstate's business *and* society."

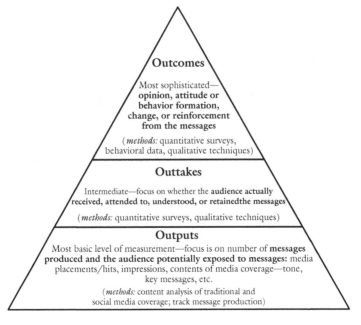

Figure 10.1 Levels of communication measurement

Setting communication goals and objectives not only serve as a foundation for measurement and evaluation, but it demonstrates to business managers and stakeholders alike that the strategic communication function wants to be held accountable for its performance.

Levels of Communication Measurement

There are many ways that strategic communicators may measure and monitor the performance of campaigns and programs. A straightforward framework introduced by Lindenmann (1993) some 20 years ago has become the basis for how many communication research experts and strategic communicators plan and evaluate communication campaigns and programs (Michaelson & Stacks, 2014; Stacks, 2010, 2013b). It is known as The Effectiveness Yardstick, and Lindenmann (1993, 2003, 2006) states that campaign and program effectiveness may be measured and evaluated with three broad levels of measurement: (1) level one: outputs, (2) level two: outtakes (originally known as outgrowths), and (3) level three: outcomes. According to Lindenmman (1993): "Like marks on a yardstick or a ruler, each level identifies or pinpoints a higher or more sophisticated plateau for the measurement of PR success or failure" (p. 8). See figure 10.1 for an adaption of this framework and the measurement tools frequently used.

Outputs

These are the short-term or immediate results of a communication campaign or program (Lindenmann, 1993, 2003, 2006). These may be the strategic communication messages actually created or distributed by an organization, such as news releases, media pitches, and social media posts, or the media content that results from these outreach efforts. This can include either traditional media coverage by journalists or the content produced by other information intermediaries, such as bloggers or analysts. Tracking the number of media placements and media impressions or analyzing the content of the key messages and affective tone of media coverage would all fall under the evaluation of outputs. This type of monitoring is relatively simple or easy to carry out but does not directly tell a communicator whether campaign or program messages actually influenced the targeted stakeholder group's thoughts, attitudes, or behaviors.

Outtakes

While outputs focus on possible message exposure and impact on third parties, outtakes are somewhat more sophisticated and are concerned with whether targeted stakeholders actually *received*, paid *attention to*, *understood*, and/or *retained* these messages (Lindenmann, 1993, 2006, 2006). Outtakes may be measured with a mix of research methods including quantitative surveys using random sampling, which allow for generalizability, and qualitative techniques like focus groups and interviews that are typically nongeneralizable but in-depth.

Outcomes

Outcomes, the most sophisticated level of evaluation, measure the *establishment, reinforcement*, or *change* in the targeted stakeholder group's opinions, attitudes, or behaviors based on the campaign or program messages (Lindenmann, 1993, 2003, 2006). The techniques used for measuring outtakes also apply to outcomes. To gauge reinforcement or change in opinions, attitudes, or behaviors, baseline data (i.e., establishing a starting point) need to have been collected before the start of the campaign or program. With outcomes, actual longitudinal online and offline behavioral data on stakeholders may be available. Advanced statistical techniques such as market mix modeling now allow researchers to ascertain the contribution that a specific communication category (e.g., advertising, public relations) has on a desired behavioral outcome, such as sales (Michaelson & Stacks, 2014; Stacks & Bowen, 2013; Weiner, 2012).

Measurement and Evaluation in Practice

Communication research and measurement experts generally recommend that strategic communication professionals place greater effort on measuring communication outtakes and outcomes rather than outputs. In fact, the second principle of the Barcelona Principles states: "Measuring the effect on outcomes is preferred to measuring outputs" (AMEC, 2010, para. 3).

Evaluating a campaign or program on only outputs makes a weak case regarding the ultimate effectiveness of the campaign or program (Michaelson & Stacks, 2014). Stacks of media clippings or social media metrics by themselves don't necessarily mean that the opinions, attitudes, or behaviors of an organization's stakeholders were influenced in a meaningful way by a communication campaign or program. Placements, impressions, and multipliers may have been the traditional language of public relations, but those metrics are not the language of business; they often mean little to colleagues in other departments or professions, business managers, or the C-suite (Motley, 2014; T. Watson, 2013).

In practice, there has indeed been a shift toward measuring campaigns and programs with more tools and techniques that get at stakeholder outtakes and outcomes. However, a variety of surveys of the communication profession (Berger, 2012; Berger & Meng, 2014; NASDAQ & Ragan, 2013; "Study Shows PR Pros Making Progress in Following the Barcelona Principles," 2013; Swerling et al., 2012; Wright, Gaunt, Leggetter, Daniels, & Zerfass, 2009) show that—both in the United States and internationally—measures of media outputs are still the most prevalent approach to campaign and program evaluation.

A global survey of nearly 4,500 public relations and communication management professionals conducted by The Plank Center for Leadership in Public Relations at the University of Alabama found that monitoring and analyzing media coverage was the most frequently mentioned approach (Berger, 2012; Berger & Meng, 2014). The second and third most frequent approaches were using business outcome metrics and nonfinancial performance indicators, respectively. Besides being ingrained in professional routines (T. Watson, 2012), communicators may still turn to media metrics to gauge performance because this approach is typically less expensive and less complex than measuring communication outtakes and outcomes (Lindenmann, 2012).

Return on Investment

Perhaps no discussion on strategic communication research, measurement, and evaluation is complete without at least briefly exploring the concept of return on investment (ROI). As the field shifts more toward demonstrating business value, the idea of ROI—traditionally a business term—has received much more attention among strategic communication professionals and the organizations they work with or represent (Weiner, 2012). It is important to remember that ROI is a financial metric that equals the profit from an investment (Stacks & Bowen, 2013). More specifically, ROI is an indicator of *net financial performance* based on a ratio of how much profit or cost savings is realized from an activity against its actual cost. A ROI metric is typically expressed as a percentage (Stacks & Bowen, 2013; T. Watson, 2005).

A particular challenge for strategic communicators is that the focus of a campaign or program may not be on directly impacting financial performance but rather may be on influencing a mix of *nonfinancial performance* indicators such as trust, relationships, reputation, credibility, or other opinion and attitude-based metrics. Calculating an ROI in the financial sense of the term may not be readily available or appropriate. The concept of "PR ROI" more broadly refers to the impact of a public relations program on business results. Some measurement and evaluation experts believe that any use of the term ROI is misleading and should be avoided all together in a strategic communication context (e.g., T. Watson, 2005, 2011; Watson & Zerfass, 2011). "The recommendation of the Coalition for Public Relations Research is that the term ROI should only be used when a researcher can vigorously measure an investment and the return from making that investment from a financial perspective," says Frank Ovaitt, president and CEO of the Institute for Public Relations, an independent research foundation (personal communication, April 25, 2014).

A related concept introduced by Don Stacks, a professor of public relations at the University of Miami and a communication measurement expert, is that of return on expectations or ROE (Stacks, 2010). ROE evaluates the performance of both financial (e.g., unit sales, gross profits, expenses) and nonfinancial variables (e.g., credibility, confidence, relationships, reputation and trust) on stakeholder expectations. In this approach, ROE serves as a moderator of ROI (Michaelson & Stacks, 2014; Stacks, 2010, 2013a, 2013c). In statistics, a moderator is a variable that strengthens or weakens the relationship between two other variables (Baron & Kenny, 1986), in this case, the influence of shifts in stakeholder expectations on the relationship between the campaign or program outputs and the actual, tangible financial outcomes.

Through the availability today of advanced statistical techniques, the strategic communication function is better positioned to demonstrate its value and improve its contribution to the bottom line (Weiner, 2012, p. 7). "The days when communicators could depend on a clip-book to represent ROI or value-for-money are over," says Mark Weiner, CEO of PRIME Research, one of the world's largest public relations and corporate communication research providers. "The return on investment of communication is quantifiable and, when managed properly, can contribute toward the organization's overall business goals and objectives."

Research, Measurement, and Evaluation in the Future

The explosion in so-called "big data," Web analytics tools, and social media monitoring systems has left communication departments and agencies literally swimming—and sometimes even drowning—in data (Ragas, 2014b). In this new digital world, a major challenge for strategic communicators is determining which metrics are valid gauges of communication's contribution to the attainment of organizational and communication goals and objectives and which metrics are simply distractions ("Are Traditional Ways of Doing Research Still Valuable in the Age of Social Media?", 2011). This more complex environment requires an "all hands on deck" approach to communication measurement and evaluation. It is no longer just research experts who need to be thinking about the role of research, measurement, and evaluation through all phases of a campaign or program (Michaelson & Stacks, 2014). While the research approach or metrics used may change from one campaign or program to the next, the general purpose of communication measurement and evaluation—to demonstrate business value and improve performance—does not. David Rockland, partner and managing director of global research at Ketchum, suggests that strategic communication professionals ask themselves the following questions when evaluating any campaign or program (personal communication, January 10, 2014):

- Did I reach the stakeholders that I was trying to reach with the messages that I wanted to convey?
- How did those stakeholders change as a result?
- Did that stakeholder change make a difference to achieving our organizational objective?
- And, we follow each of these questions with, "how would I do it better next time now that I know what's working and what's not?"

There are a growing range of educational resources available to strategic communication professionals who are interested in strengthening their competencies in communication research, measurement, and evaluation. The Measurement Commission of the Institute for Public Relations (IPR) and the International Association for Measurement and Evaluation of Communication (AMEC) provide a range of free resources on these topics on their websites. IPR, AMEC, and other professional communication organizations and groups increasingly hold conferences, webinars, and workshops on measurement and evaluation. A particularly valuable resource from IPR is the *Dictionary of Public Relations Measurement and Research*, now in its third edition, which is edited by Professors Don Stacks and Shannon Bowen. This comprehensive dictionary of research terminology is available as a free download from the IPR website.

There is also a growing range of books and guides on strategic communication research, measurement, and evaluation (e.g., Lindenmann, 2003, 2006; Michaelson & Stacks, 2014; Paine, 2007, 2011; Ruler, Vercic, & Vercic, 2008; Stacks, 2010; T. Watson & Noble, 2007). Finally, research, measurement, and evaluation is an ideal subject for promoting greater dialogue and collaboration between professionals and academicians (Grunig, Grunig, & Dozier, 2002). Many professors would be happy to share their research knowledge with professionals. After all, at the end of the day, whether professional, academician, or student, everyone in the strategic communication field has a vested interest in demonstrating that communication makes a meaningful contribution to the success of organizational strategies and beneficial stakeholder outcomes (Hon, 1997, 1998).

Key Terms

Advertising value equivalency (AVE)
Analytics
Applied research
The Barcelona Principles
Baseline
Basic research
Best practice
Case study
Content analysis
Depth interview
Ethnography
Experimental design
Focus group
Goal
Historical analysis

Institute for Public Relations (IPR)
International Association for the Measurement and Evaluation of Communication (AMEC)
Media clipping
Media impressions
Media placement
Metric
Mixed methods
Multipliers
Nonrandom sample
Objectives
Outcome

Output
Outtake
Public relations return on investment (PR ROI)
Qualitative research
Quantitative research
Random sample
Return on expectations (ROE)
Return on investment (ROI)
Standard
Statistics
Strategy
Survey

Discussion Questions

1. Review the Barcelona Principles. Which of these principles do you find the *most important* for improving the practice of communication measurement and evaluation?

2. If you were writing a new principle to add to the existing Barcelona Principles, what would you write? What motivated you to add this statement as a new principle?

3. Many communication research experts say it is important to have agreed upon measurement and evaluation standards and terms. Do you agree? Why or why not?

4. Do you think strategic communication professionals will place a greater focus on communication *outcomes* in the future or will communication *outputs* always remain an important part of measurement and evaluation? Explain your reasoning.

5. How does the rise and availability of so-called "big data," including a wide range of Web analytics data and social media conversation metrics about

current and prospective stakeholders, change communication research, measurement, and evaluation?

6. In your own experience, has it been important for the strategic communication function to demonstrate the value of communication efforts in business terms? Are there differences in the metrics valued by communication managers and managers in other departments?

Glossary

Accounting—The process of summarizing, analyzing, recording, and reporting business and financial transactions. Accounting is guided by detailed principles and procedures.

Accounts payable—A line on the balance sheet that is a liability, this figure is money the company owes to a supplier for a good or service purchased by the company, for which the company has not yet paid.

Accounts receivable—A line on the balance sheet that is an asset, this figure is money owed to the company such as from the sale of a good or service for which funds have yet to be collected.

Advertising value equivalence (AVE)—A controversial media metric that attempts to place a financial value on "earned" media coverage based on the cost to buy ad space in that publication.

Agency problem—Also known as agency costs, this problem arises when the interests of an organization's board of directors and/or management diverge from that of stakeholders.

Agency theory—Theory that conceptualizes shareholders as the "principals" of an organization and the board of directors as the "agents" that act on behalf of shareholders in creating value.

Agenda-building theory—A theory that explores the role of organizational information subsidies in influencing how information is used and interpreted by influencers and stakeholders.

Agenda-setting theory—A theory that examines how the media's presentation of topics in the news over time focuses and shapes the public's perceptions of the world around them.

Amortization—In corporate accounting, the deduction of capital expenses over the useful life of an intangible asset, such as a copyright, trademark, patent or other intellectual property.

Analyst/investor day—A half- or full-day event held in a major city or at a company facility in which management provides the financial community with a detailed look at its business.

Analytics—A collection of numeric metrics or indicators that help track the performance of a communication campaign or program in meeting a stated objective or objectives.

Annual meeting—A meeting held by a company typically after the end of its fiscal year. Many of these meetings are largely procedural with low in-person attendance, but there are exceptions.

Annual report—Document published annually that reviews the company's performance in the prior year. This document typically includes a letter from the CEO. May just be a 10-K wrap.

Applied research—Research that is conducted by or on behalf of an organization to solve a business challenge or address an opportunity. This research may be proprietary and nonpublic.

Arthur W. Page—Served as the vice president of public relations for AT&T. The first public relations executive to serve as an officer and member of the board of a major public company.

Arthur W. Page Center for Integrity in Public Communications—A research center at Penn State University dedicated to the study of ethics and responsibility in public communication.

Arthur W. Page Society—Based in New York and founded in 1983, a professional association for senior public relations and corporate communication executives with over 400 members.

Asset—A source of value for an organization. In a financial context, an asset is something that the organization owns or controls and that is expected to contribute to the creation of future profits.

Association for Education in Journalism and Mass Communication: Founded in 1912, AEJMC is the largest association of journalism and mass communication educators and students.

Balanced scorecard—Strategic management approach popularized by Robert Kaplan and David Norton that gauges organizational performance using both financial and nonfinancial metrics.

Balance sheet—This document tracks a company's assets, liabilities, and net worth on an accounting basis. It summarizes what a company owns and owes at the stated period in time.

Bankruptcy—A legal process in which an organization restructures its financial obligations to creditors (known as a Chapter 11) or liquidates its assets and shuts down (known as a Chapter 7).

The Barcelona Principles—A set of seven measurement principles agreed to at a meeting of communication measurement and evaluation experts held in Barcelona, Spain in summer 2010.

Baseline—Used in measurement and evaluation, a baseline is an initial measure of a campaign or program indicator that is used to assess future change in the performance of that indicator.

Basic research—Research that is conducted with the primary purpose of developing theory and contributing to the general body of knowledge. Academicians often conduct basic research.

Basis point—Also known as BPS, a basis point represents one one-hundredth (0.01 percent) of 1.0 percent. A unit used to track percentage changes in interest rates and bond yields. A 100 BPS equals 1.0 percent.

Bear market—A market that is declining or expected to decline in value is said to be a "bear market." This phrase refers to the symbolism of a bear's claws pulling downward.

Bearish—An expression used to convey negativity about the overall stock market or a particular security. May also be used in a broader business context to convey negativity about something.

Behavioral economics—Subfield of economics that involves the study of the effect of emotional factors and the seemingly "irrational" economic decisions made by individuals and organizations.

Behavioral finance—Subfield of finance that uses human and behavioral psychology to explain market behavior. Research in this field runs counter to the efficient market hypothesis.

Best practice—In a communication measurement context, a method or technique that has consistently demonstrated superior results compared with using other approaches.

Blackout period—The period around quarterly earnings reports in which company insiders cannot buy or sell shares of company stock. This limits the risk of insider trading charges.

Blue-chip company—A company with a high credit rating that has generated strong and predictable financial performance for years, if not decades, is said to be a "blue chip" company.

Board of directors—In a public company, the board of directors is elected by the company's shareholders. The board provides oversight and guidance to the company's senior management.

Bond—Generally considered safer than stocks, a bond is a form of debt that pays interest to the holder. Unless a convertible bond, a bond does *not* represent an ownership interest in a firm.

Book value—The stated net asset value of a company as carried on a company's accounting balance sheet (a.k.a. "the books"). Many intangible assets are not accounted for in this figure.

Bottom line—Refers to an organization's net income. The name "bottom line" comes from the fact that net income is generally a line near the bottom of an organization's income statement.

Breakup fee—This is a fee that an acquiring company agrees to pay the to-be-acquired company if the transaction is not approved or the acquirer decides to back out of the agreement.

Warren Buffett—Known as "the Oracle of Omaha," Buffett, the CEO of Berkshire-Hathaway, is regarded as one of the greatest investors of the century; also cocreated "The Giving Pledge."

Bull market—A market that is rising or expected to rise in value is said to be a "bull market." This phrase refers to the symbolism of a bull thrusting its horns upward (i.e., a rising market).

Bullish—An expression used to convey optimism about the overall stock market or a particular security. May also be used in a broader business context to convey optimism about something.

Harold Burson—Called the most influential public relations leader of the twentieth century, Burson is the founder of Burson-Marsteller, one of the world's largest communication agencies.

Business Marketing Association (BMA)—Founded in 1922, BMA is a national association of business-to-business (b-to-b) marketing and communication professionals.

Business model—A brief explanation of how a company intends to make money and create value for its stakeholders, and the factors that influence this value creation process.

Capital—Money, property and other assets of value that serve as the lifeblood of any organization. Investors provide capital to organizations with the goal of generating a profit.

Capital expenditure—Also known as CapEx, funds spent on buying or improving fixed, physical, long-term assets such as property, plants and equipment to generate future value.

Capitalized—Under accounting rules, an expenditure is capitalized if the item's useful life is believed to be longer than a year. Capitalized costs are amortized or depreciated over time.

Andrew Carnegie—Late nineteenth century industrialist and philanthropist who wrote the "Gospel of Wealth" in which he urged the wealthy to devote their resources to bettering society.

Case study—A research approach that relies on multiple sources of data to study a topic. This may include both quantitative and qualitative data sources as well as primary and secondary data.

Cash flow statement—This document literally "follows the money" and shows the amount of cash generated or spent by an organization in its course of business over the stated time period.

Cause marketing—A form of marketing in which a company partners with a nonprofit organization and agrees to donate a portion of sales to the cause supported by the nonprofit.

Chair—The chair of the board serves as the leader of the organization's board of directors. The chair serves as a key conduit between the board and senior management.

Chief communication officer—A member of the C-suite, the CCO is tasked with managing the internal and external communication of the organization. Often serves as an advisor to the CEO.

Chief executive officer—The CEO is the top executive in an organization's C-suite, tasked with setting and implementing firm strategy. Often sits on the company's board of directors.

Chief financial officer—A member of the C-suite, the CFO is increasingly tasked with overseeing not just an organization's finances but also other executive level functions like firm strategy.

Chief operating officer—A member of the C-suite, the COO is tasked with the day-to-day management of an organization's operations. This person may also carry the title of president.

Classified board—For companies that have a classified or "staggered" board of directors, all directors do not come up for shareholder vote annually, rather the directors come up for a vote over a multiyear period.

Clawback provision—A provision included in an employment contract that allows the company to "clawback" previously paid compensation on certain circumstances occurring.

Closely held—A closely held company refers to a company that has only a small number of shareholders and that is likely to be privately owned. The opposite would be a public company.

Commission on Public Relations Education—With representatives from 15 societies in public relations and communication, the commission provides recommendations on standards in public relations education.

Common stock—Security that represents an ownership interest in a firm and holds voting rights. In the event of a liquidation, creditors and preferred holders get paid before common holders.

Company insider—As defined by U.S. federal securities laws, company insiders are executive officers, members of the board of directors, large shareholders and potentially outside advisors.

Consent solicitation—Some public companies allow corporate actions to be taken outside of the annual meeting format if a written consent solicitation receives majority shareholder support.

Consumer confidence—Survey-based measures of how the public feels about current and future economic performance. Consumer confidence can be predictive of future economic behavior.

Consumer price index (CPI)—A popular gauge of the rate of inflation. The U.S. CPI measures changes in the average value of a basket of goods and services purchased by urban households.

Content analysis—A research method that may be quantitative or qualitative depending on the approach. The analysis of the frequency and contents of textual and image-based messages.

Corporate finance—Concerned with the raising and managing of funds (i.e., capital) with the goal of maximizing value for stakeholders, particularly shareholder and investor interests.

Corporate gadfly—Individual investor that attempts to affect change at public companies. Pioneering gadflies have included the Gilbert brothers and Evelyn Davis among others.

Corporate governance—The system of checks and balances that attempts to make boards of directors and management more accountable and better aligned with stakeholder interests.

Corporate reputation—An overall assessment of a company by its stakeholders using a company's various dimensions as the evaluative criteria. The *attitude* held toward a firm.

Corporate social responsibility—The voluntary actions taken by a company to fulfill perceived obligations to stakeholders that go beyond maximizing profits and following the law.

Cost of capital—A concept in corporate finance, cost of capital is the cost of obtaining funds to grow a business. Generally speaking, a lower cost of capital helps improve profitability.

Cost of goods sold—Also known as COGS or COS (for cost of sales), these are the *direct* costs that go into producing a good or service. Indirect costs are excluded from this figure.

Council of Institutional Investors (CII)—Founded in 1985, this association of investment funds with combined assets of $3 trillion dollars is a driving force in corporate governance.

Council of Public Relations Firms—With more than one hundred public relations agencies as members, the Council advocates for and advances the business of public relations firms.

Credit—Entered on the right-hand side of an accounting ledger, a credit entry is made to record changes in value due to a business transaction. A debit is the opposite of a credit.

C-suite—The C-level executives (e.g., CEO, president, CFO, CTO, CCO and the like) that collectively make up the senior leadership team and top decision makers within an organization.

Cumulative voting—At some public companies, shareholders have the right to pool their votes all for one director nominee, thereby amplifying the voice of minority shareholders in elections.

Currency exchange rate—The rate at which one currency will be exchanged for another. Exchange rates fluctuate based on shifts in the economic conditions of the various countries.

Debit—Entered on the left-hand side of an accounting ledger, a debit entry is made to record changes in value due to a business transaction. A debit is the opposite of a credit.

Debt—A bond, loan note, mortgage or other obligation, which states repayment terms on borrowed money and, if applicable, the interest owed as a condition of the borrowed money.

Declassified board—A board of directors in which all board of director seats come up for vote annually rather than a classified board where there is a staggering of terms for directors' seats.

Deflation—The opposite of inflation. Deflation is when prices for goods and services decline. Deflation leads to consumers delaying purchases and the value of assets declining.

Depreciation—In corporate accounting, the deduction of capital expenses over the useful life of a tangible asset, such as fixtures, equipment, vehicles, buildings, and improvements.

Depreciation and amortization—Also known as D&A, these related "noncash" expenses on the income statement take into account the wear and tear of assets over the life of the asset.

Depression—A severe, long-term downturn in the economy. A depression is much worse than simply a recession. The most well-known U.S. depression is the Great Depression of the 1930s.

Depth interview—A qualitative research technique in which a researcher conducts a detailed interview with a subject one participant at a time. Also known as a one-on-one interview.

Diffusion of innovation theory—Theory that seeks to explain how, why and at what rate innovations are communicated through certain channels over time through a social system.

Disclosures—In an organizational and communication context, the release of organizational information that aids stakeholders in decision making and reduces information asymmetry.

The Dodd-Frank Wall Street Reform and Consumer Protection—Passed in 2010 in the wake of taxpayer-funded bailouts of Wall Street, this landmark legislation tightens and places new regulations over corporations, particularly those operating in the financial services sector.

Dow Jones Industrial Average (DJIA)—Often known as simply the Dow, the DJIA is a widely followed stock market index comprised of 30 large, well-known U.S. companies.

Dual class stock—A type of ownership structure in place at some companies in which there are two or more classes of stock with one class having greater voting rights than the others.

Earnings—Terminology usually used with public companies that refers to the amount of money a company made or loss over a set time period. Earnings are the same at net income or net profits.

Earnings call—Generally held quarterly, a conference call at which company management discusses the company's latest financial performance and takes questions from investors.

Earnings guidance—Informational disclosures specifically focused on expectations about future company performance. The content of these forward-looking statements may vary widely.

Earnings per share (EPS)—A measure of earnings or profits. Earnings per share is calculated by dividing the net income (i.e., net earnings) of a company by its number of shares outstanding.

Earnings release—A news release, typically distributed over a paid wire service, which reports the company's quarterly financial performance. The release may also include earnings guidance.

Economic cycle—Economies go through natural periods of growth followed by decline and then growth again. This process of expansion and contraction is known as an economic cycle.

Economics—The study of the cause-and-effect relationships in an economy. While often now housed and taught in business schools around the world, economics is actually a social science.

Economists—Study the consequences of decisions that people make about the use of land, labor, capital and other resources that go into producing the products that are bought and sold.

Economy—The total aggregate sum of all goods and services produced among market participants. An economy may be studied at a local, regional, national, or even international level.

EDGAR—All public companies must file disclosure documents with the U.S. SEC's EDGAR system. The full name is Electronic Data Gathering, Analysis, and Retrieval.

Employment report—Regular reports, often issued by government agencies, providing data on the state of employment and the employment rate for a particular region, such as a country.

Enterprise value—This comprehensive valuation measure is the sum of the company's market capitalization (common stock) plus debt, any preferred stock and minority interest minus cash.

Environmental scanning—The process of monitoring the environment in which organizations and clients operate for issues, trends, and other factors that may impact future decisions.

Environmental, social, and governance (ESG)—Refers to the various disclosures and policies that comprise an organization's environmental, societal, and governance impact on its stakeholders.

Equity—A stock or other security that represents an underlying ownership interest in a company. More broadly, equity refers to ownership in an asset after all debts have been paid.

Ethnography—Drawing from anthropology, a qualitative research technique in which the researcher observes, and potentially interacts with, participants in an area of their everyday lives.

Exchange traded fund (ETF)—An investment fund that is bought and sold on an exchange like an individual stock but that tracks the performance of a pool of securities or other assets.

Executive committee—A committee comprised of the members of the C-suite, as well as senior executives and division heads across the organization. Separate from the board of directors.

Exit, voice, and loyalty—Framework developed by Albert Hirschman that explains how individuals will engage in either "exit" or "voice" when faced with declining quality in a relationship.

Expense—A cost that an organization incurs to generate revenue. This includes production, labor, leases, supplies, financing, and administration. Expenses are the opposite of revenue.

Expensed—Under accounting rules, an expenditure in which the total cost of the item is incurred all at once on the income statement. No amortization or depreciation is allowed.

Experimental design—A quantitative research method that relies on the manipulation and control of variables in a laboratory-like setting to establish causation between variables.

Federal Open Market Committee (FOMC)—An influential committee within the Federal Reserve System that makes decisions about monetary policy, including setting the fed funds rate.

Federal Reserve—Created in 1913 by the U.S. Congress, the Federal Reserve is the central bank of the United States. The Fed sets monetary policy with a goal of full employment and stable prices.

Fiduciary obligation—When referenced in the context of corporate governance, this refers to the legal duty that directors have to act in the best interest of the organization's stakeholders.

Financial Accounting Standards Board (FASB)—An independent private organization that sets the generally accepted accounting principles (GAAP) for U.S. financial reporting.

Financial asset—Assets such as stocks, bonds, and cash that lack a physical embodiment, but are not considered intangibles since they basically represent claims on organizational assets.

Financial Communication Society (FCS)—Founded in 1967, FCS is an association of financial services marketing and communication professionals. Chapters are in major financial centers.

Financial statements—Documents that state the financial health of an organization. The most well-known of these statements are the income statement, balance sheet, and cash flow statement.

Fiscal year—The 12 month period that marks one full year of operations and financial reporting for an organization. Many organizations have a fiscal year that is the same as the calendar year.

Focus group—A qualitative research approach in which a moderator leads a semistructured discussion with a group of participants that is recorded and then later analyzed.

Charles Fombrun—Leading scholar on corporate reputation, founded Reputation Institute and led the development of the Reputation Quotient and RepTrak corporate reputation measures.

Form 4—This document is required to be filed with the U.S. SEC's EDGAR system whenever there are changes in an insider's ownership (i.e., a purchase or sale) of company securities.

Form 8-K—This document is required to be filed with the U.S. SEC's EDGAR system whenever a material current event occurs in between a periodic report (i.e., 10-Qs and 10-K).

Form 10-K—This document is required to be filed with the U.S. SEC's EDGAR system. The 10-K reports a company's annual results and forms the foundation for a firm's annual report.

Form 10-Q—This document is required to be filed with the U.S. SEC's EDGAR system. The 10-Q reports a company's quarterly results. Unlike the 10-K, these financials are unaudited.

Form S-1—Also known as a prospectus, this registration document is required to be filed with the U.S. SEC's EDGAR system and is used by companies planning to go public.

***Fortune* magazine's Most Admired Companies**—Launched by *Fortune* in 1982, this annual list was the first attempt at measuring and ranking the reputations of America's largest companies.

Forward-looking statement—A statement made by a company about future expectations and performance (i.e., guidance). Safe-harbor language should accompany such a statement.

R. Edward Freeman—Business philosopher that is most closely associated with stakeholder theory, the concept of stakeholders, and the moral responsibility the firm has to stakeholders.

Milton Friedman—A winner of the Nobel Prize in Economic Sciences, this free market economist is most closely associated with shareholder theory and shareholder primacy.

Futures contract—A standardized agreement where both parties agree to buy and sell an asset, such as a physical commodity, of a specified quantity at a specified future date and price.

General and administrative expenses—Also known as G&A, these are expenses related to the day-to-day operations of a firm rather than expenses related to the direct production of goods.

Generally Accepted Accounting Principles—Set by the Financial Accounting Standards Board (FASB), these principles help guide and provide consistency in U.S. financial reporting.

Glass, Lewis & Co.—Founded in 2003, this organization is a provider of proxy advisory services and shareholder voting recommendations to institutional investors.

Global Reporting Initiative (GRI)—A nonprofit organization that develops and promotes one of the most widely used sustainability reporting standards and frameworks for CSR reporting.

GMI Ratings—A research firm that provides advisory services to institutional investors on environmental, social, and governance-related (ESG) issues to help them manage risk.

Goal—A general statement rooted in the organization's mission and vision, stating what the organization intends to achieve; a goal tells stakeholders "*where* it is trying to go."

Golden handcuffs—Special incentives provided to top executives that encourage them to remain with a company and not to go to work for a competitor. Also called golden handshakes.

Golden parachute—An agreement, typically with a top executive, which the individual will receive certain significant benefits on termination, often following a change in control.

Al Golin—The founder of the global public relations firm GolinHarris and the originator of the "trust bank" concept in which companies build up deposits of goodwill through giving back.

Goodwill—In a corporate accounting context, an asset that is based on the amount paid for a company over its stated book value. This figure places a value on the acquired firm's intangibles.

The Great Depression—Severe worldwide economic depression that started in 1930 and lasted for at least a decade. In the United States, the Great Depression sparked the first wave of federal securities laws.

Greenwashing—Derogatory term for when a company is perceived as spending more resources promoting and touting sustainable business practices than actually engaging in such behavior.

Gross Domestic Product (GDP)—Widely followed economic indicator of a country or region's economic health. GDP represents the market value of all goods produced over a certain period.

Gross profit—Also called gross income, gross profit is a company's revenue minus its cost of goods sold. In other words, it is how much money is left over after deducting the direct expenses.

Guidance—The widespread practice of public companies attempting to improve transparency and manage investor expectations by releasing forecasts about future company performance.

Harris Interactive—Best known for the Harris Poll on public opinion, this market research firm also codeveloped the Harris Reputation Quotient (RQ), which is used in the reputation field.

Historical analysis—A qualitative research method that seeks to learn from and about the past through the collection and analysis of historical artifacts related to the topic of study.

Human capital—Term that recognizes that an organization's employees are a key source of future benefits. Human capital is typically viewed as a specific type of intangible asset.

Imperfect information—In an economics context, situations in which one party to a transaction has superior information than the other party, resulting in negative pricing and other actions.

Income statement—Also known as a profit & loss statement, this document tracks how much money an organization made or lost, and spent, on an accounting basis for the stated time period.

Independent director—Also known as an outside director, this is an individual who is not an employee of the company and does not have a material relationship with the company.

Individual investor—A small, private, nonprofessional investor that typically buys small blocks of stock when making investments. Individual investors are sometimes known as retail investors.

Inflation—The opposite of deflation. Inflation is when the prices for goods and services increase. Inflation decreases the value of money and reduces its purchasing power.

Information asymmetry—A gap that occurs when one party to a potential transaction (i.e., the insider) is in possession of more and better information than the other party (i.e., the outsider).

Information intermediary—Any entity that reports, interprets, and analyzes information for broader consumption. In corporate finance, this includes financial journalists and analysts.

Information subsidy—Organizational communication vehicles and prepackaged materials that lower the cost of information thereby increasing consumption by influencers and stakeholders.

Initial public offering (IPO)—An IPO marks the first time that a company sells stock to the public and its shares are listed on a stock exchange and widely available for purchase.

Insider trading—The illegal practice of a company insider (i.e., executive or director), consultant, or related party trading on and profiting from nonpublic, material information.

Institute for Public Relations—Located at the University of Florida and founded in 1956, this independent nonprofit foundation is dedicated to the science beneath the art of public relations.

Institutional investor—A professional investor, such as a mutual fund, hedge fund, pension fund, or endowment, which typically buys large blocks of stock when making investments.

Institutional Shareholder Services (ISS)—A subsidiary of MSCI Inc., ISS is a provider of proxy advisory services and shareholder voting recommendations to institutional investors.

Intangible asset—An asset that provides a source of future benefits, but lacks a direct physical embodiment. Examples include a firm's intellectual property, reputations, and relationships.

Integrated reporting—A "one report" approach to company reporting in which financial and nonfinancial performance metrics are presented in a format conducive to all stakeholders.

Intellectual property—A class of intangible assets that is generally the result of research and development (R&D) activities. This includes patents, trademarks, copyrights, and trade secrets.

Interest rate—The rate at which interest is paid by people or organizations to borrow money from lenders, such as banks. The Federal Reserve and other central banks impact interest rates.

International Accounting Standards Board (IASB)—An independent body that is responsible for developing the International Financial Reporting Standards (IFRS) used around the world.

International Association for the Measurement and Evaluation of Communication (AMEC)—Founded in London in 1996, AMEC is a global trade group that played a lead role in the establishment of the Barcelona Declaration of Measurement Principles and other standards.

International Association of Business Communicators (IABC)—An association of approximately fifteen thousand business communication professionals based in over 80 countries.

International Communication Association (ICA)—Founded in 1950, ICA is an academic association for communication scholars with more than four thousand five hundred members in 80 countries.

International Financial Reporting Standards (IFRS)—These accounting standards are overseen by the International Accounting Standards Board and used in more than one hundred countries.

Investment bank—Financial organization that helps a company go public, sell stock or bonds, and advise it on financial transactions, such as mergers, acquisitions or divestitures.

Investment conference—These are typically organized by an investment bank. Public companies are invited to make a presentation to professional investors and analysts. They are often offered by webcast.

Investor relations—A strategic communication function that in most public companies serves as the primary interface between the financial community and company management.

Jawboning—The planned, purposeful use of statements by government actors, such as the Federal Reserve, to try to influence economic behavior and conditions in the financial markets.

Jumpstart Our Business Startups Act—Passed in 2012 and known as the JOBS Act, this legislation loosened securities regulations on smaller companies and helped promote growth.

Key performance indicator (KPI)—A measure designed to gauge the performance of an organization or business unit at advancing or achieving a stated strategy, goal, or objective.

Lead director—Also called a "presiding director," the lead director presides over meetings of the independent directors of the board; this position's level of power varies by company.

Leveraged buyout (LBO)—Typically associated with "going private" transactions and private equity firms. An LBO involves the use of a mix of debt and equity to acquire a company.

Liability—The opposite of an asset, a liability is an obligation that an organization takes on during the course of business, such as debt, accounts payable, or future incomes taxes payable.

Liquidity—A concept in corporate finance, liquidity is concerned with the ability to buy and sell a security, such as a stock, quickly and at a low cost with a limited effect on the market price.

Macroeconomics—Concerned with the study of the economy as a whole. Assesses the economy at a *macro-level* and studies the interactions of its various market participants.

Majority voting—In the context of board of director elections, majority voting stipulates a director must receive majority shareholder support or otherwise tender their resignation.

Management, Discussion & Analysis (MD&A)—A section of a company's proxy statement in which management discusses the company's prior year performance and discusses future plans.

Market capitalization—Also known as market cap, this valuation measure is calculated by multiplying the company's stock price times the total number of shares of stock outstanding.

Market maker—Specialists that stand ready to buy and sell a particular stock on a regular basis at the publicly quoted price. Market makers are essential to the functioning of stock exchanges.

Market-to-book ratio—A valuation ratio calculated by taking a public company's total market capitalization and dividing it by the company's accounting book value (i.e., net asset value).

Materiality—In a public company context, information is considered material if a typical investor would likely view such information as important in affecting their investment decision.

Media clipping—Also known as a media placement or hit. The term goes back to when strategic communicators would "clip" articles and maintain records of media coverage in clip books.

Media impressions—The maximum size of an audience that might have been exposed to a communication message as the result of a placement. Based on the publication's circulation size.

Media placement—Also known as a hit or a clip. A placement is a news item or story that is attributed to strategic communication efforts, such as interactions with a journalist or influencer.

Metric—An informal term for a campaign or program measure or indicator. More specifically, a numeric value that should help determine whether a stated objective is being met.

Microeconomics—Concerned with the study of individual firms and households. Approaches economics from a *microlevel*, assessing the economic decisions of specific organizations.

Mission—A brief description of why an organization exists and how it creates value for stakeholders. The organizational mission may be codified in a mission statement.

Mixed methods—A research approach in which multiple research techniques, specifically both quantitative methods and qualitative methods, are used to study and evaluate a topic of interest.

Multiple-step flow theory—Also known as the two-step flow theory, identifies the role of opinion leaders in the spread of information from the mass media to the general public.

Multipliers—The disputed notion that earned media coverage is worth more than or a "multiple of" paid advertising space in the same publication. Often used with ad value equivalencies.

NASDAQ—Founded in 1971, the NASDAQ is the second largest stock exchange in the United States and the world, behind only the NYSE. The NASDAQ is owned by the NASDAQ OMX Group.

National Investor Relations Institute (NIRI)—Founded in 1969 and based in the United States, it is the world's largest professional association of corporate investor relations officers and consultants.

Need for orientation—Concept that finds that news media reporting has the greatest impact on shaping perceptions when people have high *relevance* and high *uncertainty* regarding a topic.

Negative equity—Also known as negative shareholders' equity, this occurs when total liabilities exceed total assets at a company. This indicates the firm may have trouble funding its operations.

Net income—Also known as net profit, net earnings, or the bottom line, this figure shows how much money a firm made after taking into account both operating and *non*operating expenses.

Net margin—A ratio of profitability calculated as net income or net profit divided by *all* expenses (both operating and nonoperating expenses, such as interest and taxes).

New York Stock Exchange—Also known as the Big Board, the NYSE is the oldest and largest stock exchange in the world. The NYSE is operated by NYSE Euronext.

Nondeal road show—A series of meetings held in various financial center cities in which company management meets with current and prospective large shareholders.

Nonfinancial information—Information that companies are generally not required to disclose but that provides insights into the management and performance of intangible assets.

Nongovernmental organization (NGO)—An organization that operates independently of government and has a mission committed to advancing environmental or social issues.

Nonorganic growth—In a business context, "nonorganic" refers to business growth that is generated through acquisitions rather than through ownership of existing business operations.

Nonrandom sample—A sample in which every member of a target population *does not* have an equal chance of being selected. Also known as a nonprobability sample.

Objectives—Specific statements emerging from a goal presented in clear, measurable, realistic, and time-bounded terms; tells us "how we will know *if* and *when* we have gotten there."

Open outcry—Also called pit trading, this form of trading relies on verbal bids, offers, and hand signals, unlike electronic trading, which is fully computerized. The NYSE still has open outcry.

Operating income—Also called operating profit or income from operations, this figure shows how much money a firm made or lost after taking into account all of its operating expenses.

Operating margin—A ratio of profitability calculated as operating income or operating profit divided by net revenue. This measure does not take into account nonoperating expenses.

Options contract—A contract that offers the buyer the right—but not the obligation—to buy ("call") or sell ("put") a security at a specified future date and price during a certain time period.

Organic growth—In a business context, "organic" refers to growth that is generated internally via a company's existing operations rather than growth that comes through acquisitions.

Outcome—The most sophisticated level of evaluation; measures the establishment, change, or reinforcement in stakeholders' opinions, attitudes, or behaviors based on campaign messages.

Output—The most basic level of evaluation; measures the distribution of and possible exposure to campaign messages by stakeholders. Media analysis of third party content falls under outputs.

Outtake—An intermediate level of evaluation; measures whether targeted stakeholders actually received, paid attention to, understood, and/or or retained the campaign messages.

Over the counter (OTC)—A security, such as a stock, which is available for purchase, but is not listed on a formal stock exchange. Stocks traded "over the counter" are usually of higher risk.

Page Up—Affiliated with the Arthur W. Page Society, this organization is for Page members' most senior staff leaders. It is committed to developing the next generation of CCOs.

P&L—An informal name for a profit and loss statement. The P&L is simply another name for the income statement, which tracks a company's revenue and expenses on an accounting basis.

Pink sheets—Originally a list of securities printed on sheets of pink paper, the securities quoted on the pink sheet system are not listed on a formal exchange and generally are speculative.

Plank Center for Leadership in Public Relations—Named after Betsy Plank, this center housed at The University of Alabama supports leadership in public relations education and practice.

Poison pill—A type of antitakeover provision, a poison pill limits the amount of stock that any one shareholder can own beyond a certain threshold, thereby giving more power to the board.

Preferred stock—A special class of stock that has priority over common stock holders in the event of liquidation. Preferred shares generally have a fixed dividend, but no voting rights.

Profit margin—A measure of operational efficiency that shows how much a company makes (i.e., earnings) on a percentage basis for each dollar of sales it generates after various expenses.

PR Return on Investment (PR ROI)—The impact of a public relations program on business results. The outcome variable that demonstrates the impact of a PR investment on business.

Public company—A public company is a company whose shares are listed on a stock exchange and is widely available for purchase by the public. May also be called a listed company.

Publicity Club of Chicago—Founded in 1941, it is the nation's largest independent public relations membership organization with a focus on Chicagoland and the Midwest.

Public Relations Society of America (PRSA)—With twenty-one thousand members across the United States, it is the world's largest professional association for public relations and communication professionals.

Private company—A private company is a company whose shares are *not* listed on a stock exchange and has a small number of shareholders. May also be called a closely held company.

Private equity firm—A type of professional investor that invests in large, more established companies using a mix of debt and equity. May hold ownership stakes in public companies.

Property, plant, and equipment (PP&E) —This line on the balance sheet records the estimated value of this broad category of physical assets, ranging from company real estate to equipment.

Prospectus—A legal document that offers for sale securities, such as stock in a company. The prospectus outlines the business, its financial performance, its risks factors, and the use of funds.

Proxy adviser—A specialized investment research firm hired by institutional investors to advise them on how to vote on corporate ballot issues, such as elections for board of director seats.

Proxy contest—Also known as a proxy fight, such situation typically occurs when there is a contested election between a dissident investor and the company for one or more board seats.

Proxy solicitor—A specialized communication and research firm hired by public companies or large shareholders to predict and influence the voting outcomes on corporate ballot issues.

Proxy statement—Formally known as a DEF 14A filing with the SEC, this governance-oriented document is distributed annually in advance of a public company's annual meeting.

Qualitative research—A general research approach that collects nonnumeric textual or image-based data (i.e., soft data) from relatively small samples to uncover deep, rich insights.

Quantitative research—A general research approach that collects numeric data from random samples often with a goal of using statistics to generalize findings to a larger population.

Quiet period—As mandated by U.S. federal securities law, a company that has registered to sell stock (e.g., IPO) is limited in the public statements it can make. Many public companies also choose to voluntarily adopt "quiet periods" around the release of quarterly earnings.

Random sample—A sample in which every member of a target population has an equal chance of being selected. Also known as a probability sample. Statistics assume random samples.

Recession—A period of economic decline and contraction during an economic cycle. A recession is officially defined as two consecutive quarters (six months) of negative GDP growth.

Regulation Fair Disclosure—Also known as Reg. FD, this federal regulation adopted by the SEC in August 2000 promotes the full and fair disclosure of information by companies.

RepTrak®—Launched in 2005, an annual measure of corporate reputation designed by scholars Charles Fombrun and Cees van Riel of Reputation Institute, a research and consulting firm.

Reputation management—The strategic communication and actions taken by a company to manage its reputation—an intangible asset that is co-owned by the company and its stakeholders.

Reputation Quotient (RQ)®—Launched in 1999, the RQ® is an annual measure of corporate reputation designed by scholar Charles Fombrun and market research firm Harris Interactive.

Research and development (R&D)—An expense line on the income statements that tracks spending on the development of new products, processes, procedures or related innovations.

Retained earnings—Also known as retained profits or retained income. The profits left in an organization's bank accounts to invest back in the business after paying out any dividends.

Return on expectations (ROE)—A metric that assesses the combined impact of financial and nonfinancial variables on stakeholder expectations, which leads to public relations ROI.

Return on investment (ROI)—An indicator of net financial performance based on a ratio of how much profit or cost savings is realized from an activity against its actual cost.

Revenue—The amount of money received for the sale of a good. Also known as sales, revenue is referred to as the "top line" since this figure appears near the top of the income statement.

Road show—A series of meetings held in financial centers in which a company's management team, investment bankers, and other advisors meet with prospective large shareholders.

Rule 14(a)8—A rule passed by the SEC in 1943, which allowed shareholders for the first time to submit some shareholder proposals for inclusion in public company's proxy materials.

Russell 2000—A widely followed stock market index, the Russell 2000 is comprised of 2,000 small capitalization U.S. companies. This index is a key measure of "small cap" performance.

Safe harbor language—As part of the Securities Litigation Reform Act of 1995, firms may list current risk factors when making forward statements to protect against frivolous lawsuits.

The Sarbanes-Oxley Act—Nicknamed SOX or SarbOx, this U.S. federal accounting reform and investor protection legislation was passed in 2002 in response to corporate scandals.

Say on frequency—A provision in the Dodd-Frank Act of 2010 gives shareholders the right to cast an advisory vote on how frequently shareholders should vote on executive compensation.

Say on pay—A provision in the Dodd-Frank Act of 2010 gives shareholders the right to cast an advisory vote on executive compensation packages. This nonbinding vote is known as say on pay.

Schedule 13D—A filing that is required to be made with the U.S. SEC's EDGAR system within ten days of whenever anyone acquires a more than 5 percent voting stake in a public company.

Schedule 13G—An alternative to the Schedule 13D, the 13G filing connotes that the investor tends to have only a passive (rather than active) ownership position in the public company.

Secondary offering—Occurs when an already public company decides to sell additional shares of stock in order to raise money for the company and/or allow company insiders to sell shares.

Securities—Financial instruments that represent some type of financial value such as an ownership interest in a company (stock) or money that is borrowed and must be repaid (bond).

Securities Act of 1933—Also known as the Truth in Securities Act, this U.S. federal legislation regulates the offer and sale of securities. The act promoted better disclosures.

Securities Exchange Act of 1934—This landmark U.S. legislation governs the secondary trading of securities. The Securities and Exchange Commission was formed through this act.

Securities laws—The laws that govern the offer and sale of securities. This includes the mandatory and voluntary disclosure of material, nonpublic, information to the market.

Selective disclosure—Illegal practice in which select market participants are made aware of material, nonpublic information about a public company ahead of the broader market.

Selling, general, and administrative (SG&A)—Broad expense category line that appears on a company's income statement. Spending on strategic communication falls under SG&A.

Shareholder activism—Attempt by one or more company shareholders to affect change at an organization through a variety of strategies, ranging from private meetings to proxy contests.

Shareholder primacy—A perspective embedded in classic agency theory in which the board of directors first and foremost makes decisions based on how such actions affect shareholder value.

Shareholder proposal—A proposal submitted by a shareholder for inclusion in a public company's proxy statement. Votes on shareholder proposals are typically advisory/nonbinding.

Shareholder theory—Most closely associated with economist Milton Friedman, this theory posits that a company should maximize profits for shareholders, while following the rules.

Shareholders' equity—Also known as net worth or book value, this line on the balance sheet is equal to total assets minus total liabilities. This is share capital invested plus retained earnings.

Shares outstanding—Shown on a company's balance sheet, this figure represents the total number of shares currently outstanding and owned by shareholders, including insiders.

Signaling theory—A theory into the process of how and why market participants engage in costly and observable behaviors, known as "signals," which reduce information asymmetry.

Adam Smith—A father of modern economics and the author of *The Wealth of Nations*, which argues that by operating out of self-interest individuals and firms inadvertently benefit others.

Socially responsible companies (SRC)—Moving beyond corporate social responsibility (CSR) initiatives and programs towards embedding CSR into the very core of a firm's business model.

Sovereign wealth fund—A government owned investment fund or entity that is funded by a country's foreign currency reserves. These funds invest in securities and other assets.

Special meeting—When a major corporate event occurs, such as a pending merger or acquisition, a special meeting of shareholders may be called before the next annual meeting.

Spin-off—In a corporate context, refers to when a company separates off one or more of its operating units into a newly established standalone business. This is also known as a "spin-out."

Staggered board—A board of directors is said to be "staggered" when board seats come up for vote over a multiyear period rather than all seats coming up for vote on an annual basis.

Stakeholder—Individuals or groups that have a shared interest or "stake" in the performance of an organization. This includes customers, employees, suppliers, investors, and the community.

Stakeholder theory—Most closely associated with business ethicist R. Edward Freeman, this theory posits that firms have a responsibility to all stakeholder groups, not just shareholders.

Standard—In a communication measurement context, an agreed upon approach, process or idea used as a norm or model that facilitates comparative evaluations against and across campaigns.

Standard & Poor's 500 (S&P 500)—A widely followed broad measure of the U.S. market, the S&P 500 stock market index is comprised of 500 large capitalization or "large cap" companies.

Statistics—A field of mathematics concerned with the collection and analysis of numeric data, often for purposes of making inferences from a sample data set onto the population of study.

Stock—A security that represents an ownership interest in a company and its future earnings. The two main classes of stock are common stock and preferred stock.

Stock exchange—A market where securities, such as shares of stock in a company, are bought and sold. A company must meet listing requirements to have its stock listed on an exchange.

Stock index—A collection of stocks that represent the change in value of a particular industry, sector, or the overall stock market. The DJIA and S&P 500 are widely tracked indexes.

Stock option—An instrument that gives someone, whether a company employee or an investor, the right to buy a specific number of shares of stock at a particular price on a future date.

Stock split—An action in which a company divides its existing shares outstanding into additional shares. A stock split in itself does not change the total dollar value of the company.

Stock ticker symbol—In the U.S. market, a series of unique letters (or single letter) used to identify the publicly traded stock of a company. Goes back to the days of ticker tape machines.

Strategic communication—The purposeful use of communication to advance an organization's mission. Strategic communicators employ persuasion, relational, and informational approaches.

Strategic Communication and Public Relations Center—Housed at the University of Southern California, the center seeks to bridge the gap between the public relations profession and academia.

Strategy—An overall plan or method employed to achieve an organizational goal; not to be confused with *tactics*, which are specific elements implemented in support of a strategy.

Supermajority voting—In the context of corporate governance, a provision that states that proposed bylaw amendments must receive a high percentage (67 percent or greater) of total votes.

Supply and demand—A core tenet of economic theory and the pricing of goods and services. In a free market environment, shifts in supply and demand play a key role in affecting prices.

Survey—A quantitative research method that uses a standard series of questions to collect data from respondents to gauge the sample and/or population's beliefs, attitudes and/or behaviors.

Sustainability—In a corporate context, refers to business practices and performance that meet current needs, while not compromising the environment and society for future generations.

Sustainability reporting frameworks—Standards developed by nonprofit organizations to guide company sustainability reporting practices so that they are comparable across firms.

Tangible asset—An asset that has a direct physical embodiment such as real estate, factories and fixtures, equipment, vehicles or product inventory. Also known as "hard" assets.

Third-party endorsement—Recommendation, verification, or similar action provided by a seemingly independent, objective third party, whether the news media or another influencer.

Top line—Refers to an organization's revenue or sales. The name "top line" comes from the fact that revenue is generally the first line at the top of an organization's income statement.

Transparency—In a communication context, the proactive efforts taken by an organization to be open, visible, and accessible to stakeholders about organizational policies and actions.

Triple bottom line—A core concept of corporate social responsibility; companies have a responsibility to profits, people, and the planet rather than solely the traditional bottom line.

Trust Barometer—An annual global survey conducted by public relations firm Edelman into the concept of trust by country on institutions, industry sectors and informational sources.

Underwriter—An investment bank that is responsible for the distribution, pricing and sale of securities by a company, such as during an initial public offering of a company's stock.

Unemployment rate—A percentage calculated from employment report data, which represents the ratio of unemployed people looking for work versus those that are currently employed.

U.S. Securities and Exchange Commission (SEC)—U.S. federal government agency tasked with enforcing federal securities laws and regulating the securities industries and stock market.

Values—In an organizational context, these are the guiding ethical ideals and principles that an organization holds as important. Should guide the organization's mission and vision.

Cees van Riel—Leading scholar and consultant on corporate communication and reputation management. Cofounder and vice chair of the Reputation Institute with Charles Fombrun.

Venture capital firm—A type of professional investor that typically invests in private, fast-growing companies. Venture capital firms are often investors in pre-IPO companies.

Vesting period—In the context of corporate finance, refers to the time that an employee must wait until they are able to exercise stock incentives. Vesting encourages loyalty by employees.

Vision—The core tenets and values driving what an organization hopes to become and achieve.

Wall Street—A street in Lower Manhattan that is the heart of New York's financial district. Wall Street or simply "the street" is used to refer to the U.S. financial industry as a whole.

Warrant—Similar to an option, only that a warrant is a longer-dated instrument that gives the holder the right to purchase a security, usually a stock, at a specific price within a certain time.

Written consent—In the context of corporate governance, written consent allows shareholders to take various corporate actions without having to wait for voting at the next annual meeting.

References

Achieve. (2013). *The 2013 millennial impact report.* Indianapolis, IN: Author.

Ackerman, A. (2013, August 21). SEC is set to propose new rule on CEO pay. *The Wall Street Journal.* Retrieved September 15, 2013, from http://on.wsj.com/16eDoet

Adams, R. B., Licht, A. N., & Sagiv, L. (2011). Shareholders and stakeholders: How do directors decide? *Strategic Management Journal, 32*(12), 1331–1355.

AFL-CIO. (2011). *Dodd-Frank Section 953(b): Why CEO-to-worker pay ratios matter for investors.* Washington, DC: AFL-CIO Office of Investment.

Aguinis, H., & Glavas, A. (2012). What we know and don't know about corporate social responsibility: A review and research agenda. *Journal of Management, 38*(4), 932–968.

Ahern, L., & Bortree, D. S. (Eds.). (2012). *Talking green: Exploring contemporary issues in environmental communications.* New York, NY: Peter Lang.

Akerlof, G. A. (1970). The market for "lemons": Quality uncertainty and the market mechanism. *The Quarterly Journal of Economics, 84*(3), 488–500.

Akerlof, G. A., & Shiller, R. J. (2009). *Animal spirits: How human psychology drives the economy, and why it matters for global capitalism.* Princeton, NJ: Princeton University Press.

Altman, D., & Berman, J. (2011). *The single bottom line.* New York, NY: Department of Economics, Stern School of Business, New York University.

Amihud, Y., & Mendelson, H. (2003). The liquidity route to a lower cost of capital. In J. M. Stern & D. H Chew (Eds.), *The revolution in corporate finance* (4th ed., pp. 70–88). Malden, MA: Blackwell.

Amihud, Y., & Mendelson, H. (2006). Stock and bond liquidity and its effect on prices and financial policies. *Financial Markets and Portfolio Management, 20,* 19–32.

Amihud, Y., & Mendelson, H. (2008). Liquidity, the value of the firm, and corporate finance. *Journal of Applied Corporate Finance, 20*(2), 32–45.

Amihud, Y., & Mendelson, H. (2012). Liquidity, the value of the firm, and corporate finance. *Journal of Applied Corporate Finance, 24*(1), 17–32.

Amir, E., Lev, B., & Sougiannis, T. (2003). Do financial analysts get intangibles? *European Accounting Review, 12*(4), 635–659.

Anderson, F. W., Hadley, L., Rockland, D., & Weiner, M. (2009). *Guidelines for setting measurable public relations objectives: An update.* Gainesville, FL: Institute for Public Relations.

Appleby, J. (2010). *The relentless revolution: A history of capitalism.* New York, NY: Norton.

Are traditional ways of doing research still valuable in the age of social media? (2011, June). *PRWeek* (U.S. ed.), 51–52.

Arthur W. Page Society. (2007). *The authentic enterprise: An Arthur W. Page Society report.* New York, NY: Author.

Arthur W. Page Society. (2012). *Building belief: A new model for activating corporate character & authentic advocacy.* New York, NY: Author.

Arthur W. Page Society. (2013a). *The CEO view: The impact of communications on corporate character in a 24×7 digital world.* New York, NY: Author.

Arthur W. Page Society. (2013b). *Corporate character: How leading companies are defining, activating & aligning values.* New York, NY. Author.

Arthur W. Page Society. (2013c). The Page principles. Retrieved May 20, 2013, from http://www.awpagesociety.com/about/the-page-principles/

Arthur W. Page Society. (2013d). *Teaching strategic communication in business schools: New evidence from the c-suite.* New York, NY: Author.

Associated Press. (2005, September 14). Health care takes its toll on Starbucks: Company to spend more on benefits than raw materials to brew coffee. Retrieved March 29, 2014, from http://nbcnews.to/1paiBaZ

Aud, S., Hussar, W., Johnson, F., Kena, G., Roth, E., Manning E., . . . Zhan, J. (2012). *The condition of education 2012* (NCES Publication No. 2012045). Washington, DC: Institute of Education Sciences, U.S. Department of Education.

Auletta, K. (2011, July 11). A woman's place. *The New Yorker.* Retrieved September 13, 2013, from http://www.newyorker.com/reporting/2011/07/11/110711fa_fact_auletta

Babbie, E. (2013). *The practice of social research* (13th ed.). Belmont, CA: Wadsworth.

Ball-Rokeach, S. J. (1985). The origins of individual media system dependency: A sociological framework. *Communication Research, 12*(4), 485–510.

Ball-Rokeach, S. J., & DeFleur, M. L. (1976). A dependency model of mass-media effects. *Communication Research, 3*(1), 3–21. Barnett, M. L., & Pollock, T. G. (2012, August/September). Building and maintaining a strong corporate reputation: A broad look at a core issue. *The European Financial Review, 6*–9.

Baron, R. M., & Kenny, D. A. (1986). The moderator–mediator variable distinction in social psychological research: Conceptual, strategic, and statistical considerations. *Journal of Personality and Social Psychology, 51*(6), 1173–1182.

Bauer, T. N. (2010). Looking back: Reputation research published in the Journal of Management. *Journal of Management, 36*(3), 585–587.

Bebchuk, L. A., Brav, A., & Jiang, W. (2013). *The long-term effects of hedge fund activism.* Retrieved from http://www.shareholderforum.com/access/Library/20130709_Bebchuk-Brav-Jiang.pdf

Bebchuk, L. A., & Weisbach, M. S. (2010). The state of corporate governance research. *The Review of Financial Studies, 23*(3), 939–961.

Bender, R. (2014, February 27). WPP misses margin target, hurt by pound strength. *The Wall Street Journal.* Retrieved March 11, 2014, from http://on.wsj.com/1i91Don

Berger, B. (2012, November). *Key themes and findings: The cross-cultural study of leadership in public relations and communication management.* Paper presented at the Plank Center Leadership Summit, Chicago, IL.

Berger, B. K., & Meng, J. (Eds.). (2014). *Public relations leaders as sensemakers: A global study of leadership in public relations and communication management.* New York, NY: Routledge.

Berr, J. (2012, August 27). Change the "quiet period" rule. Retrieved July 2, 2013, from http://on-msn.com/12ckzXz

Bhagat, S., & Bolton, B. (2008). Corporate governance and firm performance. *Journal of Corporate Finance, 14*(3), 257–273.

Bissland, J. H. (1990). Accountability gap: Evaluation practices show improvement. *Public Relations Review, 16*(2), 25–35.

Blankespoor, E., Miller, G. S., & White, H. D. (2012). *Dissemination, direct-access information technology and information asymmetry* (Research Paper No. 2106). Stanford, CA: Stanford Graduate School of Business.

Blood, D. J., & Phillips, P. C. B. (1997). Economic headlines news on the agenda: New approaches to understanding causes and effects. In M. McCombs, D. L. Shaw, & D. Weaver (Eds.), *Communication and democracy: Exploring the intellectual frontiers in agenda-setting theory* (pp. 97–114). Mahwah, NJ: Erlbaum.

Bloom, K. (2011, March 9). Salary survey provides more bullish news. Retrieved May 2, 2013, from Culpwrit website: http://bit.ly/g048v7

BNY Mellon. (2009). *Global trends in investor relations: A survey analysis of IR practices worldwide* (5th ed.). New York, NY: Author.

BNY Mellon. (2012). *Global trends in investor relations: A survey analysis of IR practices worldwide* (8th ed.). New York, NY: Author.

Board of Governors of the Federal Reserve System. (2005). *The Federal Reserve system: Purposes & functions* (9th ed.). Washington, DC: Author.

Board of Governors of the Federal Reserve System. (2014). Open market operations. Retrieved July 31, 2014, from http://www.federalreserve.gov/monetarypolicy/openmarket.htm

Bobkoff, D. (2013, February 20). For the publicly traded, going private can be risky business. Retrieved July 2, 2013, from http://n.pr/17RUDtA

Bosker, B. (2012, February 8). Facebook's all-male board draws investor scrutiny—But don't count on change. Retrieved September 13, 2013, from http://www.huffingtonpost.com/2012/02/08/facebook-all-male-board-_n_1263278.html

Botan, C. H. (2006). Grand strategy, strategy, and tactics in public relations. In C. H. Botan & V. Hazelton (Eds.), *Public relations theory II* (pp. 223–247). Mahwah, NJ: Erlbaum.

Botan, C. H., & Taylor, M. (2004). Public relations: State of the field. *Journal of Communication, 54*(4), 645–661.

Bowen, S. A. (2004). Expansion of ethics as the tenth generic principles of public relations excellence: A Kantian theory and model for managing ethical issues. *Journal of Public Relations Research, 16*(1), 65–92.

Bowen, S. A. (2005). A practical model for ethical decision making in issues management and public relations. *Journal of Public Relations Research, 17*(3), 191–216.

Bowen, S. A. (2008). A state of neglect: Public relations as "corporate conscience" or ethics counsel. *Journal of Public Relations Research, 20*(3), 271–296.

Bradford, J., & Gordy, B. (1963). Money (that's what I want) [Recorded by the Beatles]. On *With the Beatles* [record]. London, England: Parlophone.

Brancaccio, D. (2012, August 21). Some companies compare—and cap—the CEO-to-worker pay ratio. Retrieved September 15, 2013, from Marketplace website: http://bit.ly/NfbOvp

Brandau, M. (2013, January 25). McDonald's fish certified as sustainable. *Nation's Restaurant News*. Retrieved October 17, 2013, from http://bit.ly/19PnjO2

Bromley, D. B. (2000). Psychological aspects of corporate identity, image, and reputation. *Corporate Reputation Review, 3*(3), 240–252.

Brown, A. (2013, April 18). CEO compensation growth slows amid say on pay. Retrieved September 15, 2013, from Inside Investor Relations website: http://bit.ly/147a6SD

Brown, C. (2013, October 15). Consumers demand supply chain transparency: Where did it come from? *Forbes*. Retrieved October 17, 2013, from http://onforb.es/1gHTWVi

Brusch, M. (2014, March). Shareholder value: A myth? *IR Update*, 6–9.

Bryant, J., & Cummins, G. (2007). Traditions of mass media theory and research. In R. Preiss, B. Gayle, N. Burrell, M. Allen, & J. Bryant (Eds.), *Mass media effects research: Advances through meta-analysis* (pp. 1–13). Mahwah, NJ: Erlbaum.

Bryant, J., Thompson, S., & Finklea, B. W. (2013). *Fundamentals of media effects* (2nd ed.). Long Grove, IL: Waveland Press.

Bryman, A. (2007). Barriers to integrating quantitative and qualitative research. *Journal of Mixed Methods Research, 1*(1), 8–22.

Burton, K., Grates, G., & Learch, C. (2013). *Best-in-class practices in employee communication: Through the lens of 10 global leaders*. Gainesville, FL: Institute for Public Relations.

Bushee, B. J., Core, J., Guay, W., & Hamm, S. (2010). The role of the business press as an information intermediary. *Journal of Accounting Research, 48*(1), 1–19.

Bushee, B. J., Matsumoto, D. A., & Miller, G. S. (2003). Open versus closed conference calls: The determinants and effects of broadening access to disclosure. *Journal of Accounting & Economics, 34*(1–3), 149–180.

Bushee, B. J., & Miller, G. S. (2012). Investor relations, firm visibility, and investor following. *The Accounting Review, 87*(3), 867–897.

Bushee, B., & Noe, C. (2000). Corporate disclosure practices, institutional investors, and stock return volatility. *Journal of Accounting Research, 38*, 171–202.

Byrum, K. (2013). *PRSA MBA program: Bridging the gap between strategic communications education and master of business administration (MBA) curriculum*. New York, NY: Public Relations Society of America.

Carnegie, A. (1901). *The gospel of wealth*. New York, NY: The Century Co.

Carroll, C. E. (2010). Should firms circumvent or work through the news media? *Public Relations Review, 36*(3), 278–280.

Carroll, C. E. (Ed.). (2011). *Corporate reputation and the news media: Agenda-setting within business news coverage in developed, emerging, and frontier markets*. New York, NY: Routledge.

Carroll, C. E. (Ed.). (2013). *The handbook of communication and corporate reputation*. Malden, MA: Wiley-Blackwell.

Carroll, C. E., & McCombs, M. (2003). Agenda-setting effects of business news on the public's images and opinions about major corporations. *Corporate Reputation Review, 6*(1), 36–46.

Carter, N. M., & Wagner, H. M. (2011). *The bottom line: Corporate performance and women's representation on boards (2004–2008).* New York, NY: Catalyst.

Chan, L. K. C., Lakonishok, J., & Sougiannis, T. (2001). The stock market valuation of research and development expenditures. *The Journal of Finance, 56*(6), 2431–3456.

Chareonsuk, C., & Chansa-ngavej, C. (2008). Intangible asset management framework for long-term financial performance. *Industrial Management & Data Systems, 108*(6), 812–828.

Chasan, E. (2012, November 13). New benchmarks crop up in companies' financial reports. *The Wall Street Journal.* Retrieved November 4, 2013, from http://on.wsj.com/1ahgtDb

Chin, M. K., Hambrick, D. C., & Trevino, L. K. (2013). Political ideologies of CEOs: The influence of executives' values on corporate social responsibility. *Administrative Science Quarterly, 58*(2), 197–232.

Christian, R. C. (1997). Foreword. In C. L Caywood (Ed.), *The handbook of strategic public relations and integrated communications* (pp. iii–v). Boston, MA: McGraw-Hill.

Clark, L., & Master, D. (2013). *2012 corporate ESG/sustainability/responsibility reporting—Does it matter?* New York, NY: Governance & Accountability Institute.

Claussen, D. (2008). On the business and economics education of public relation students. *Journalism & Mass Communication Educator, 63*(3), 191–194.

Clinton, B. (2004). *My life.* New York, NY: Alfred A. Knopf.

CNNMoney.com. (2006, January 6). Martha Stewart's conviction upheld. Retrieved August 19, 2013, from http://money.cnn.com/2006/01/06/news/newsmakers/martha/index.htm

CNNMoney.com. (2002, September 25). Buffett bullish on stocks. Retrieved July 2, 2013, from http://money.cnn.com/2002/09/25/news/buffett/

Commission on Public Relations Education. (1999). *Public relations education for the 21st century: A port of entry.* New York, NY: Author.

Commission on Public Relations Education. (2012). *Standards for a master's degree in public relations: Educating for complexity.* New York, NY: Author.

Cone Communications, & Echo Research. (2013). *2013 Cone Communications/Eco Global CSR study.* Boston, MA: Author.

Cone Inc., & AMP Agency. (2006). *The 2006 Cone millennial cause study: The millennial generation: Pro-social and empowered to change the world.* Boston, MA: Author.

Connelly, B. L., Certo, S. T., Ireland, R. D., & Reutzel, C. R. (2011). Signaling theory: A review and assessment. *Journal of Management, 37*(1), 39–67.

Constable, S., & Wright, R. E. (2011). *The Wall Street Journal guide to the 50 economic indicators that really matter.* New York, NY: Harper Business.

Coombs, W. T., & Holladay, S. J. (2007). *It's not just PR: Public relations in society.* Malden, MA: Blackwell.

Coombs, W. T., & Holladay, S. L. (2010). *PR strategy and application: Managing influence*. Malden, MA: Blackwell.

Coombs, W. T., & Holladay, S. L. (2012). *Managing corporate social responsibility: A communication approach*. Malden, MA: Wiley-Blackwell.

Corporate Board Member. (2012). America's best corporate law firms. Retrieved July 2, 2013, from NYSE Governance Services website: http://bit.ly/JmdXTJ

Costco Wholesale Corporation. (2010). Costco mission statement and code of ethics. Retrieved October 9, 2013, from http://bit.ly/foG6Qw

Creswell, J., & Creswell, J. (2005). Mixed methods research: Developments, debates and dilemmas. In R. Swanson & E. Holton III (Eds.), *Research in organizations: Foundations and methods of inquiry* (pp. 313–326). San Francisco, CA: Berrett-Koehler.

Cripps, K. (2013, April 24). Building bridges between academia and business: A report from the council's "taking flight" event in Chicago. Retrieved May 3, 2013, from Council of Public Relations Firms website: http://bit.ly/ZIJSTS

Daily, C. M., Dalton, D. R., & Canella, A. A. (2003). Corporate governance: Decades of dialogue and data. *Academy of Management Review, 28*(3), 371–382.

Daines, R. M., Gow, I. D., & Larcker, D. F. (2010). Rating the ratings: How good are commercial governance ratings? *Journal of Financial Economics, 98*(3), 439–461.

Daniels, C. (2013, March). Salary survey 2013: Building momentum. *PRWeek*, 32–38.

Daniels, C. (2014, March). Salary survey 2014: Investment strategy. *PRWeek*, 28–36.

Davidoff, S. M. (2011, April 5). In corporate disclosure, a murky definition of material [Blog post]. Retrieved August 19, 2013, from http://dealbook.nytimes.com/2011/04/05/in-corporate-disclosure-a-murky-definition-of-material/?_php=true&_type=blogs&_r=0

Davies, J. (2013, August 19). Why CDP, GRI, DJSI stand out among sustainability frameworks. Retrieved October 9, 2013, from http://www.greenbiz.com/print/53693

Deephouse, D. L. (2000). Media reputation as a strategic resource: An integration of mass communication and resource-based theories. *Journal of Management, 26*(6), 1091–1112.

De La Merced, M. J., & Creswell, J. (2013, August 30). With huge war chests, activist investors tackle big companies. *The New York Times*. Retrieved September 21, 2013, from http://nyti.ms/1dzNNLODeloitte. (2013). *Director 360: Degrees of progress* (2nd ed.). New York, NY: The Deloitte Global Center for Corporate Governance.

Deloitte. (2014). *Directors' alert 2014: Greater oversight, deeper insight: Boardroom strategies in an era of disruptive change*. New York, NY: The Deloitte Global Center for Corporate Governance.

Di Leo, L. (2011, March 25). Bernanke to speak out more to explain, bolster policies. *The Wall Street Journal*. Retrieved June 13, 2013, from http://on.wsj.com/ih0pj0

DiPiazza, S. A., McDonnell, D., Parrett, W. G., Rake, M. D., Samyn, F., & Turley, J. S. (2006). *Serving global capital markets and the global economy: A view from the CEOs of the international audit networks*. London, England: IFRS Foundation.

DiStaso, M. W. (2012). The annual earnings press release's dual role: An examination of relationships with local and national media coverage and reputation. *Journal of Public Relations Research, 24*(2), 123–143.

DiStaso, M. W., & Bortree, D. S. (2012). Multi-method analysis of transparency in social media practices: Survey, interviews and content analysis. *Public Relations Review, 38*(3), 511–514.

Doh, J. P., Howton, S. D., Howton, S. W., & Siegel, D. S. (2010). Does the market respond to an endorsement of social responsibility? The role of institutions, information, and legitimacy. *Journal of Management, 36*(6), 1461–1485.

Doorley, J., & Garcia, H. F. (2011). *Reputation management: The key to successful public relations and corporate communication* (2nd ed.). New York, NY: Routledge.

Dowse, J. (2012, May). *ESG—Why now?* Manly, New South Wales, Australia: Dowse CSP.

Dozier, D. M. (1992). The organizational roles of communications and public relations practitioners. In J. E. Grunig (Ed.), *Excellence in public relations and communication management* (pp. 395–417). Hillsdale, NJ: Erlbaum.

Dozier, D. M., & Broom, G. M. (2006). The centrality of practitioner roles to public relations theory. In C. H. Botan & V. Hazelton (Eds.), *Public relations theory II* (pp. 137–170). New York, NY: Erlbaum.

Dozier, D. M., & Grunig, L. A. (1992). The organization of the public relations function. In J. E. Grunig (Ed.), *Excellence in public relations and communication management* (pp. 395–417). Hillsdale, NJ: Erlbaum.

Duckworth, A., Goltz, J., & Trayner, G. (2009, Winter). Are analysts and investors engaging with new media? *Brunswick Review, 2.* Retrieved August 23, 2013, from http://bit.ly/14qohTn

Duhé, S. (2013, December 12). Teaching business as a second language. Retrieved December 12, 2013, from Institute for Public Relations website: http://bit.ly/1cGKcsw

Dupont, S. (2013, Winter). Understanding the language of economics is critical to communicating effectively. *The Public Relations Strategist*, 10–11.

Ebenstein, L. (2007). *Milton Friedman: A biography.* New York, NY: Palgrave Macmillan.

Eberhart, A. C., Maxwell, W. F., & Siddique, A. (2004). An examination of long-term abnormal stock returns and operating performance following R&D increases. *Journal of Finance, 59*(2), 623–650.

Eccles, R. G., & Krzus, M. P. (2010). *One report: Integrated reporting for a sustainable strategy.* Hoboken, NJ: Wiley.

Edmans, A. (2011). Does the stock market fully value intangibles? Employee satisfaction and equity prices. *Journal of Financial Economics, 101*(3), 621–640.

Einwiller, S. A., Carroll, C. E., & Korn, K. (2010). Under what conditions do the news media influence corporate reputation? The roles of media dependency and need for orientation. *Corporate Reputation Review, 12*(4), 299–315.Ernst & Young. (1997). *Measures that matter.* Boston, MA: Ernst & Young.

Ernst & Young. (2012). *Ernst & Young's guide to going public.* London, England: Ernst & Young.

Ernst & Young. (2014). *Tomorrow's investment rules: Global survey of institutional investors on non-financial performance.* London, England: Ernst & Young.

Esterl, M., & Bauerlein, V. (2011, June 28). PepsiCo wakes up and smells the cola. *The Wall Street Journal.* Retrieved October 8, 2013, from http://on.wsj.com/18LwRga

Fabrigar, L. R., Krosnick, J. A., & MacDougall, B. L. (2005). Attitude measurement: Techniques for measuring the unobservable. In T. C Brock & M. C. Green (Eds.), *Persuasion: Psychological insights and perspectives* (2nd ed., pp. 17–40). Thousand Oaks, CA: Sage.

Fair Labor Association. (2013, May 16). *Fair Labor Association verifies ongoing progress at Apple supplier Foxconn* [Press release]. Retrieved August 19, 2014, from http://bit.ly/16C9oik

Fama, E. F. (1980). Agency problems and the theory of the firm. *Journal of Political Economy. 88*(2), 288–307.

Fama, E. F., & Jensen, M. C. (1983). Agency problems and residual claims. *Journal of Law and Economics, 26*(2), 327–349.

Fazio, R. H., & Roskos-Ewoldsen, D. R. (2005). Acting as we feel: When and how attitudes guide behavior. In T. C Brock & M. C. Green (Eds.), *Persuasion: Psychological insights and perspectives* (2nd ed., pp. 41–62). Thousand Oaks, CA: Sage.

Financial Executives Research Foundation Inc. (2009). *Earnings guidance: The current state of play.* Danvers, MA: Author.

Financial Times. (2013). League tables—Top 10 banks. Retrieved July 2, 2013, from http://markets.ft.com/investmentBanking/tablesAndTrends.asp

FINRA Investor Education Foundation. (2013). *Financial capability in the United States: Report of findings from the 2012 national financial capability study.* Washington, DC: FINRA Investor Education Foundation.

Fombrun, C. J. (1996). *Reputation: Realizing value from the corporate image.* Boston, MA: Harvard Business School Press.

Fombrun, C. J., Gardberg, N. A., & Sever, J. M. (2000). The Reputation Quotient[sm]: A multi stakeholder measure of corporate reputation. *Journal of Brand Management, 7*(4), 241–255.

Fombrun, C., & Shanley, M. (1990). What's in a name? Reputation building and corporate strategy. *Academy of Management Journal, 33*(2), 233–258.

Fombrun, C., & van Riel, C. B. M. (2004). *Fame & fortune: How successful companies build winning reputations.* Upper Saddle River, NJ: FT Prentice Hall.

Francis, T., & Lublin, J. S. (2014, May 27). CEO pay rises moderately; a few reap huge rewards. *The Wall Street Journal.* Retrieved June 1, 2014, from http://on.wsj.com/U5Ymi7

Freeman, R. E. (2010). *Strategic management: A stakeholder approach.* New York, NY: Cambridge University Press.

Freeman, R. E., Harrison, J. S., & Wicks, A. C. (2007). *Managing for stakeholders: Survival, reputation, and success.* New Haven, CT: Yale University Press.

Freeman, R. E., Harrison J. S., Wicks, A. C., Parmar, B. L., & de Colle, S. (2010). *Stakeholder theory: The state of the art.* New York, NY: Cambridge University Press.

Friedman, M. (1965, August 24). Social responsibility: A subversive doctrine. *National Review,* 721–723.

Friedman, M. (1970, September 13). The social responsibility of business is to increase its profits. *The New York Times Magazine*.

Friedman, M., Mackey, J., & Rodgers, T. J. (2005, October). Rethinking the social responsibility of business. *Reason*. Retrieved August 19, 2014, from http://bit.ly/3gxNgE

Gandy, O. H. (1982). *Beyond agenda setting: Information subsidies and public policy*. Norwood, NJ: Ablex.

Gentry, J. K. (2011). Lecture on *Understanding financial statements* . Personal collection of J. Gentry, University of Kansas, Lawrence, KS.

Gentry, J. K. (2012, January). *Understanding markets*. Presentation to the Business Journalism Professors Seminar at The Donald W. Reynolds National Center for Business Journalism in the Walter Cronkite School of Journalism and Mass Communication at Arizona State University, Phoenix, AZ.

Georgeson. (2011). *2011 annual corporate governance review*. New York, NY: Author.

Georgeson. (2012). *2012 annual corporate governance review*. New York, NY: Georgeson.

Georgeson. (2013a). Facts behind 2013 failed say on pay votes. Retrieved September 15, 2013, from http://bit.ly/17Zlvp2

Georgeson. (2013b). *2013 annual corporate governance review*. New York, NY: Georgeson.Geron, T. (2013, May 8). The top ten in venture capital today—Midas list. *Forbes*. Retrieved July 2, 2013, from http://onforb.es/18u3zVf

Gerpott, T. J., Thomas, S. E., & Hoffmann, A. P. (2008). Intangible asset disclosure in the telecommunications industry. *Journal of Intellectual Capital, 9*(1), 37–61.

Gillan, S. L., & Starks, L. T. (1998). A survey of shareholder activism: Motivation and empirical evidence. *Contemporary Finance Digest, 2*(3), 2–38.

Gillan, S., & Starks, L. (2007). The evolution of shareholder activism in the United States. *Journal of Applied Corporate Finance, 19*(1), 55–73.

Glinton, S. (2011, August 14). Weak dollar? That's good for U.S. exports. Retrieved June 13, 2013, from http://m.npr.org/story/139611423

Global Alliance for Public Relations and Communication Management. (2013). Measurement in public relations. Retrieved February 2, 2014, from http://www.globalalliancepr.org/website/page/measurement-public-relations

Global Reporting Initiative. (2013). About GRI. Retrieved October 10, 2013, from https://www.globalreporting.org/Information/about-gri/Pages/default.aspx

Goldstein, S. (2013, April 2). SEC backs social media for disclosing corporate information. *The Wall Street Journal*. Retrieved August 22, 2013 from http://on.wsj.com/YQZ8xP

Golin, A. (2006). *Trust or consequences: Build trust today or lose your market tomorrow*. New York, NY: AMACOM.

Golz, J., Zivin, S., & Spero, R. (2012). *2012 analyst and investor survey: Trends in the use of digital & social media by the investment community*. San Francisco, CA: Brunswick Group.

Goodman, M. B., & Hirsch, P. B. (2010). *Corporate communication: Strategic adoption for global practice*. New York, NY: Peter Lang.

Greenhouse, S. (2012, February 13). Critics questions record of monitor selected by Apple. *The New York Times*. Retrieved October 17, 2013, from http://nyti.ms/yTjolH

Grondstedt, A. (1997). The role of research in public relations strategy and planning. In C. L. Caywood (Ed.), *The handbook of strategic public relations and integrated communications* (pp. 34–59). Boston, MA: McGraw-Hill.

Grunig, L. A., Grunig, J. E., & Dozier, D. M. (2002). *Excellent public relations and effective organizations: A study of communication management in three countries.* Mahwah, NJ: Erlbaum.

Gunther, M. (2013, May 23). Unilever's CEO has a green thumb. Retrieved October 8, 2013, from http://fortune.com/2013/05/23/unilevers-ceo-has-a-green-thumb/

Hagerty, J. R. (2013, January 4). Flextronics CEO sees hope for U.S. tech production. *The Wall Street Journal.* Retrieved November 7, 2013, from http://on.wsj.com/1hRhmIo

Hallahan, K., Holtzhausen, D., van Ruler, B., Vercic, D., & Sriramesh, K. (2007). Defining strategic communication. *International Journal of Strategic Communication, 1*(1), 3–35.

Hamburger, J. M. (2014). 2013 market review: Irrational exuberance in restaurant land. *Restaurant Finance Monitor, 25*(1), 4.

Hand, R. M., & Lev, B. (Eds.). (2003). *Intangible assets: Values, measures, and risks.* New York, NY: Oxford University Press.

Harris Interactive. (2009). *A record number of Americans (88%) says the reputation of corporate America is "not good" or "terrible," but the public rewards companies that concentrate on building their reputations with "excellent" reputation scores* [Press release]. Retrieved March 29, 2014, from http://bit.ly/1jlb5Wn

Harris Interactive. (2013). *The Harris Poll 2013 RQ summary report: A survey of the U.S. general public using the Reputation Quotient®* [Press release]. Retrieved March 29, 2014, from http://bit.ly/1gbuP9u

Hester, J. B., & Gibson, R. (2003). The economy and second-level agenda setting: A time-series analysis of economic news and public opinion about the economy. *Journalism & Mass Communication Quarterly, 80*(1), 73–90.

Hill & Knowlton. (2006). *Return of reputation: Corporate reputation watch 2006.* London, England: Author.

Hilsenrath, J. (2011, April 21). Bernanke to open up as Fed embarks on era of Glasnost. *The Wall Street Journal.* Retrieved June 13, 2013, from http://on.wsj.com/eM8Np7

Hirschman, A. (1971). *Exit, voice, and loyalty: Responses to decline in firms, organizations, and states.* Cambridge, MA: Harvard University Press.

Hodges, C. (2012, September 1). Don't forget to update those forward looking statements occasionally. Retrieved August 23, 2013, from Alpha IR Group website: http://bit.ly/18OYP9O

Hoffmann, C., & Fieseler, C. (2012). Investor relations beyond financials: Nonfinancial factors and capital market image building. *Corporate Communications: An International Journal, 17*(2), 138–155.

Holmes, E., & Lublin, J. S. (2011, June 15). Penney picks boss from Apple. *The Wall Street Journal.* Retrieved December 19, 2013, from http://on.wsj.com/IYp7Pw

Holmes Report. (2013, January 20). Brunswick leads M&A rankings, Sard enjoys strong 2012. Retrieved July 2, 2013, from http://bit.ly/14LViGS

Holton, G. A. (2006). Investor suffrage movement. *Financial Analysts Journal, 62*(6), 15–20.

Holton, K. (2014, February 27). Currency swings and ad competition hit WPP's shares. Retrieved March 11, 2014, from http://reut.rs/1qsTLSy

Holtzhausen, D., & Zerfass, A. (Eds.). (2014). *The Routledge handbook of strategic communication.* New York, NY: Routledge.

Hon, L. C. (1997). What have you done for me lately? Exploring effectiveness in public relations. *Journal of Public Relations Research, 9*(1), 1–30.

Hon, L. C. (1998). Demonstrating effectiveness in public relations: Goals, objectives and evaluation. *Journal of Public Relations Research, 10*(2), 103–135.

House, C. H., & Price, R. L. (1991). The return map: Tracking product teams. *Harvard Business Review, 69*(1), 92–100.

Human, T. (2010, November 5). Office Depot case highlights value of Reg. FD policies. *IR Magazine.* Retrieved August 21, 2013, from http://bit.ly/174yenS

Hutton, J. G., Goodman, M. B., Alexander, J. B., &, Genest, C. M. (2001). Reputation management: The new face of corporate public relations? *Public Relations Review, 27*(3), 247–261.

Institute for Public Relations. (2013). *Four major corporations adopt public relations research standards* [Press release]. Retrieved February 2, 2014, from http://bit.ly/1aggmwB

Institute for Public Relations. (2014). Pledge commitment to PR research standards. Retrieved June 1, 2014, from http://bit.ly/1kfSI7F

Interbrand. (2001). *FASB statements no. 141 & 142: The impact on intangible assets, including brands.* New York, NY: Author.

International Association for the Measurement and Evaluation of Communication. (2010). Barcelona declaration of measurement principles. Retrieved August 18, 2014, from http://amecorg.com/2012/06/barcelona-declaration-of-measurement-principles/

IRRC Institute, & Sustainable Investment Institute. (2013, April). *Integrated financial and sustainability reporting in the United States.* New York, NY: IRRC Institute.

Isaac, M. (2012, June 25). Facebook names COO Sheryl Sandberg to board of directors.. Retrieved September 13, 2013, from All Things D website: http://dthin.gs/OlWZXS

Isaac, M. (2013, March 6). Former Genentech exec Susan Desmond-Hellmann joins Facebook's board of directors. Retrieved September 13, 2013, from All Things D website: http://dthin.gs/XRp7Uc

Isdell, N., & Roberts, C. (2013, August 19). Do all the good you can. Retrieved October 9, 2013, from Skoll World Forum website: http://bit.ly/1gqtiA8

Jargon, J. (2013, September 26). McDonald's to offer alternatives to fries, sodas. *The Wall Street Journal.* Retrieved October 8, 2013, from http://on.wsj.com/1hxQp9z

Jargon, J. (2014, May 15). Chipotle shareholders vote down executive pay plan. *The Wall Street Journal.* Retrieved June 1, 2014, from http://on.wsj.com/1jKGdLg

Jarzemsky, M. (2013, December 12). Hotelier Hilton gains in trading debut after $2.35B IPO. Retrieved April 13, 2014, from Dow Jones Newswires http://on.wsj.com/1jChg82

Jensen, M. C., & Chew, D. (2000). *A theory of the firm: Governance, residual claims and organizational forms.* Cambridge, MA: Harvard University Press.

Jensen, M. C., & Meckling, W. F. (1976). Theory of the firm: Managerial behavior, agency costs, and ownership structure. *Journal of Financial Economics, 3*(4), 305–360.

Johnson & Johnson Services Inc. (2013). Our credo values. Retrieved October 9, 2013, from http://www.jnj.com/about-jnj/jnj-credo

Jones, R. W., & Kostyak, C. (Eds.). (2011). *Words from a page in history: The Arthur W. Page speech collection.* University Park, PA: The Arthur W. Page Center for Integrity in Public Communications, College of Communications, Pennsylvania State University.

Joshi, P. (2013, June 29). Golden parachutes are still very much in style. *The New York Times.* Retrieved September 14, 2013, from http://nyti.ms/18gQCIz

Joy, L., Carter, N. M., Wagner, H. M., & Narayanan, S. (2007). *The bottom line: Corporate performance and women's representation on boards.* New York, NY: Catalyst.

Judd, E. (2013, April 3). Guiding principles: Earnings guidance remains popular despite tough economic conditions. *IR Magazine.* Retrieved August 18, 2013 from http://bit.ly/14Up0i0

Kaplan, D. A. (2011, November 17). Howard Schultz brews strong coffee at Starbucks. *Fortune.* Retrieved March 29, 2014, from http://bit.ly/1h6VFQs

Kaplan, R. S., & Norton, D. P. (1992). *The balanced scorecard: Translating strategy into action.* Cambridge, MA: Harvard Business Review Press.

Kaplan, R. S., & Norton, D. P. (1996, January–February). Using the balanced scorecard as a strategic management system. *Harvard Business Review, 74*(1), 75–85.

Kaplan, R. S., & Norton, D. P. (2001). Transforming the balanced scorecard from performance measurement to strategic management: Part I. *Accounting Horizons, 15*(1), 87–104.

Kaplan, R. S., & Norton, D. P. (2004a). Measuring the strategic readiness of intangible assets. *Harvard Business Review, 82*(2), 52–63.

Kaplan, R. S., & Norton, D. P. (2004b). *Strategy maps: Converting intangible assets into tangible outcomes.* Cambridge, MA: Harvard Business Review Press.

Kaplan, R. S., & Norton, D. P. (2007, July–August). Using the balanced scorecard as a strategic management system. *Harvard Business Review, 85*(7/8), 150–161.

Kaplan, R. S., & Norton, D. P. (2008). *Alignment: Using the balanced scorecard to create corporate synergies.* Cambridge, MA: Harvard Business Review Press.

Katz, E., & Lazarfeld, P. F. (2009). *Personal influence: The part played by people in the flow of mass communications.* Brunswick, NJ: Transaction.

Keynes, J. M. (2011). *The general theory of employment, interest, and money.* Seattle, WA: CreateSpace.

Kieffer, B. (2013, September 1). Shareholder activism rising, big companies in crosshairs. *PRWeek.* Retrieved September 26, 2013, from http://bit.ly/18CNp77

Kiernan, M. J. (2007). Universal owners and ESG: Leaving money on the table? *Corporate Governance: An International Review, 15*(3), 478–485.

Kim, S. (2014, January 23). 11 companies offering health care benefits to part-time workers. Retrieved March 29, 2014, from http://abcn.ws/1gbeMbK

Kim, Y. (2000). Measuring the bottom-line impact of corporate public relations. *Journalism & Mass Communication Quarterly, 77*(2), 273–291.

Kim, Y. (2001). Measuring the economic value of public relations. *Journal of Public Relations Research, 13*(1), 3–26.

Kiousis, S., Kim, S., McDevitt, M., & Ostrowski, A. (2009). Competing for attention: Information subsidy influence in agenda building during election campaigns. *Journalism & Mass Communication Quarterly, 86*(3), 545–562.

Kiousis, S., Popescu C., & Mitrook, M. (2007). Understanding influence on corporate reputation: An examination of public relations efforts, media coverage, public opinion, and financial performance from an agenda-building and agenda-setting perspective. *Journal of Public Relations Research, 19*(2), 147–165.

Kiousis, S., & Strömbäck, J. (2010). The White House and public relations: Examining the linkages between presidential communications and public opinion. *Public Relations Review, 36*(1), 7–14.

Klein, A., & Zur, E. (2009). Entrepreneurial shareholder activism: Hedge funds and other private investors. *The Journal of Finance, 64*(1), 187–229.

Koehler, D. A., & Hespenheide, E. J. (2013). Finding the value in environmental, social, and governance performance. *Deloitte Review, 12*(1), 99–111.

Kolberg, B. (2014, March). Getting down to business at public relations agencies. *PR Update, 49*(2), 6–7.

Krantz, M. (2006, February 13). There's no set time for an IPO. *USA Today.* Retrieved July 2, 2013, from http://usat.ly/12kfVru

Krantz, M. (2013, March 17). Investors face a shrinking stock supply. *USA Today.* Retrieved April 12, 2014, from http://usat.ly/1gmrNjl

Krause, R., & Semadeni, M. (2013). Apprentice, departure, and demotion: An examination of the three types of CEO-board chair separation. *Academy of Management Journal, 56*(3), 805–826.

Lan, L. L., & Heracleous, L. (2010). Rethinking agency theory: The view from law. *Academy of Management Review, 35*(2), 294–314.

Laskin, A. V. (2008). *Investor relations: A national study of the profession* (Unpublished doctoral dissertation). University of Florida, Gainesville.

Laskin, A. (2008). *Investor relations.* Gainesville, FL: Institute for Public Relations.

Laskin, A. V. (2009). A descriptive account of the investor relations profession: A national study. *Journal of Business Communication, 46*(2), 208–233.

Laskin, A. V. (2011). How investor relations contributes to the corporate bottom line. *Journal of Public Relations Research, 23*(3), 302–324.

Leder, M. (2003). *Financial fine print: Uncovering a company's true value.* Hoboken, NJ: Wiley & Sons.

Ledingham, J. A. (2003). Explicating relationship management as a general theory of public relations. *Journal of Public Relations Research, 15*(2), 181–198.

Ledingham, J. A. (2006). Relationship management: A general theory of public relations. In C. H. Botan & V. Hazleton (Eds.), *Public relations theory II* (pp. 1–18). Mahwah, NJ: Erlbaum.

Letzing, J., & Lublin, J. S. (2012, February 8). California pension fund challenges Facebook over diversity on board. *The Wall Street Journal.* Retrieved September 13, 2013, from http://on.wsj.com/w8yck6

Lev, B. (2001). *Intangibles: Management, measurement, and reporting*. Washington, DC: Brookings Institution Press.

Lev, B. (2004, June). Sharpening the intangibles edge. *Harvard Business Review, 82*(6), 109–116.

Lev, B. (2005). Intangible assets: Concepts and measurements. *Encyclopedia of Social Measurement, 2*, 299–305.

Lev, B. (2011). How to win investors over. *Harvard Business Review, 89*(11), 53–62.

Lev, B. (2012a, February 27). The case for guidance. *The Wall Street Journal*. Retrieved August 18, 2013, from http://on.wsj.com/wUn7hW

Lev, B. (2012b). *Winning investors over: Surprising truths about honesty, earnings guidance and other ways to boost your stock price*. Boston, MA: Harvard Business Review Press.

Levine-Weinberg, A. (2014, May 25). Chipotle's CEOs deserve their millions. Retrieved August 19, 2014, from The Motley Fool website: http://bit.ly/1tzQL5H

Levitt, A. (2011, April 2). A word to Wall Street: "Plain English," please. *The Wall Street Journal*. Retrieved August 19, 2013, http://on.wsj.com/eW1TVA

Library of Congress. (2011). *Financial literacy among retail investors in the United States*. Washington, DC: Federal Research Division, Library of Congress.

Lieber, P. S., & Golin, G. (2011). Political public relations, news management, and agenda indexing. In J. Strömbäck & S. Kiousis (Eds.), *Political public relations: Principles and applications* (pp. 54–74). New York, NY: Routledge.

Liebowitz, J., & Wright, K. (1999). Does measuring knowledge make "cents"? *Expert Systems with Applications, 17*(2), 99–103.

Light, D. A. (1998, November). Performance measurement: Investors' balanced scorecards. *Harvard Business Review, 76*(6), 17–20.

Lindemann, J. (2004, April 27). Brand valuation: The financial value of brands. Retrieved November 5, 2013, from http://www.brandchannel.com/papers_review.asp?sp_id=357

Lindenmann, W. K. (1993, Spring). An "effectiveness yardstick" to measure public relations success. *The Public Relations Strategist, 38*(1), 7–9.

Lindenmann, W. K. (2003). *Guidelines for measuring the effectiveness of PR programs and activities*. Gainesville, FL: Institute for Public Relations.

Lindenmann, W. K. (2006). *Public relations research for planning and evaluation*. Gainesville, FL: Institute for Public Relations.

Lofgren, K.-G., Persson, T., & Weibull, J. W. (2002). Markets with asymmetric information: The contributions of George Akerlof, Michael Spence and Joseph Stiglitz. *The Scandinavian Journal of Economics, 104*(2), 195–211.

Low, J., & Siesfield, T. (1998). Measures that matter: Wall Street considers non-financial performance more than you think. *Strategy & Leadership, 26*(2), 24–30.

Lowenstein, R. (2009, June 2). A seat at the table. *The New York Times Magazine*. Retrieved September 25, 2013, from http://nyti.ms/18WJ2t1

Lublin, J. S. (2013, May 8). Job split doesn't always work magic. *The Wall Street Journal*. Retrieved September 14, 2013, from http://on.wsj.com/12fboc0

Lublin, J. S., & Grind, K. (2013, May 22). For proxy advisers, influence wanes. *The Wall Street Journal*. Retrieved July 2, 2013, from http://on.wsj.com/185SVDF

Lucchetti, A. (2011, May 26). U.S. falls behind in stock listings. *The Wall Street Journal*, p. A1.

Luk, L. (2013, November 27). iPhone5S wait time drops as Foxconn boost production [Blog post]. Retrieved December 12, 2013, from http://on.wsj.com/1j0S5hQ

Lynn, D. (2012, September 12). Regulatory: Happy anniversary Regulation FD: Is it time to revisit your Regulation FD policy? Retrieved August 19, 2013, from Inside Counsel website: http://bit.ly/Qju3MM

Machan, T. R. (2011, February 12). Profit: The right standard for business. *Barron's*. Retrieved August 19, 2014, from http://on.barrons.com/hAGqpL

Mackey, J., & Sisodia, R. (2013). *Conscious capitalism: Liberating the heroic spirit of business*. Boston, MA: Harvard Business Review Press.

Manning, A., & Rockland, D. B. (2011). Understanding the Barcelona Principles. *The Public Relations Strategist, 17*(1), 30–31.

Marempudi, A., & Wolff, M. (2012, August). *The guidance effect: Improving valuation*. Princeton, NJ: IntelliBusiness/eventVestor.

Marens, R. (2002). Inventing corporate governance: The mid-century emergence of shareholder activism. *Journal of Business and Management, 8*(4), 365–389.

Margolis, J. D., Elfenbein, H. A., & Walsh, J. P. (2009). *Does it pay to be good . . . and does it matter? A meta-analysis of the relationship between corporate social and financial performance*. Retrieved August 19, 2014, from the Social Science Research Network website: http://papers.ssrn.com/sol3/papers.cfm?abstract_id=1866371

McCombs, M., & Shaw, D. (1972). The agenda-setting function of the media. *Public Opinion Quarterly, 36*, 176–187.

Meijer, M., & Kleinnijenhuis, J. (2006a). Issue news and corporate reputation: Applying the theories of agenda setting and issue ownership in the field of business communication. *Journal of Communication, 56*(3), 543–559.

Michaelson, D., & Macleod, S. (2007). The application of "best practices" in public relations measurement and evaluation systems. *Public Relations Journal, 1*(1), 1–14.

Michaelson, D., & Stacks, D. (2011). Standardization in public relations measurement and evaluation. *Public Relations Journal, 5*(2), 1–22.

Michaelson, D., & Stacks, D. W. (2014). *A professional and practitioner's guide to public relations research, measurement and evaluation* (2nd ed.). New York, NY: Business Expert Press.

Mitchell, B., & Fitzpatrick, J. (2013, August 10). NYSE opening bell: Where fame, finance collide. *USA Today*. Retrieved August 13, 2013, from http://usat.ly/15mOspx

Mizruchi, M. S. (1983). Who controls whom? An examination of the relation between management and board of directors in large American corporations. *Academy of Management Review, 8*(3), 426–435.

Molina-Azorin, J. (2010). The use and added value of mixed methods in management research. *Journal of Mixed Methods Research, 5*(1), 7–24.

Monks, R. A. G., & Minow, N. (2011). *Corporate governance* (5th ed.). Hoboken, NJ: Wiley & Sons.

Morrill, D. C. (1995). Origins of NIRI—Chapter I. Retrieved August 16, 2013, from National Investor Relations Institute website: http://www.niri.org/FunctionalMenu/About/Origins/originsch1cfm.aspx

Motley, A. (2014, April). The measurement movement. *IR Update,* 10–14.

Murphy, A. (2012, November 28). America's largest private companies. *Forbes.* Retrieved June 28, 2013, from http://onforb.es/TqYfqk

Murphy, M. (2012, April 24). Going-concern warnings hang over IPOs [Blog post]. Retrieved August 9, 2013, from http://on.wsj.com/Iuv1nK

Murphy, M. (2014, February 18). Confidential discussions of IPO plans kept brief [Blog post]. Retrieved March 14, 2014, from http://on.wsj.com/1fx2lH6

NASDAQ OMX, & Lawrence Ragan Communications Inc. (2013). *PR measurement.* New York, NY: NASDAQ OMX Corporate Solutions.

National Bureau of Economic Research. (2013). US business cycle expansions and contractions. Retrieved June 11, 2013, from http://www.nber.org/cycles.html

National Investor Relations Institute. (2010). *NIRI survey sheds light on trading blackout and quiet period practices.* Vienna, VA: Author.

National Investor Relations Institute. (2011). *NIRI survey reveals current analyst/investor day practices.* Vienna, VA: Author.

National Investor Relations Institute. (2012a). *Guidance practices and preferences 2012 survey report.* Alexandria, VA: Author.

National Investor Relations Institute. (2012b). *Standards of practice for investor relations: Vol. III. Disclosure.* Alexandria, VA: Author.

National Investor Relations Institute. (2013a). *Social media use in investor relations 2013 survey results.* Alexandria, VA: Author.

National Investor Relations Institute. (2013b). *Standards of practice for investor relations: Earnings release content.* Alexandria, VA: Author.

National Investor Relations Institute. (2014). *Standards of practice for investor relations: Disclosure.* Alexandria, VA: Author.

Ocean Tomo, LLC. (2014). Intellectual capital equity. Retrieved August 4, 2014, from http://www.oceantomo.com/about/intellectualcapitalequity

O'Reilly, G. (2008, October 10). Profile: Harold Burson. *PRWeek* (UK ed.), 18–19.

Ovaitt, F., & Geddes, D. (2014). Bringing measurement up to standard: Ready comparison of results across programs, business units and research partners. In L. Cooper (Ed.), *PR Measurement Guidebook* (Vol. 8). New York, NY: PR News Press.

Pagliery, J. (2013, August 27). Starbucks CEO: We won't cut benefits because of Obamacare. Retrieved March 29, 2014, from http://cnnmon.ie/1k7CHN2

Paine, K. D. (2007). *Measuring public relationships: The data-driven communicator's guide to success.* Berlin, NH: KDPaine & Partners.

Paine, K. D. (2011). *Measure what matters. Online tools for understanding customers, social media, engagement, and key relationships.* Hoboken, NJ: Wiley.

Park, D.-J., & Berger, B. K. (2004). The presentation of CEOs in the press, 1990–2000: Increasing salience, positive valence, and a focus on competency and personal dimensions of image. *Journal of Public Relations Research, 16*(1), 93–125.

Pasadeos, Y., Lamme, M., Gower, K., & Tian, S. (2011). A methodological evaluation of public relations research. *Public Relations Review, 37*(2), 163–165.

Peloza, J. (2009). The challenge of measuring financial impacts from investments in corporate social performance. *Journal of Management, 35*(6), 1518–1541.

Pesta, A. (2012, May 23). Facebook comes under increasing fire for its white-male board. Retrieved September 13, 2013, from http://thebea.st/JTjfEA

Phair, J. (2013, Winter). Developing a new generation of PR-savvy business leaders. *The Public Relations Strategist,* 28–29.

Pieczka, M. (2000). Objectives and evaluation in public relations work: What do they tell us about expertise and professionalism? *Journal of Public Relations Research, 12*(3), 211–233.

Pincus-Roth, Z. (2009, July 6). Best weekend never: Why journalists don't account for inflation when they report box office records. Retrieved June 13, 2013, from http://slate.me/1bzZHyV

Piper, M. (2013). *Accounting made simple: Accounting explained in 100 pages or less.* Lexington, KY: Simple Subjects.

Pound, J. (1992). Raiders, targets, and politics: The history and future of American corporate control. *Journal of Applied Corporate Finance, 5*(3), 6–18.

Preston, J. (2011, January 30). Pepsi bets on local grants, not the Super Bowl. *The New York Times.* Retrieved October 18, 2013, from http://www.nytimes.com/2011/01/31/business/media/31pepsi.html?_r=0

Private Equity International. (2013). The 2013 PEI 300. Retrieved July 2, 2013, from https://www.privateequityinternational.com/PEI_300_%E2%80%93_Top_50/#

Public Relations Society of America. (2011, December). *PRSA business leaders survey.* Retrieved May 1, 2013, from http://bit.ly/sUp6tf

Quinn, M. (2010, June 17). How to choose a calendar or fiscal year. Retrieved August 8, 2013, from Inc. website: http://bit.ly/cEuHy4

Ragas, M. (2010). *Agenda-building and agenda-setting in corporate proxy contests: Exploring influence among public relations efforts, financial media coverage and investor opinion* (Unpublished doctoral dissertation). University of Florida, Gainesville.

Ragas, M. W. (2012). Issue and stakeholder intercandidate agenda setting among corporate information subsidies. *Journalism & Mass Communication Quarterly, 89*(1), 91–111.Ragas, M. W. (2013a). Agenda-building and agenda-setting theory: Which companies we think about and how we think about them. In C. E. Carroll (Ed.), *The handbook of communication and corporate reputation* (pp. 153–165). New York, NY: Wiley-Blackwell.

Ragas, M. W. (2013b). Agenda building during activist shareholder campaigns. *Public Relations Review, 39*(3), 219–221.

Ragas, M. (2013c, January 22). Reputation and the news: 5 research-driven insights. *PR News.* Retrieved August 30, 2013, from http://bit.ly/XVECYd

Ragas, M. (2013d, February 8). Require business 101 for every student. *The Chronicle of Higher Education, 59*(22), p. A25.

Ragas, M. W. (2014a). Agenda-setting in the corporate sphere: Synthesizing findings and identifying new opportunities in this growing domain. In T. Johnson (Ed.),

Agenda setting in a 2.0 world: A Tribute to Maxwell McCombs (pp. 256–280). New York, NY: Routledge.

Ragas, M. W. (2014b). Intermedia agenda setting in business news coverage. In R. Hart (Ed.), *Communication and language analysis in the public sphere* (pp. 332–354). Hershey, PA: IGI-Global.

Ragas, M., & Culp, R. (2013, Spring). How PR pros and academics can build a stronger profession. *The Public Relations Strategist, 15–16.*

Ragas, M. W., Kim, J., & Kiousis, S. (2011). Agenda-building in the corporate sphere: Analyzing influence in the 2008 Yahoo–Icahn proxy contest. *Public Relations Review, 37*(3), 257–265.

Ragas, M. W., & Laskin, A. V. (2014). Mixed-methods: Measurement and evaluation among investor relations officers. *Corporate Communications: An International Journal, 19*(2), 166–181.

Ragas, M. W., Laskin, A. V., & Brusch, M. D. (2014). Investor relations measurement and evaluation: A survey of professionals. *Journal of Communication Management, 18*(2), 176–192.

Ragas, M. W., & Roberts, M. S. (2009). Communicating corporate social responsibility and brand sincerity: A case study of Chipotle Mexican Grill's "food with integrity" program. *International Journal of Strategic Communication, 3*(4), 264–280.

Rassart, C., & Miller, H. (2013). *Lead or be led: Time to take advantage of the new business reality.* New York, NY: The Deloitte Global Center for Corporate Governance.

Rawlins, B. L. (2005). Corporate social responsibility. In B. Heath (Ed.), *Encyclopedia of public relations* (Vol. 1, pp. 210–214). Thousand Oaks, CA: Sage.

Rawlins, B. L. (2006a). Measuring the relationship between organizational transparency and trust. In M. W. DiStaso (Ed.), *Proceedings of the 10th International Public Relations Research Conference* (pp. 425–439). Miami, FL: International Public Relations Research Conference.

Rawlins, B. L. (2006b). *Prioritizing stakeholders for public relations.* Gainesville, FL: Institute for Public Relations.

Rawlins, B. L. (2008). Measuring the relationship between organizational transparency and employee trust. *Public Relations Journal, 2*(2), 1–21.

Rawlins, B. L. (2009). Give the emperor a mirror: Toward developing a stakeholder measurement of organizational transparency. *Journal of Public Relations Research, 21*(1), 71–99.

Reputation Institute. (2013a). *Global RepTrak® 100: The world's most reputable companies in 2013. Reputation intelligence.* New York, NY: Author.

Reputation Institute. (2013b). *Global RepTrak® 100: The world's most reputable companies, a reputation study with consumers in 15 countries.* New York, NY: Author.

Reputation Institute. (2013c). *2013 CSR RepTrak® 100 study.* New York, NY: Author.

Reputation Institute. (2014). *Global RepTrak® 100: The world's most reputable companies: A reputation study with consumers in 15 countries.* New York: NY: Author.

Rigby, D., & Bilodeau, B. (2013). *Management tools & trends 2013.* Boston, MA: Bain & Company.

Rindova, V. P., Williamson, I. O., & Petkova, A. P. (2010). Reputation as an intangible asset: Reflections on theory and methods in two empirical studies of business school reputations. *Journal of Management, 36*(3), 610–619.

Rindova, V. P., Williamson, I. O., Petkova, A. P., & Sever, J. M. (2005). Being good or being known: An empirical examination of the antecedents, and consequences of organizational reputation. *Academy of Management Journal, 48*(6), 1033–1049.

Ritter, J. R., & Welch, I. (2002). A review of IPO activity, pricing, and allocations. *Journal of Finance, 57*(4), 1795–1828.

Roach, G. (2013, March 26). What do investors want from guidance? *IR Magazine.* Retrieved November 4, 2013, from http://bit.ly/1cJDhNQ

Roberts, P. W., & Dowling, G. R. (2002). Corporate reputation and sustained superior financial performance. *Strategic Management Journal, 23*(12), 1077–1093.

Rogers, E. M. (1997). *A history of communication study: A biographical approach.* New York, NY: Free Press.

Rogers, E. M. (2003). *Diffusion of innovations* (5th ed.). New York, NY: The Free Press.

Rosenbaum, J., & Pearl, J. (2013). *Investment banking: Valuation, leverage buyouts, and mergers & acquisitions* (2nd ed.). Hoboken, NJ: Wiley.

Roush, C. (2006). The need for more business education in mass communication schools. *Journalism & Mass Communication Educator, 61*(2), 195–204.

Roush, C. (2011). *Show me the money: Writing business and economics stories for mass communication* (2nd ed.). New York, NY: Routledge.

Roush, C., & Cloud, B. (2012). *The SABEW stylebook: 2,000 business and financial terms defined and rated* (2nd ed.). Portland, OR: Marion Street Press.

Rudolf, J. C. (2010, May 4). Slogans and facts [Blog post]. Retrieved May 21, 2013, from http://green.blogs.nytimes.com/2010/05/04/bps-green-credentials/

Ruler, B., Vercic, A., & Vercic, D. (Eds.). (2008). *Public relations metrics: Research and evaluation.* New York, NY: Routledge.

Sadowski, M., Whitaker, K., & Buckingham, F. (2010, October). *Rate the raters: Phase two, taking inventory of the ratings universe.* London, England: SustainAbility.

Schnurr, L. (2013, March 5). Analysis: The Dow—old, yes, but hardly irrelevant in march to record. Retrieved July 2, 2013, from http://reut.rs/YU4oP0

Seltzer, T., & Zhang, W. (2011). Debating healthcare reform: How political parties' issue specific communication influences citizens' perceptions of organization-public relationships. *Journalism & Mass Communication Quarterly, 88*(4), 753–770.

Servaes, H., & Tamayo, A. (2013). The impact of corporate social responsibility on firm value: The role of customer awareness. *Management Science, 59*(5), 1045–1061.

Sherk, D. M. (2004). Investor relations for the IPO. In B. M. Cole (Ed.), *The new investor relations: Expert perspectives on the state of the art* (pp. 119–135). New York, NY: Bloomberg Press.

Shiller, R. J. (2005). *Irrational exuberance* (2nd ed.). New York, NY: Broadway Books.

Silvestrelli, P. (2010). Market-driven management and intangible assets in global television set manufacturers. *Symphonya Emerging Issues in Management, 2,* 86–96.

Skonieczny, M. (2012). *The basics of understanding financial statements*. Schaumburg, IL: Investment.

Slavin, S. (1999). *Economics: A self-teaching guide* (2nd ed.). New York, NY: Wiley & Sons.

Smith, A. (2009). *An inquiry into the nature and causes of the wealth of nations*. New York, NY: Digireads.

Smith, E. B., & Kuntz, P. (2013). CEO pay 1,975-to-1 multiple of wages skirts U.S. law. Retrieved September 15, 2013, from http://bloom.bg/ZhG20Y

Smith, R. D. (2013). *Strategic planning for public relations* (4th ed.). New York, NY: Routledge.

The Social Media Measurement Conclave. (2013). Complete social media measurement standards, June 2013. Retrieved February 2, 2014, from #SMMStandards website: http://bit.ly/1fOXinh

Solomon, G. (2008). BP: Coloring public opinion? Retrieved May 21, 2013, from Adweek website: http://www.adweek.com/news/advertising/bp-coloring-public-opinion-91662

Solomon, R. C. (1992). *Ethics and excellence: Cooperation and integrity in business*. New York, NY: Oxford University Press.

Sorkin, A. R. (2013, June 24). Economists are asking: Did Bernanke tip Fed's hand? *The New York Times*. Retrieved June 25, 2013, from http://nyti.ms/19mINbf

Sorkin, A. R. (2011, May 2). Buffett lets the facts bury Sokol. *The New York Times*. Retrieved May 20, 2013, from http://nyti.ms/lUZ3qQ

Sowell, T. (2011). *Basic economics: A common sense guide to the economy*. New York, NY: Basic Books.

Spangler, J. (2014, June 2). Valued communicators understand the business [Blog post]. Retrieved June 6, 2014, from Institute for Public Relations website: http://bit.ly/1xiYB8n

Spangler, T. (2013, May 28). Clawbacks becoming fashionable on Wall Street. *Forbes*. Retrieved September 14, 2013, from http://onforb.es/153DIiO

Spence, M. (1973). Job market signaling. *Quarterly Journal of Economics, 87*(3), 355–374.

Spence, M. (2002). Signaling in retrospect and the informational structure of markets. *American Economic Review, 92*(3), 434–459.

Spicer, J. (2012, January 25). In historic shift, Fed sets inflation target. Retrieved June 13, 2013, from http://reut.rs/xqFVp1

Stacks, D. (2010). *Primer of public relations research* (2nd ed.). New York, NY: Guilford Press.

Stacks, D. (2013a, January 29). Stacks on research [Blog post]. Retrieved February 2, 2014, from http://www.instituteforpr.org/2013/01/stacksonresearch/

Stacks, D. (2013b, March 13). Stacks on research [Blog post]. Retrieved February 2, 2014, from http://www.instituteforpr.org/2013/03/stacks-on-research/

Stacks, D. (2013c, June 11). Thoughts on the passing of Jack Felton [Blog post]. Retrieved February 2, 2014, from http://www.instituteforpr.org/2013/06/thoughts-on-the-passing-of-jack-felton/

Stacks, D. W., & Bowen, S. A. (Eds.). (2013). *Dictionary of public relations measurement and research* (3rd ed.). Gainesville, FL: Institute for Public Relations.

Starbucks Coffee Company. (2014). *Starbucks annual shareholders meeting spotlights record performance driven through the lens of humanity* [Press release]. Retrieved March 29, 2014, from http://bit.ly/1i4y4lG

Stern, J. M., & Chew, D. H. (Eds.). (2003). *The revolution in corporate finance* (4th ed.). Malden, MA: Blackwell.

StevensGouldPincus LLC. (2012). *PR agency industry 2012 billing rates & utilization report: By agency size, region and specialty.* New York, NY: Author.

Stiglitz, J. E. (2000). The contributions of the economics of information to twentieth century economics. *Quarterly Journal of Economics, 115*(4), 1441–1478.

Stiglitz, J. E. (2002). Information and the change in the paradigm in economics. *American Economic Review, 92*(3), 460–501.

Stone, B. (2013, June 6). Costco CEO Craig Jelinek leads the cheapest, happiest company in the world. *Bloomberg Businessweek.* Retrieved September 16, 2013, from http://buswk.co/19KnopY

Stout, L. (2012). *The shareholder value myth: How putting shareholders first harms investors, corporations, and the public.* San Francisco, CA: Berrett-Koehler.

Strasburg, J., & Das, A. (2012, December 20). NYSE to sell itself in $8.2 billion deal. *The Wall Street Journal.* Retrieved June 28, 2013, from http://on.wsj.com/XOQeNc

Strömbäck, J., & Kiousis, S. (2011). Political public relations research in the future. In J. Strömbäck & S. Kiousis (Eds.), *Political public relations: Principles and applications* (pp. 314–323). New York, NY: Routledge.

Study shows PR pros making progress in following the Barcelona Principles. (2013, April 1). *PR News.* Retrieved February 2, 2014, from http://bit.ly/1gEkGbU

Stumpf, D. (2014, February 5). U.S. public companies rise again. *The Wall Street Journal.* Retrieved April 5, 2014, from http://on.wsj.com/1sWlVGF

Sveiby, K. E. (1997). The intangible assets monitor. *Journal of Human Resource Costing & Accounting, 2*(1), 73–97.

Swerling, J., Thorson, K., Tenderich, B., Ward, N., O'Tierney, B. C., Becker, M., . . . Li, Y. (2012). *Seventh communication and public relations generally accepted practices study.* Los Angeles, CA: Strategic Communication & Public Relations Center, Annenberg School for Communication and Journalism, University of Southern California.

Talner, L. (1983). *The origins of shareholder activism.* Washington, DC: Investor Responsibility Research Center.

Taparia, J. (2004). *Understanding financial statements: A journalist's guide.* Portland, OR: Marion Street Press.

Tashakkori, A., & Teddlie, C. (Eds.). (2010). *Sage handbook of mixed methods in social & behavioral research* (2nd ed.). Thousand Oaks, CA: Sage.

Thomas, C., & Corrigan, S. (2013, July 3). Ratings and rankings: How competition promotes corporate sustainability. Retrieved October 17, 2013 from GreenBiz website: http://bit.ly/12FxqBw

Thomson Reuters. (2013, February 6). Top private equity-backed leverage buyouts. Retrieved July 2, 2013, from http://bit.ly/YDe7cw

Thomson Reuters. (2013, February 6). Top private equity-backed leverage buyouts. Retrieved July 2, 2013, from http://bit.ly/YDe7cw

Thurm, S. (2013, May 15). What's a CEO worth? More firms say $10 million. *The Wall Street Journal*. Retrieved September 15, 2013, from http://on.wsj.com/10rtB6n

Trading Economics. (2013). List of countries by GDP annual growth rate. Retrieved June 13, 2013, from http://www.tradingeconomics.com/country-list/gdp-annual-growth-rate

Tseng, N.-H. (2010, December 1). Who is an insider, anyway? Retrieved August 19, 2013, from CNN website: http://bit.ly/fypYDM

Turk, J. V. (1985). Information subsidies and influence. *Public Relations Review*, *11*(3), 10–25.

Turk, J. V. (1986). Information subsidies and media content: A study of public relations influence on the news. *Journalism Monographs*, *100*, 1–29.

upper 90 consulting, & Holton Research. (2014). *Professional development in corporate communications today: Key insights from in-depth interviews with chief communications officers*. Grand Rapids, MI: upper 90 consulting.

U.S. Bureau of Labor Statistics. (2012). *Occupational outlook handbook, 2012–2013 edition*. Washington, DC: U.S. Bureau of Labor Statistics.

U.S. Department of Education. (2012). *The condition of education 2012*. Washington, DC: Institute of Education Sciences, U.S. Department of Education.

U.S. Securities and Exchange Commission. (1998). *A plain English handbook: How to create clear SEC disclosure documents*. Washington, DC: Office of Investor Education and Assistance, U.S. Securities and Exchange Commission.

U.S. Securities and Exchange Commission. (2011). Quiet period. Retrieved July 2, 2013, from http://www.sec.gov/answers/quiet.htm

U. S. Securities and Exchange Commission. (2012a). *Investor bulletin: How to read an 8-K*. Washington, DC: Office of Investor Education and Advocacy, U.S. Securities and Exchange Commission.

U.S. Securities and Exchange Commission. (2012b). Plain writing initiative. Retrieved August 18, 2013, from http://www.sec.gov/plainwriting.shtml

U.S. Securities and Exchange Commission. (2012c). Spotlight on proxy matters— Corporate elections generally. Retrieved September 13, 2013, from http://1.usa.gov/16r6xYn

U.S. Securities and Exchange Commission. (2012d). *Study regarding financial literacy among investors*. Washington, DC: Office of Investor Education and Advocacy, U.S. Securities and Exchange Commission.

U. S. Securities and Exchange Commission. (2013). *Investor bulletin: Insider transactions and forms 3, 4, and 5*. Washington, DC: Office of Investor Education and Advocacy, U.S. Securities and Exchange Commission.

U.S. SIF Foundation (2012). *Report on sustainable and responsible investing trends in the United States: 2012*. Washington, DC: U.S. SIF Foundation, The Forum for Sustainable and Responsible Investment.

van Riel, C. B. M., & Fombrun, C. J. (2007). *Essentials of corporate communication: Implementing practices for effective reputation management.* New York, NY: Routledge.

Veronis Suhler Stevenson. (2012, September 26). *New VSS forecast 2012–2016.* Retrieved May 2, 2013, from http://www.vss.com/NewsDetails.aspx?ID=272

Vlad, T., Becker, L. B., Simpson, H., & Kalpen, K. (2013). *2012 annual survey of journalism and mass communication enrollments.* Athens: The Cox Center, The Grady College of Journalism and Mass Communication, University of Georgia.

Vogel, D. (1983). Trends in shareholder activism: 1970–1982. *California Management Review, 25*(3), 68–87.

Watson, E. S. (1936, November 12). The truth about that "public be damned." *Weston County Gazette.* Retrieved May 20, 2013, from http://bit.ly/16AEPWR

Watson, T. (2005). ROI or evidence-based PR: The language of public relations evaluation. *PRism, 3*(1), 1–10.

Watson, T. (2011). An initial investigation on the use of 'Return on Investment' in public relations practice. *Public Relations Review, 37*(3), 314–317.

Watson, T. (2012). The evolution of public relations measurement and evaluation. *Public Relations Review, 38*(3), 390–398.

Watson, T. (2013). Advertising value equivalence—PR's orphan metric. *Public Relations Review, 39*(2), 139–146.

Watson, T., & Noble, P. (2007). *Evaluating public relations: A best practices guide to public relations planning, research and evaluation.* London, England: Kogan Page.

Watson, T., & Zerfass, A. (2011). Return on investment in public relations: A critique of concepts used by practitioners from communication and management science perspectives. *PRism, 8*(1), 1–14.

Weaver, D. H. (1980). Audience need for orientation and media effects. *Communication Research, 7*(3), 361–373.

Weiner, M. (2012). *PR and meaningful business outcomes: Demonstrating and generating a positive return on your PR investment.* New York, NY: PRIME Research Americas.

Weise, K. (2012, February 21). Why Facebook must stay quiet. *Bloomberg Businessweek.* Retrieved July 2, 2013 from http://www.businessweek.com/technology/why-facebook-must-stay-quiet-02212012.html

Wheelan, C. (2010). *Naked economics: Undressing the dismal science.* New York, NY: Norton.

Wimmer, R. D., & Dominick, J. R. (2014). *Mass media research: An introduction* (10th ed.). Boston, MA: Wadsworth.

Wingfield, N. (2012, April 1). Apple's chief puts stamp on labor issues. *The New York Times.* Retrieved October 8, 2013 from http://nyti.ms/H8J7cA

World Bank Group. (2014). GDP (current US$). Retrieved August 19, 2014, from http://bit.ly/VDmvMI

World Federation of Exchanges (2014). *2013 WFE market highlights.* London, England: Author.

Wright, D. (2007). *2007 Arthur W. Page Society distinguished service award acceptance remarks: Thoughts on ethics, education and friendship.* Laguna Niguel, CA: Arthur W. Page Society.

Wright, D., Gaunt, R., Leggetter, B., Daniels, M., & Zerfass, A. (2009). *Global survey of communication measurement 2009 – final report.* London, England: Benchpoint Ltd. and the International Association for Measurement and Evaluation of Communication (AMEC).

Yang, J. L. (2013, August 26). Maximizing shareholder value: The goal that changed corporate America. *The Washington Post.* Retrieved September 21, 2013, from http://bit.ly/1a7jtqs

Young, A. (1998). *Measuring intangible investment. Towards an interim statistical framework: Selecting the core components of intangible investment.* Paris, France: OECD Secretariat.

Zilka, J., Myers, R., & Gomes, P. (2013). *What the new SEC rule on disclosure in social media means for IR.* Chicago, IL: Edelman.

Index

Printed in the United States
By Bookmasters